CULTURE **SHIFT**

CULTURE **SHIFT**

*Communicating God's Truth
to Our Changing World*

David W. Henderson

Foreword by Haddon Robinson

Baker Books

A Division of Baker Book House Co
Grand Rapids, Michigan 49516

Published by Baker Books
a division of Baker Book House Company
P.O. Box 6287, Grand Rapids, MI 49516-6287

Printed in the United States of America

Library of Congress Cataloging-in-Publication Data

Henderson, David W., 1959–
    Culture shift : communicating God's truth to our changing world / David W. Henderson : foreword by Haddon Robinson.
        p.   cm.
    Includes bibliographical references.
    ISBN 0-8010-9059-8 (pbk.)
    1. Evangelistic work—United States. 2. Christianity and culture—United States.   I. Title.
BV3793.H46   1998
269'.2—DC21   98-27281

For current information about all releases from Baker Book House, visit our web site:
http://www.bakerbooks.com

To the glory of God
and for the sake of his kingdom

CONTENTS

Part 7:   How We Think: *Beyond Meaning and Purpose*

FOREWORD

A man by the name of Paul planted the cross of Christ in the soil of the first century. As we face obstacles in our day, so did he. Demons infested the culture. The population was hostile to the Good News. The pagans caricatured the Christians. They accused the believers of being atheists because they did not worship the ordinary gods. Since the Christians met in secret and talked about "feeding on Christ" and loving one another, the pagans accused the Christians of cannibalism and incest. The gentiles themselves lived in a moral sewer. Throughout the society from the highest to the lowest, prostitution, homosexuality, adultery, and the killing of infant girls were the order of the day. Paul ministered in a culture that despised his ethic based on love and purity. Although the Jews separated themselves from the immorality of the gentiles and based their religion on the Old Testament, they were often bitter enemies of the apostle. They came to believe that Paul, a fellow Jew, was a traitor, someone who trifled with their law.

Yet Paul won great spiritual victories. Granted that the Wind of God was at his back, but so it is with every Christian. How could Paul have penetrated the thinking of the society of his day? In the first letter of his Corinthian correspondence, Paul spelled out his strategy. "Though I am free and belong to no man, I make myself a slave to everyone, to win as many as possible. To the Jews I became like a Jew, to win the Jews. To those under the law I became like one under the law (though I myself am not under the law), so as to win those under the law. To those not having the law I became like one not having the law (though I am not free from God's law but am under Christ's law), so as to win those not having the law. To the weak I became weak, to win the weak. I have become all things to all men so that by all possible means I might save some" (1 Cor. 9:19–22). Paul is saying, "I will identify with anyone's way of thinking and anyone's way of living in order to communicate my message. I will do anything short of sinning to win men and women to Jesus Christ."

Christians today are not far from the first century. In effect, we live in a pre-Christian culture. A majority of men and women in our society have little knowledge of God. Christians are written off as political radicals who are devoted to bashing lesbians and homosexuals and who show no sympathy for women carrying babies they had not planned. We live with inhabitants of a culture which now approves and embraces lifestyles that thirty years ago moral people condemned. We cringe at the way the media misunderstands and misrepresents us.

When we weren't looking, the world changed, and we weren't ready for it. Christians may be nostalgic for "the good old days" when society endorsed Christian values and believed churches were important. But we will wait in vain for the culture to turn back its thinking so we can speak to it again as we did in a more "Christian" period.

Like Paul in the ancient world, Christians today must understand and adjust to the mindset of our neighbors. We must be willing to adapt to other people's way of thinking in order to win them to the Savior. That is risky and painful business. It demands that we pursue uncomfortable questions: How do they think? What do they value? How do we accommodate to their beliefs without abandoning our own? What is negotiable and what is not? How do we speak to moderns so they will understand? Those are the questions David Henderson tackles in ways thoughtful Christians can grasp.

Invest a few hours and lots of thought in this book. By doing so, you will be better able to tell the good news about Jesus to your neighbors, to your children, and to your grandkids. What might be most surprising is that somewhere in these pages you might also come to a keener understanding of yourself.

–Haddon Robinson

ACKNOWLEDGMENTS

If Thou dost give me honour, men shall see, the honour doth belong to Thee.

George Herbert

ore than I would like to admit, I find myself relating with eighteenth-century historian Edward Gibbon, who, in the opening pages of his first book, wrote: "Unprovided with original learning, unformed with the habits of thinking, unskilled in the arts of composition, I resolved to write a book."

Fortunately, no one writes a book alone. As dozens of brooks converge to form a single stream, which in turn joins others to form a river, so this book represents the gathered influences of numerous others. Apart from their contributions—their characters, their examples, their insights, their encouragement—this book would be no more than a few drops of water in a dry streambed.

My passion to understand and reach our world with biblical truth was forged by several important influences for which I am deeply grateful.

Three teachers of preaching—Dr. Roy Clements, Dr. Haddon Robinson, and the late Dr. Gwyn Walters—have, through their artful proclamation as well as through their insightful instruction, given me an appetizing picture of what it looks like to engage our world with truth. I write this book in honor of these godly mentors and friends, celebrating their faithful ministry of the Word as well as their profound impact on my own.

A course with Dr. David Wells, who modeled a piercing inquisitiveness about the thought-world in which we find ourselves, first infected me with the desire to make sense of the culture around me. Subsequent interactions with him have only fueled the bug.

I also owe thanks to the anonymous benefactor of the Parish Pulpit Graduate Fellowship Award, whose vision and generosity made possible a year of study in Cambridge, where the understandings of my own culture that shape this book first began to crystalize.

As this book took shape, it was mightily helped along by many hands and minds.

Thanks go especially to Dr. Haddon Robinson, whose gracious honesty sank a less-than-effective first approach at this material and whose patient advice helped transform a lump of ideas into a sculpted whole. What an encouragement you have been to me!

Great thanks are also due to Dr. Sid Buzzell, Dr. William Dyrness, Dr. George Gallup, Dan Smick, Lon Allison, Steve and Lois Rabey, and Jon Graf for wading through those early drafts of the manuscript and offering both affirmation of its content and valuable suggestions for its improvement.

Along the way, Dr. David Wells also took time to interact with some of the material and generously pointed me toward a bundle of valuable bibliographic resources. I'm grateful to you, as well as to the wonderful staff at McKinzey-White Booksellers in Colorado Springs, who provided ever-gracious help in tracking down one obscure book after another!

Jeff Behan, Geoff Paddle, Matt Muehlhausen, Malcolm Springs, and Scott Blanchard all gave patient technical (and moral) support as the book haltingly took shape. Thanks for the readiness with which you dropped what you were doing to give me a hand. I'm also grateful for the never-ending encouragement that poured in from so many, especially from two great families—the Royals and the Boths—and from good chum Glenn Paauw. You buoyed my spirits again and again, pulling me along with your unflagging interest and enthusiasm.

That this book exists at all is tribute to the gracious support of scores of people at Covenant Presbyterian Church in Colorado Springs. In particular, Pastor Bill Tibert and the elders at Covenant not only provided me with a wonderful ministry platform on which to build my understanding of our changing world and the challenges of reaching it but also enthusiastically (and generously) supported my studies and freed me from my ministerial responsibilities for three months to allow me to write this book.

To Paul Engle I extend deep thanks for seeing in those early drafts the makings of a book that might make a difference and for taking a risk with an unknown writer—as well as for your gracious encouragement and patient direction along the way. Thanks also to Brian Phipps in editorial, Cheryl Van Andel in art, and the many others at Baker who make it such a joy to do a book project with you. In a publishing world driven so often by profit considerations alone, Baker Book House is to be applauded for its refreshing eagerness to see its work first as a kingdom ministry and only secondarily as a business.

Brandon, Sean, Molly, Corrie—what great sports you were as I tucked myself away in the basement day after day, clattering away at my computer while surrounded by all those piles of books. Thanks for your patience—and for all the snuggles and smooches along the way. Finally, for words of encouragement unceasingly spoken, for time together sacrificially set aside, for love notes and understanding looks and back rubs and cups of tea, I thank my wife, Sharon Joy. This book was written in honor of my mentors and for the sake of the kingdom, but it was written because of you. I love you tons and tons.

Soli Deo Gloria.

PROLOGUE

Return to Sender

Last fall a friend in Cincinnati was having a birthday, and I wanted to get him a present.

Now, I'm usually the guy who's in line at the post office the week after Christmas with a pile of packages under my arms. And birthdays have a way of not even registering until they are weeks past.

But this time was going to be different. I went out well ahead of time and, after considerable looking, found a gift I *knew* he'd like. I packed it up, addressed the box, and sent it on its way.

It never showed up.

I called my friend on his birthday and he said there was no sign of it.

I called him again a week later. Still not a trace. Drat!

After another week went by, the package finally turned up . . . on *my* doorstep. "Return to sender. Addressee unknown."

Oh, for crying out loud! I had copied the address straight from my address book. The gift should have gotten there. I checked the book. Yep. I had copied it correctly. Then, just to convince myself how right I was and how wrong the postal service was, I pulled out the last letter from my friend and looked for the address.

It was different! My friend had moved, and somehow I'd missed it altogether.

The package delivery business has become a blur of trucks, planes, and people crisscrossing the world hundreds of times over in a pattern that, if it were traced out, would rival the scribbles of even the most determined toddler. But complex as the delivery business is, it still boils down to a surprisingly simple task—picking up a package and asking two questions: Where is it going and how do we get it there?

This book sets out to answer the same questions.

We've done our work, carefully unfolding God's spoken Word. Now we pack up our insights into well-chosen phrases and send them out across this nation's pulpits and restaurant tables and neighborhood fences. The perfect gift.

But the address of the world around us has changed. Dramatic shifts in the fabric of American culture have nudged the world out of reach of the words we've so carefully selected.

A good friend of mine was invited to speak to a gathering of distinguished church leaders from across the state. When he finished the message and came over to where I sat, his expression was a mixture of frustration and futility. He leaned over and whispered, "I feel like that one went out about two feet and . . ." His hand went into a dive like a Fokker triplane shot out of the French skies. He didn't need to finish his sentence.

The world has moved, but it neglected to send a change of address card. We keep delivering the same words to the old address, but no one is home.

"How, then, can they call on the one they have not believed in?" asks Paul in Romans 10:14. "And how can they believe in the one of whom they have not heard? And how can they hear without someone preaching to them?"

To this cascade of questions Paul could have added another: "And how can they understand if they haven't a clue what we're saying?"

What follows is an attempt to help us discover where the world has moved, and how to meet it there.

Part 1 considers the process of communication. What is at work whenever we try to make ourselves understood? How does relevant communication happen, and what does that have to do with the way we present the Bible when we share our faith, teach, and preach? After presenting the two most common ways we can overstep the line in our efforts to communicate the Bible faithfully, I conclude these two chapters by laying out a model for biblical communication in the contemporary world. It is based on the life and ministry of Jesus, and I believe it can help us bring timeless Word and ever-changing world together.

As I write, there swirls around evangelical circles a great debate about the issue of relevance. What about this church-growth and seeker-sensitive business? On one side are those who argue that what matters most is getting the Word out, regardless of what it takes. Meeting felt needs, adapting our message to our audience, making our message positive, brief, encouraging, and nonconfrontational: church-growth advocates argue that these are valid and crucial steps to communicating biblical truth effectively today.

On the other side are those who argue that a felt-needs, audience-adapted message compromises the true character of Christianity. We shouldn't be so eager to go chasing after the surrounding world. We should wait and let it come to us. The line between orthodoxy and heresy is a fine one and

16

easy to trip over. We should be more concerned with the purity than the popularity of our message.

Part 1 reflects both voices and points to a view of communication that answers the concerns on both sides.

The main portion of the book, parts 2–7, describes the crucial changes that have shifted Western culture out of the reach of our words. This interpretive survey describes the six most important features of our culture when it comes to communicating biblical truth. More than any other aspect of our culture, they shape how we see, hear, think, relate, and believe. This portion looks at each of these culture shifts and explores what to do about them.

Much of what I am talking about in these pages is so familiar to us that it has become tough for us to recognize its impact. We simply don't notice whole features of our culture, not because they are hidden, but because we see them all the time. Sometimes we have to take a couple of steps back from our culture to really see them.

The seeds of this book were planted during two such experiences: a summer mission trip to West Africa and a year of study in Cambridge, England. Only after I was out of the United States and immersed in another culture for an extended time could I begin to see in a new way some of the things we take so much for granted.

Each of these six qualities of our culture should dramatically impact the way we go about our business as communicators of biblical faith. Our commitment to the authority of the Bible will press us to ask *what* we should communicate in the face of these characteristics, while our commitment to be sensitive to our audience will nudge us to ask *how* best to communicate it.

For that reason, each part ends with practical suggestions about how to speak, how to share our faith, and what to communicate. To make these parts as helpful as possible, I've divided each into two chapters. The first gives some background about a particular characteristic—our consumerism, say, or postmodernism—explaining how we got where we are and how it affects us today. A second chapter presents practical suggestions about what and how to communicate in the face of that feature of our culture. You can use this book in whatever way will be most beneficial for you: reading the whole or focusing on the analysis or beelining to the practical suggestions.

Whether you are a pastor, a parachurch minister, a student, or a thoughtful Christian, one of my greatest hopes is for you to become more a student of the world at your doorstep. And one of the best ways is to step out of my book and straight into somebody else's. Books are like lenses that bring our world into focus, and there are so many worth reading. At the end of each section and at the back of the book are suggestions for further reading. Track down some of these gems and dig in. You will be richly rewarded as you jump into the works of other authors who can shed light on different aspects of our culture far more effectively than I ever could.

This book maps the cultural landscape of our country and our world. But the question only you can answer is, How do these broad cultural shifts play out in the congregations, the relational circles, and the individual lives of those you're working hard to reach? And how does that affect the way you set about speaking God's Word? I believe you will be better able to answer those questions than I will. And that is the whole point of this book—to walk you through the changing cultural landscape so you can see how to be more effective right where God has placed you.

God's grace to you as you strive to bring Word and world together.

Part **1**

GAINING A HEARING

Dear God,
Want to hear a joke? What is red, very long, and you hear it right before you go to sleep? Give up? Answer is a sermon.
Your friend,
Frank (age 11)

I have come closer to being bored out of the Christian faith than being reasoned out of it. . . . I think we underestimate the deadly gas of boredom. It is not only the death of communication, but the death of life and hope.

Haddon Robinson

1

Walking the Narrow Ledge of Relevance

Dr. Emmett Brown, a research scientist and inventor of sorts, was in a bit of a pinch. Perched on a crumbling masonry ledge fifty feet above the ground, he was trying as hard as he could to bring two electrical cords together. The upper cord, which hung just out of his reach, ran up to the roof of the Hill Valley Clock Tower. There it was attached to a lightning rod where, in a few seconds, at precisely 10:04 P.M., a bolt of lightning would strike. The other cord, the one he held in his right hand, hung down across the courtyard and ran over to an exposed wire stretched ten feet high across the adjoining street.

Everything hung on Doc Brown's ability to connect the two cords in time. For as Brown wrestled in the wind and rain, a converted DeLorean sports car accelerated toward the overhead cable. If the current from the coming lightning strike failed to reach the car the instant it passed by, then Marty McFly, the driver, would be stuck forever in 1955. And everything—lightning strikes, clock-tower bells, crumbling concrete, curious policemen, falling trees, balky starter motors—*everything* seemed to conspire against Marty's attempt to get back to the future where he belonged.

The drama that drives this scene in the movie *Back to the Future* is at work every time a pastor steps behind a pulpit or a neighbor opens her Bible with a non-Christian friend. God has spoken. Words of life-inverting grace and world-transforming power spill out into human history like a bolt from heaven. They are words direct from God's heart, each carefully chosen to speak truth and love to the world God created. And the world—

distracted, bored, and restless—yawns as it streaks by. Bringing ever-moving humanity into contact with the eternal while all of existence seems to conspire against it: Isn't that what we are about?[1]

What does it mean to communicate biblical truth with relevance? How do we, the Doc Browns of the kingdom, bring heaven within hearing of busy and bored earth?

American experience is punctuated by talking heads—David Letterman, Dan Rather, Barbara Walters, Oprah Winfrey, Rush Limbaugh, Tom Brokaw—on and on goes the list. Groomed, polished, and powdered, they flash before us nonstop, pitching, selling, probing, persuading. Day in and day out. Blah, blah, blah.

In a world where everybody is talking, what happens to the person who really has something to say? How does the Christian gain a hearing for biblical truth?

The issue is the same regardless of the setting. Sitting across from a businessman in a hot uptown restaurant that throbs with talk of weekday conquests and weekend escapades. Chatting over a splintery cedar fence, trying to be heard above the growl of a neighbor's lawnmower. Or standing at the pulpit before a familiar group of half-attentive pew potatoes.

How do we do an E. F. Hutton? How do we speak so people will listen? How do we bridge the chasm that stands between God's Word and the stockbrokers and students and store clerks who occupy the world with us?

We can't make the world believe. But we sure can speak in such a way that the world cannot help but listen.

Sorry, Wrong Number

Paul had a great smile, and it broke across his face as we talked. He shook his head in disbelief as he slid my roast beef sandwich across the counter to me. "I still don't understand, David. You left Procter and Gamble and all that money to become a *minister?* Why? I don't get it."

Almost every time I stopped at the roast beef place on the way to the seminary (which was often), there was Paul. He worked nonstop, but not because his heart was in the sandwich business. Paul wanted to "make it," to step out of the hard, lower-class life of a Greek immigrant and to hit the big time, make the big bucks. So my story of leaving a cushy position in marketing and management at P&G headquarters to go into ministry made absolutely no sense to him. And he asked me about it nearly every time I saw him.

But I was never able to give Paul what he wanted. I couldn't provide a simple, clear explanation for the transformation in my life when, as an atheist in college, I gave my life to Christ. Nor was I able to explain what it would mean for him to become a follower of Christ. I tried—across that countertop late at night and in our home across the dining room table—but it kept coming out sideways and muddled.

Not that Paul wasn't interested. He was. The failure was mine. I couldn't find the right way to express to him what this thing called Christianity was all about. Again and again I'd fall into talking about the Christian life on *my* terms, from reference points that were meaningful to me but meant nothing to Paul.

Whole segments of our culture are missed by our efforts to speak. It is not that they don't hear the gospel. Few people in America can escape hearing some account of the basics of Christianity. The problem is that they, like Paul, don't hear it put meaningfully.

They are not just "out there," these untouched pockets of people. Many of these men and women occupy the pews with us on Sunday morning. They are well-meaning, God-fearing people who file in faithfully each week, eager to hear a word of encouragement that will zing home to their hearts, or a word of wisdom that will help them make sense of their lives. But they leave empty handed. For them, the words are irrelevant, meaningless.

Where does the breakdown occur? Why is it that eyes close when the Bible is opened?

Society has changed. And if we speak tomorrow as we did yesterday, our words will become just one more sound in a noisy world, addressed to everyone, heard by no one.

Two women head out for a cappuccino after a long day at the office. They commiserate about their low wages, the never-ending demands of the job, and the challenges of juggling full-time work and full-time parenting. As they settle into their conversation, one says to the other, "Listen, Anne, I've got to ask you . . . I don't know what it is, but it seems like there's something that you have that I don't. Life just seems so hard to me. I don't feel like I'm gonna make it sometimes. But there's a peace about you; you just seem to be able to handle life better than I do. What is it?"

Anne responds warmly, "You know, Sue, I'm really glad you asked. It takes courage to be that vulnerable. As it turns out, this is something I've been meaning to talk with you about for some time. You know that I go to church pretty often, and you've seen my Bible on my desk at work. I think whatever you're seeing in me is probably the result of my faith in Jesus Christ. Can I tell you about it?"

"Sure!" Sue leans forward in her chair, interested in what her friend has to say. But what comes next sounds to her like a foreign language.

"Well, I guess it was about four years ago now that I was saved. You see, I was in the middle of some real trials, and a friend of mine helped me to see that the tribulations I was having were because I was a sinner and I was rebelling against God. As Isaiah 53:6 says, 'We all like sheep have gone astray. Each of us has turned to his own way.'"

Anne had a genuine experience of God's grace in Jesus Christ. Her life was turned inside out. And Sue was interested. But now she is no longer listening. "Saved? Trials? Sinner? Isaiah?" Those things mean nothing to her. Because of the words Anne chooses, Sue is unable to make the connection between Anne's explanation of Christianity and her own life struggles. She's left tapping her nails on the tabletop, looking at her watch, and glancing impatiently around the coffee shop.

Or meet Bill, a tool-and-die worker ground down by the hassles of a difficult workplace and the constant struggle to make ends meet. Suppose some Sunday morning he wakes up—with more than a little guilt about the way he has been wasting away his days and drowning away his nights—and decides it's time to give God another chance. So he pulls his dusty suit from the back of the closet, squeezes into it, and heads down to the church on the corner. He finds an empty seat next to white-haired Mrs. Smith and slides in. When the pastor stands up to preach, Bill listens, eager to hear something—anything—that will address the growing inner turbulence he's been feeling.

The pastor opens the Bible, takes out his notes, and begins. "Today in our series through the Epistle of James we come to a passage that talks about Christian fellowship. In particular, James is talking about a schismatic attitude that can so easily divide the body of Christ. Turn with me to James 3:13. . . ."

Bill scrunches up his face in disappointment. Then, kicking himself for making the mistake of giving church yet another try, he mentally begins to head for lunch, and Mrs. Smith, a regular for some thirty years, isn't far behind. Little do they know that the morning's passage has everything to do both with Bill's difficulty in getting along with his hard-nosed boss and Mrs. Smith's power struggles with gray-haired Mrs. Jones in the Women's Guild.

The issue here is one of relevance. Sue had no way of knowing that Anne's words did hold the answer to her inner hollowness, those nagging longings and unmet expectations of her heart. And Bill had no way of knowing that the pastor's words would apply with great timeliness to some of his biggest struggles at work. By the time the pastor got there, Bill was gone.

Words Brought Home

Great communication, it is rightly said, is relevant communication. But what does it mean to be relevant?

The word traces back to a medieval Latin word, *relevaré,* which means "to bear upon." Something is relevant when it has to do with my circumstances, when it bears upon my questions and struggles.

For something to be relevant for me, two things need to be true. First, whatever it is—a talk, a book, a letter, an instruction guide—needs to be pertinent to my life. It has to address the issues I'm wrestling with, answer the questions I'm asking, meet my needs.

But that is not enough. Something is not relevant for me unless I see and understand its pertinence. Unless I can make the connection, unless I see how this book or conversation connects with my life, it really isn't helpful; it isn't relevant at all.

I call these two aspects *actual relevance* and *functional relevance.* Actual relevance gets at whether a message has anything to do with my life, while functional relevance has to do with whether I am able to see the connection.

So if something I'm saying seems irrelevant to someone, it could be because of one of two things. Either it *is* irrelevant, or it merely *seems* to be irrelevant. For Bill and Sue, the words they were hearing seemed to have nothing to do with their experience. The words were functionally irrelevant, words that may just as well not have been said.

An airline safety card tucked in the seat in front of me on a recent flight read, "If you are sitting in an exit row and you cannot understand this card or cannot see well enough to follow these instructions, please tell a crew member." That's important information communicated in a very unhelpful way. It may as well not have been said at all.

Paul recognized this distinction between actual and functional relevance nearly two thousand years ago. In his first letter to the Corinthians, Paul teaches that whatever is spoken in the church should strengthen the church. But that can't happen if no one understands the words. "Unless you speak intelligible words with your tongue, how will anyone know what you are saying? . . . If then I do not grasp the meaning of what someone is saying, I am a foreigner to the speaker, and he is a foreigner to me" (1 Cor. 14:9, 11).

The Relevance of the Bible

One of the convictions that unites Christians is that the Bible speaks to our issues. The Bible has actual relevance.

We believe that God has spoken, and what he has said is incredibly important because it is in the Bible that we encounter God himself. And it is there that we see ourselves clearly for the first time.

For nearly twenty centuries we have shared the conviction that the Bible is what we turn to for answers to questions about faith and life. Our experience, reflections, musings, insights, and intellectual conclusions are not enough. We speak from the Word, for only biblical truth truly addresses the needs and longings of the human heart. Only God's Word reveals truth sufficient for the task of transforming lives. And only biblically based communication—speaking and writing which spills from the pages of God's vast self-disclosure—is truly relevant.

But here's the rub: its relevance is not always obvious to the men and women of today's world. In light of the earth-shaking shifts taking place in our culture, I would argue that the Bible's relevance is harder and harder for the world to see. The Bible strikes many as extraneous, irrelevant, a relic of no particular value today. While the Bible is off the top of the chart in terms of actual relevance, its functional relevance sinks lower and lower.

The recognition that the world is tuning out our efforts to communicate biblical truth has led to two opposite reactions from Christian communicators. Both bubble up out of right concerns but boil over into huge messes. And they both result in the same thing: distortion of the heart of Christianity.

Have I Got a Deal for You

The first mistake comes when concern for the audience eclipses concern for the message. It happens when, out of an intense desire for our hearers to benefit from and be attracted to Christianity, we adjust the message to suit whomever we are addressing. Figure 1 pictures this.

Those who fall into this mistake think that Christianity is encumbered by too much baggage to draw a response from contemporary people and that it badly needs editing. So they accommodate the Bible to fit modern audiences, modifying what it says in an effort to make, or keep, it relevant. They change it, streamlining its message.

One of the more obvious ways people in the church have accommodated the Bible is by reducing it to a set of universal, timeless biblical principles. Peace. Justice. Love. Freedom from oppression. Believers of a liberal or progressive bent think that many of the concepts found in the particulars—notions such as Christian exclusivity, the holy otherness of

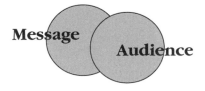

Fig. 1: Accommodation
Concern for the audience eclipses concern for the message.

God, sin, lifelong marriage commitment—are outdated carryovers from the Middle Ages and offensive to modern, enlightened ears. So they whittle away many of the specifics, and what is left is a collection of ethical and spiritual guidelines.

The assumption—a wrong one—is that if something is unfamiliar, uncomfortable, or difficult to understand, it must be irrelevant and needs to be clipped. But this abridgment merely reflects the prevailing mood of the times. We don't meet God in these biblical principles. We merely see ourselves.

Christians of a more orthodox bent are quick to point a finger on this one. But some of us have gotten so caught up in our efforts to communicate the relevance of Christianity that we've inadvertently done exactly the same thing.

Really?

Really. You and I can lop off whole portions of the Bible to make the message more palatable to "seekers." Consider this: If our number one goal is to make it easy for non-Christians to come to Christ, think how easy it is to omit discussion of such things as repentance, submission, obedience, community, and accountability. This business of taking up crosses or squeezing through eyes of needles—it just doesn't carry with today's audience. In our effort to present a winsome message, we can very easily reduce the message to a few self-serving platitudes. Although we gain an audience—sometimes a very big one—when we accommodate the content of the Bible to suit the contemporary climate, we inevitably lose the message.

The church needs to be mindful of the difference between being audience sensitive and audience driven. To be audience sensitive is to ask what can be done to make the words of Scripture better *understood* by today's unchurched audiences. Audience sensitivity begins with a commitment to the authority of God's Word. It is God who has the final say about what is and what isn't said.

To be audience driven, on the other hand, is to ask what needs to change to make the message more *acceptable*—inoffensive for the unchurched person, easy, safe, comfortable, nonconfrontational. Audience drivenness begins and ends with the authority of the audience. It is the listener who has the final say.

The line between these two disparate approaches is easily crossed. Here are some of the ways we can inadvertently slip into accommodation.

Fortune Cookies and Encyclopedias

One subtle way we accommodate is to talk about the Bible as if it were a giant fortune cookie. Crack it open anywhere and you'll find wise and useful sayings, pithy insights to better your life, marriage, business, or finances. But whenever we give principles for life without threading them through what it means to lay down our lives and deny ourselves and follow Christ, we distort Christianity. We flip it around, and suddenly the self is at the center.

We also often treat the Bible as if it were the ultimate how-to book, an encyclopedia of practical wisdom and insight. But the Bible is more like a novel. I can dip into my *Encyclopedia Britannica* wherever I want, read a few paragraphs, pick out the information that will benefit me, and then close it. But with a novel I can't do that. I must relate every passage, every description or conversation or turn of events to the overall plot. Otherwise, it makes no sense. At least, not its intended sense.

The Bible is not a collection of Confucian proverbs, each of which can stand alone. It is all of a piece. Nor is it a collection of stories. It is one story, the story of how God in Jesus Christ came to indifferent and self-absorbed humanity with the sole notion that those cold and callous men and women should be made right with him.

The term *biblical* needs to be redefined. It cannot mean merely "from somewhere within the pages of Scripture." In light of the way the Bible is written, as a single fabric of thought stretching from front to back, biblical must mean "in keeping with what the Bible is about." And the Bible is about God's unstoppable passion to be known, loved, and served—through Jesus Christ—by those he has made.

Many well-meaning people in the evangelical church have missed this. They will isolate a need, then reach into the Bible for insights that seem to address that need. But the individual is left untouched. The course of his or her life is left unchallenged, ambitions are left unchecked, the sinful nature is left unaddressed, and the fiber of his or her character is left unexposed.

But isn't this more a picture of us laying hold of practical helps than God laying hold of us? Of being consumers of the faith rather than being consumed by Christ? Is it possible to communicate biblical truth and leave people unconfronted by Jesus Christ at the core of who they are?

From the perspective of God's purposes being worked out in history, what good does it do if a person manages his business more effectively but remains untouched in the heart? What ultimately is served by helping a woman deal with her dysfunctional family of origin if her rebellion against a loving God goes unaddressed? How does it help if we bolster a person's self-esteem without pointing that person toward God's purposes for her life?

Does it please God when we present portions of the Bible to people in such a way that it reinforces their self-centered bent? Or that encourages them to think they have no real need of God but are doing just fine on their own, thank you very much? Isn't that exactly what we do when we boil down whole portions of the Bible into a series of easy self-help steps for better careers, stronger self-images, or closer friends?

That's not to say every time we preach or share our faith we need to lay out God's entire plan for humankind, or have an altar call. We don't.

Nor do I mean to suggest that the Bible doesn't contain many helpful, practical suggestions for the living of daily life. It does.

But well-meaning pastors, speakers, and laypeople, eager to show how relevant Christianity is, inadvertently can sever the cord of thought that holds the message of the Bible together.

A church I once served had an outreach event called PrimeTime. Each PrimeTime program revolves around a central theme, some issue we believe unchurched people are wrestling with. We've had shows about the environment, health and fitness, self-esteem, the workplace, dating and marriage, and so on.

Each show is a ninety-minute blend of skits, contemporary music, and a message, all aimed at accomplishing three things: introduce the topic or issue, show the world's perspective on it, and then share, in a brief closing message, what Christianity has to say to the same issue.

It could be tempting in the message to jump from what the world says about an issue to what the Bible says about it without ever dealing with the topic in a "biblical" way. In a program on friendship I could highlight several of the great passages in 1 Samuel 18 or Titus that provide practical suggestions about how to be a friend: Don't nag, listen well, take advice, keep short accounts, think about the other person first, watch your tongue. And the people could leave with some tips that could make a real difference in their friendships.

But will I have spoken biblically? I've just given a message that has nothing to do with the real plot line of the Bible and the heartbeat of Christianity.

What would happen if I took the time to talk about a carpenter of old who redefined what it is to be a friend? I could introduce Jesus as God with Us, the great and gracious friendmaker. I could describe the lengths he went to make us his friends, laying down his life to bring us back to God. I could also tell about the work of turning us upside down and inside out that he has in mind for us: transforming us into friends fit to share eternity with him by making us like himself.

Then I could talk about what it means for us to be friends from a biblical perspective. Not self-serving men and women applying a few principles to make our friendships go more smoothly, but people transformed by the living God and sent into the world, free to lay down our lives for others because of the one who has done the same for us. People with nothing at stake, with nothing to lose, ready to go out of their way for the sake of others. Then—once I had talked about what it is from a biblical perspective that gives me freedom to be a true friend—then I could share some of those practical tips.

See the difference? Both approaches are from the Bible, but only one is really biblical, staying true to the whole, faithful to the plot.

The Bible is not a self-help guide packed with helpful pointers. It is a door that brings self-absorbed humanity face to face with self-giving God. Presenting it as anything less falls short of communicating what the Bible is all about.

Vending Machine Deity

It is also a great temptation to make Christianity attractive to seekers by misrepresenting the faith as a relationship through Christ with a God who is the divine vending machine in the sky, there to meet our every need. "Unhappy? Unattractive? Unsuccessful? Unmarried? Unfulfilled? Come to Christ and he'll give you everything you ask for."

We forget God is not primarily in the business of meeting needs. When we make him out to be, we squeeze him out of his rightful place at the center of our lives and put ourselves in his place. God is in the business of being God. Christianity cannot be reduced to God meeting people's needs, and when we attempt to do so, we invariably distort the heart of the Christian message.

God's agenda is to display his glory and to further his kingdom around the globe. It's to call humanity to bended knee, bowing before him in adoration and devotion and dependence and service. It's to invite men and women out of the hollow pursuit of living for themselves and into a life consumed by him. It's to make of his followers men and women of deep trust and character, the kind of Christlike individuals with whom God is pleased to spend eternity.

The trend in the church to address the felt needs of our audience is at the heart of some of this. When we become consumed by identifying and speaking to these needs, our communication becomes audience driven. Every nugget of our conversation is pressed through that filter, and the 75 percent of Scripture that doesn't seem to speak to the needs of our audience . . . well, there's not really a place for that.

Merely using need as our main basis for making sense of the Christian life automatically knocks us away from the way believers have understood the faith for centuries. Why? Because God no longer occupies center stage. Terms like self-love, self-expression, self-confidence, and self-fulfillment, none of which graces the pages of the Scriptures, begin to dominate the church's conversations. Meanwhile, other "self" words straight from the Bible like self-surrender, self-sacrifice, self-denial, and self-control slip into disuse. Self, great big and smack dab in the middle, squeezes out the notions of a holy God, a fallen self, an undeserved gift of grace in Jesus Christ, and a divine call on the whole of one's life. When that happens, we may be preaching, we may be sharing faith, but what we are communicating is not genuine Christianity. In Christianity, the one place the self cannot be is at the center. That is the rightful place of God alone.

There's a fine line here. It is important to begin where our audiences are. It is a fundamental communication principle: begin where people are, not where you wish they were. Our words should intersect with the issues and concerns of their daily lives. Only then is it possible for our hearers to get a sense of the functional relevance of the Bible. As Haddon Robinson has said, we need to preach our audience from the text, not the text to the audience.[2]

But this is key. While we need to start with the pressing issues of our hearers, we cannot stay there. We must move on from a person's experience to God's view of the issue, and then set that in the frame of God's larger purposes. What are the things most on God's heart? What are the things God has clearly called us to in his Word? What is God up to? What is God's purpose for us as Christians? And how do those considerations shape how and why we set goals, or how we go about raising a family, or how we deal with the past?

As long as our sensitivity to felt needs drives us to ask those harder, deeper questions about God's overall plan for us, no problem. It is when we let felt needs drive all that we say that we set ourselves up to compromise the basic Christian message. We must let the Bible determine the direction and flow of the conversation.

Thus Saith the Lord

The second mistake is the reverse of the first. It happens when concern for the purity of our message eclipses concern for our audience (fig. 2).

This mistake is one of being so confident of the relevance of the Bible that we fail to translate what it says into language that is meaningful to

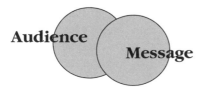

Fig. 2: Failure to Translate
Concern for the message eclipses concern for the audience.

Average Joe and Average Josephine. And there it goes—*zing*—right over the person's head.

God's Word speaks with relevance to all humans, crossing every cultural line. But not until it has been translated into words and concepts that speak with particular meaning to each particular culture. You will not overhear many conversations at McDonald's in which words like repentance, tithe, sanctified, or fellowship figure prominently. We redeem bottles, save dying trees, give testimony in the courtroom, have stewards on cruises, and give justification for showing up late for meetings, but what do those words mean when we use them in church?

The content of our witness needs to be biblical. But it is not automatic that if we speak from the Bible the pertinence of our words will be obvious. If we don't show the connection, walking a person from his or her experiences to God's revealed truth, then our efforts to share Scripture are a waste of time. We need to bring those words home, fitting them to the circumstances and to the people we address.

But wait! What about those passages that talk about the power of God's Word? They say the Word of God is God-breathed (2 Tim. 3:16), living and active (Heb. 4:12), and stands forever (1 Peter 1:25). And God through Isaiah promises that his Word will not return empty "but will accomplish what I desire and achieve the purpose for which I sent it" (Isa. 55:11).

Fortified by these passages, we assume we needn't try to make sense of the words of Scripture for contemporary audiences. The Bible speaks for itself, with no help from me, thank you very much. Our job is to preach it, to share it, to speak it, but surely not to change it.

But I'm not talking about changing it. I'm talking about packing it into the words and images and experiences and idioms of everyday life.

You can see this concept at work in a passage from Nehemiah. After long years away, the Israelite exiles have been freed to return to their homeland. Now they've finished rebuilding the walls circling Jerusalem and, eager to begin anew, they've gathered expectantly at one of the city gates. Ezra and the Levites stand, open God's Word, and begin to read it to a group of people who are largely unfamiliar with it. What they did is a perfect example for us. "They read from the Book of the Law of God, making it clear and giving the meaning so that the people could understand what was being read" (Neh. 8:8).

Is that compromise? Or merely effective communication?

Consider the problem we were thinking about a bit earlier. Why is it that, when people come in from outside the church, they often just don't get it? And why is it that in door-to-door evangelism the most common response is poorly hidden irritation, followed by a closed door?

Certainly one explanation is that a person's heart is hard, sealed off to God's thawing, convicting, and remaking power.

But to conclude that a calloused heart is the only factor involved when people are unresponsive to our efforts to share faith misses a crucial element in the communication process. It is just as likely that what the person heard made no sense because our choice of words was so poor it was nearly impossible for the hearer to make a connection between our words and real life.

For fifty years, students of the communication process have pointed out that the words that go into another person's ears do not magically carry the precise meaning we have in mind. Words are more like scoops of snow than laser beams. We throw them in the direction of our hearers, but what makes it through all the filters may be only a small part of what we first tossed. Words are fuzzy, nuanced, gray, vague. Like Silly Putty, they take on something of their color and shape from what's around them.

Communication always includes a translation process, even the communication of God's living, active, inspired Word. Everything we say invariably is retranslated into the language and filtered through the experience of whomever we're addressing.

If the Word of God needed no translation, no rephrasing, we would all still be using the first translation of the Bible into English, which came out in 1384. The fact that Wycliffe's translation now is virtually unreadable is a good reminder that each generation within a given culture needs to receive biblical truth in its own vernacular. As P. T. Forsyth put it, "The changeless Gospel must speak with equal facility the language of each new time."[3]

Enter a Different World

Why is it that translating is necessary? The Bible is a world of ideas all of its own. It's a self-contained, self-referential world that is enormously confusing to someone who is unfamiliar with it. It has its own history, its own geography, its own cast of characters, its own worldview, its own vocabulary. It only truly makes sense to those who have been steeped in its history and literature, raised with its unique emphases and nuances, taught its unique perspective on life and faith. It is an alternative way of making sense of our universe, and virtually everything it communicates runs against the way we see, think, speak, and make sense of what is going on around us.

Take a word as simple and seemingly straightforward as *grace.* On one level it's plain enough for my preschool daughter to understand. It describes the movements of a ballerina or a gazelle. But when the Bible uses it, I don't believe there is a word that hits more at the heart of the Christian message. If we breeze past it without explanation, we've missed a boatload of content. That's why virtually every time we come to a word like grace we need to flesh it out. We might say, "God is always taking the initiative in our relationship with him. Always. It always starts with him. And that is grace. God taking the first step." Or we could say, "Grace means that God pours out on us what we don't deserve and withholds from us what we do deserve."

It's not enough merely to speak the Bible word for word, regardless of whether those words are in the King James version or eighth-grade equivalent English. There has to be some sort of explanation, some way of undressing the biblical ideas from their traditional garb and outfitting them in words that communicate the same ideas meaningfully to the people who hear us. Haddon Robinson, one of the freshest biblical communicators today, puts it this way: "The language of the pulpit needs to be the language of the Volkswagen ad, not of the academy."[4]

We must find familiar ways to faithfully express unfamiliar ideas.

One goal in my preaching, writing, and sharing of faith is to strip out of my language as much Christian lingo as possible. But there's a challenge here, because most of the jargon we use comes straight from the Bible. Think about it. Born again, saved, testimony, fellowship, sovereignty—you could make a list a couple of miles long of words that come straight from the Bible but mean nothing to unchurched people today.

What do we say to people when, without explanation, we use dated words and illustrations that mean little or nothing to them? Aren't we saying that Christianity is out of touch, that it has nothing of benefit to say to people today? Even worse, aren't we saying that Christianity is only for folks on the inside, for those who grew up walking its hallways and speaking its secret language?

We couldn't distort Christianity more. Christianity is for sharing. Its message, if it has come only to me, has not come far enough. If it stops with me, it stops short of fulfilling its purpose. For Paul, and in fact for all of the early believers, sharing was axiomatic. Paul writes, "It is written: 'I believed; therefore I have spoken.' With that same spirit of faith we also believe and therefore speak" (2 Cor. 4:13).

It is ironic that, in the name of faithfulness to God's Word, we can chase away the very people who need most to hear what we're saying—and misrepresent the faith in the process. Communicating that the doors of Christianity are closed to outsiders is as serious a perversion of the faith as lopping off portions of its message in the name of relevance.

So what should we do? Every time we preach, every time we share our faith, we need to ask questions like these:

- What can I do to help this person understand what this passage is saying?

- How can I translate the unfamiliar concepts into familiar terms?
- How can I begin communicating where my hearer is, not where the Bible is?

It is not our place to make the Bible relevant, but it is unquestionably our place to communicate the relevance of the Bible. Only then is it really heard. And isn't that what we are about every time we preach or teach or share the faith?

Words That Hit Home

Relevant communication of the Bible comes down to two things:

1. *Biblical authority:* We need to allow the Bible, in its entirety, to provide the direction and substance of our messages. Only in this way will our words have *actual* relevance, speaking to the longings and desires of the human heart.
2. *Audience sensitivity:* At the same time, we need to speak in such a way that the Bible's message is brought to bear on the needs and circumstances of our hearers in language they understand. We need to begin where they are, with the things that are familiar and meaningful to them. That will ensure that our hearers will be able to see the *functional* relevance of the Bible.

Relevant biblical communication looks like figure 3, both concerns held in creative tension and neither eclipsing the other.

Let's return to our examples. The pastor's opening words failed to make the connection for Bill between his experiences and the words read from the Bible. And Anne's explanation of the basics of Christianity simply made no sense to Sue.

How might it have stirred Sue's heart if Anne had said something like this? "Sue, you've told me that things aren't really going so well for you these days. Well, you know, about four years ago I was in a similar place. The pieces just weren't fitting together. I mean, they should have been. My marriage with Lee was good, work was all right, the kids seemed to be doing okay, but there was still something missing. It felt like no matter

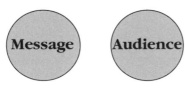

Fig. 3: Relevant Communication
Concern for the audience is held alongside concern for the message.

how hard I tried, I just wasn't—you know—happy, content, whatever. I had this sense that there was more to life than what I was experiencing, but I didn't know what it was.

"That was when a friend of mine took some time to explain what this Christianity thing is all about. She said that, according to the Bible, God made us, and he made us to live for him. That's the whole point of our lives. That's why he brought us into existence, to enjoy his presence and to put him at the center of our lives—to live for God. But every one of us, well, we decided to say to him, 'Hey, God, this is great. Thanks for life, breath, and everything else. But I'm going to live my life for me, not for you. Later.'

"We've all done it. We've all made the same choice. It's what the Bible is talking about when it says that we are like a bunch of sheep that have wandered off, every one of us heading off in a different direction, and all of us winding up lost.

"And that's when our troubles began. Because we weren't made to live for ourselves, just like sheep aren't made to run wild. We were made to live for God, with him at the center, and unless we do, we'll never experience the kind of joy and contentment that God made us to enjoy. That's what sin is. It's when we choose to push God out of the center of our lives and wind up with all the wrong thoughts and attitudes and actions that spill out from that one big choice. And that sin, that rebellion and independence and indifference, it keeps us from God and from enjoying all that God has for us. It throws a wrench in the works, because it comes between us and the one who made us, and it destroys our relationship with him. So unless we're living for God, with him at the center, we are always going to fail to live the kind of life that God intends for us to live."

All Anne needed to do was unpack the words of the Bible in a way that made sense to Sue. Can you picture the look of attentiveness on Sue's face?

And imagine the difference the sermon could have made for Bill, and Mrs. Smith, and the rest of the congregation if these had been the first words out of the pastor's mouth.

"Have you ever noticed how much life is complicated by other people? At every turn we get thrown together with people whose personalities we don't like, whose opinions we don't agree with, and whose agendas run up against our own. Have you ever thought about how much easier it would be to run the church if there were no other people to think about? How much easier it would be to go to school if you didn't have to worry about getting along with your locker partner? Or how much better work would be if you didn't have to spend all your time figuring out how to get along with everybody else? In my wearier moments

I've joked and said, 'You know, ministry would be so much easier if it wasn't for people.'

"So much of life is spent just trying to get along with, and get something done with, other people. Well, in our darker moments, it's fun to daydream about a planet without other people to feud and bicker with, but the reality is that God has put us on this planet together, and he has done so for a good reason. That means we're pretty much stuck with each other. So now the question is: How do we get along? We need wisdom and understanding to live side by side, some approach to life that will see us through as we deal with the challenge of getting along.

"Well, the Bible has a lot to say about that. According to James, one of Jesus' followers, there are two main alternatives when it comes to this struggle of sharing the planet with each other. Let's look at them and see what we can make of them. Turn with me to page 1164 in the Bible you'll find in the rack in front of you, to James chapter three. We'll be looking at verses thirteen through sixteen."

In this approach, the pastor would know he was leading his congregation into a tough passage. But he would prepare Bill and the others to hear the message by showing its practical relevance to their daily lives. His opening words would say that a commitment to Christ makes a difference this week, today, now! I don't know about you, but I suspect there's a good chance Bill not only would listen hard to what followed, but would return the next Sunday to hear more.

Relevance is standing on a masonry ledge and bridging the gap between heaven and earth, doing our best not to lose sight of either the lightning bolt about to strike at our left hand or the sports car about to speed by at our right. We're working to communicate the relevance of the Bible to contemporary culture without compromising our message on the one hand, or compromising our audience on the other.

2

Bringing the Truth
to Bear on Our World

very time we refer to the Bible, whether preaching before a congregation of familiar faces or citing a passage from memory in a conversation
with an unchurched friend, we have one goal: to gain a hearing. What
we're trying to do, ultimately, is speak God's Word in such a way that a
person is compelled to weigh it and respond to it. We can't make people
believe God's Word, or make them live it, but we can encourage them to
listen to it, to take it seriously, and to weigh its claims and promises.

So how do we communicate a high-voltage message in a way that
ensures contact? How do we let the electricity of God's spoken Word
flow through us with power?

Look how God did it. First, he knew the world. He understood it. He
knew it inside and out: its triumphs and its tragedies, its needs and its
longings, the hollow in its heart. But he didn't remain aloof from the
world. He entered it. He rolled up his sleeves and waded in. He touched
the world, and the world touched him. Then he brought truth and heavenly wisdom from outside the world to bear on human hearts. He said
what the world needed to hear, not what it wanted to hear.

Using this incarnational approach as my model, I've come up with a
simple strategy for biblical communication that I call the *relevaré* model
of communication, from the Latin word meaning "to bear upon." I believe
the method has the potential to transform our effectiveness as biblical
communicators.

The Relevaré Model of Communication

1. Understand Your World

In "The Open Boat," Stephen Crane tells the story of four men stranded in a tiny, unsteady lifeboat in the open sea. The opening lines capture the intensity with which the men watched the waves that rolled toward them: "None of them knew the colour of the sky. Their eyes glanced level, and were fastened upon the waves that swept toward them. These waves were of the hue of slate, save for the tops, which were of foaming white, and all of the men knew the colours of the sea."[1]

Nothing else mattered to them. They had become students of the sea, scrutinizing every new swell because each rising wave threatened to swamp their tiny boat.

The world around us throbs and churns like the open sea. It is always changing, blown and tossed by the winds of every new cultural bent, every new way of thinking or making sense of life.

As pastors and laypeople who want to communicate God's Word with effectiveness and power, we need to be students of our world. We need to "know the colours of the sea." What are the new swells beginning to loom, the new waves of thought?

Consider some of the changes that have swept our shores in recent years: the rise of the men's movement, the growth of computer on-line services, the press toward multiculturalism, the attraction of Eastern spirituality, the arrival of home entertainment centers. Each, when understood, provides a window to the world at our doorstep. All point to the slide away from a commitment to truth with a capital *T*, the further retreat into the distracted aloneness of one's own home, the relentless and sometimes panicky search for identity and fulfillment, and so much more.

Only when we understand what makes the world tick, what gives shape to its impulses and convictions, can we speak with any relevance.

To understand our surrounding world means we can at least begin to answer questions like these.

- What drives the world around you?
- What makes it different from other places and times?
- How do people spend their time and money?
- What is most on the heart of people who share the freeway and the supermarket with you?
- What are people thinking about, dreaming about, longing for?
- How do people make sense of life?

- What worldviews are you most likely to encounter among your acquaintances?
- Who or what has the ear of the people around you?
- How does sin most often express itself?

Here are some ways to become a student of the world around you.

- *Read everything you can get your hands on.* Look for clues to what's going on in the hearts of people in your world. The newspaper, news magazines, comics, best-sellers, airline magazines, even the headlines on the glamour magazines at the grocery store can yield treasures.

    One day I was standing in line at the grocery store, gallon of milk in hand, when I saw this headline on the cover of a *Cosmopolitan* magazine: "The Kinkiest, Wildest Turn-On of All Time Is (Would You Believe It?) Mutual Trust." What an astounding admission from those who would have us believe that looks and technique are all that matter!

    Nearly every page in print, from the comic page to the *Wall Street Journal,* can point to important waves rising on the horizon of our culture. I'm forever tearing articles out of papers or magazines and photocopying copies of articles and chapters for my files; the joke during one stay with my wife's parents was that all I left of the paper were a few shreds.

- *Watch TV and go to the movies.* The screen, whether it be in the privacy of our homes or at the local twenty-four-screen theater, has more influence on our generation than any other voice. Know what it is saying.

- *Be a quiet observer of what makes your friends' and neighbors' lives tick.* Dr. Leith Anderson likes to take advantage of the times he is invited into the homes of others as an opportunity to learn about their world. What could you learn by walking through people's homes like a detective? Now, I'm not talking about excusing yourself from the dinner table, sneaking upstairs, and rummaging around in your host's medicine cabinet. There's a lot to be learned simply by keeping your eyes open. Which room is the center of the home? How is it arranged? What does that say? What books are on the shelves, if any? What magazines are stacked for browsing in the bathroom? What videotapes are piled up by the entertainment system? What new purchases fill the garage and den?

- *Make the most of every conversation.* I don't know about you, but there's nothing I dislike more than a cocktail party. Cocktail parties can be goldmines, though. Just ask a lot of questions: Where do you work? Do you like what you do? What drew you into the field? How would you separate the winners from the losers in your profession? What do you like to do when you have some free time? Had a vacation lately? Where'd you go? How'd you pick that? Who do you like to spend time with? Who are your heroes? Why?

Put your fingertips on the pulse of the world. Know the colors of the sea around you.

2. Enter Your World

The movie *The Mission* begins with one of the most powerful scenes in recent moviemaking. Tribal people in the jungles of Brazil have just killed a Jesuit missionary who came to them. Imitating the curious figure that hung on a chain around his neck, they tie his body to a cross and shove it over a huge waterfall. Moments later his body washes up against the banks of the river where his fellow missionaries wait downstream. But they are not deterred by this grisly welcome. After burying the body of his good friend and fellow priest, another member of the order immediately sets out to reach the natives. The only way to get to them, however, is to climb straight up the enormous rock face over which his friend has just been thrown. With the mist from the waterfall blasting against his face and threatening his grip, this priest nearly doesn't make it. But he presses on and, after hours of climbing, eventually manages to reach the top. Once there, he sits down on a rock, and—knowing that these people love music—takes a recorder out of his pocket and begins to play. At great cost and risk to himself, this man steps out of his world and into theirs.

We must walk our hearers from where they are to where God's Word calls them to be. But lots of barriers make it hard for us even to get within hearing distance of non-Christians, let alone be heard and understood. Today Westerners are slow to hear and quick to lock their doors and crank up their stereos when Christians arrive on the scene.

Most people simply don't buy the idea that Christians have the answers. They see too much evidence to the contrary. We Christians have been caught, in more ways than one, with our zippers down. Our sin, our selfishness, our spiritual smugness, the inconsistency of our beliefs and our lives—those things speak much louder than our words. When the watching world sees pedestals being put under Christians, it begins to look for bowling balls . . . or earplugs.

Add to that the fact that people are subjected to a ridiculous barrage of words on a daily basis. It sends them withdrawing turtle-like into the locked-door privacy of their three-bedroom, two-bath fortresses. Little wonder we have trouble getting even a sound bite past the defenses of most non-Christians.

The days of effective street-corner and door-to-door evangelism in the United States are waning. People have had enough of words addressed to "Occupant." They are weary of being bombarded by messages "to whom it may concern." Who needs one more assault on the senses and sensibilities?

It is not enough for us to understand our world from afar. We need to wade into it and rub shoulders with those we desire to reach. We need to be willing to get our cuffs smudged by the world, living life with non-Christians on their terms, not ours. When we enter the world of the men and women around us who don't know Christ, we lay the groundwork for real communication to take place.

When I live that close to my neighbors and office mates, I know them. I know which TV shows they plan their schedules around, which radio stations they tune their car radios to, which movies they've seen seven times. I know what they spent half of their last paycheck on.

I know their hearts. I begin to understand the pressures that would lead a teen to have sex or an unfulfilled woman to divorce her husband or a man in a dead-end career to drink heavily. I know what they are looking for when they hang out at a bar during happy hour every day and what they are avoiding when they watch four hours of television a night.

And when I know their hearts, I can begin to speak their language. I'm aware of where my interests and experiences overlap with theirs, and that helps me speak biblical truth with grace and understanding. I know what words to use, what stories to tell, what images to evoke, what life experiences to draw on in ways that will make sense to them.

At the same time, when we live that close to others, they start seeing us as real persons with real struggles, but with a faith big enough to provide real answers in the midst of real challenges.

They hear what we say when a hammer hits our fingers, see how we relate to our kids when we're running on four hours of sleep, look into the bags we bring home from the mall, notice which channel our cable is left on from the night before. We need to live in such a way that, if Jesus really does make a difference in our lives, people around us cannot help but see it.

When we let others in on our lives, we earn the right to be heard.

Wasn't this Jesus' way? He knew humanity. He knew what made people tick. And he entered their world. That's what the incarnation was all about: Jesus jumping in. He didn't keep his office in the holy of holies, away from the masses. He walked the earth, not the hallways of heaven. He lived in the alleys and homes of the common people. His feet got

41

splattered with the same muck as everyone else. He hung out, so to speak, at the beer halls and bowling alleys and betting tracks of his day. Jesus spent so much time with "unchurched" people that he was accused of wining and dining too much with the wrong crowd (Matt. 11:19).

"As the Father has sent me," Jesus says to us, "so I am sending you" (John 20:21). Into the world.

3. Bring Truth to Bear from Outside Your World

Consider this.

- Jesus always began where people were, but he never allowed them to stay there.
- Jesus always listened to people's questions, but he rarely answered what they asked.
- Jesus spoke the truth people needed to hear, not what they wanted to hear.

Whenever he spoke with men and women, Jesus was not content merely to echo back to them their own insight, their own limited perspective. To do so would have been like giving salt water to a man dying of thirst. Jesus always brought truth to bear from outside a person's world and applied it to his or her life.

We are called to do the same. Across the pages of the Bible God unfolds his perspective, shows his priorities, explains his purposes. There he tells us what is real, what is important, what is true. God tells us about himself, about us, and about the relationship he desires to have with us. So it is there we must turn.

But that means conflict, because God's ways are not our ways. At least, not anymore. Not since a little conversation in a garden some years back when a man and a woman decided that they would like to apply for the position of lord of the universe. Ever since then, humanity has been at odds with God. So every time we bring people in contact with biblical truth, there is—or should be—conflict. How we think and act, the things we pursue and care about, all need to be brought back in keeping with what God has for us.

One summer during college I worked at a diesel engine dealership. Part of my job was to deliver diesel engines to other dealers around the state. I vividly remember the old truck I had to drive. It was a big, worn-out flatbed that was a bear to control. The link between the steering wheel and the rest of the steering mechanism had worn down. The steering wheel could move back and forth about four inches without affecting the steering at all. In the meantime, the front wheels would decide for themselves where they wanted to go. The truck would drift right, so I'd have to swing the wheel across and nudge it back to the left. Then it would go too far to the left, and I'd have to throw the wheel back to the right to get back on course. Sure made for an interesting job of driving down narrow city streets!

Humans are like that truck. The fall in the garden broke the connection between us and the Lord's direction for us, and we wander off course repeatedly. We all need to be nudged, and in some cases vigorously tugged, back on track.

The Bible corrects our steering. Paul gets at this when he writes in his second letter to Timothy that the Bible teaches us what to think and shows us how to live. But, he writes, it also corrects our false thinking and exposes our wrong living. Only then, as we are repeatedly corrected and challenged by God's Word, will we be prepared and equipped for life as followers of Christ (2 Tim. 3:16–17).

Because of that, true biblical communication cannot mean saying only those things that sit well, that reinforce a person's current condition. We must be about the business of bringing truth to bear from outside our hearer's world.

Jesus' words are hard words, even when they speak life. He studied the moonlit face of a religious leader and said, "You must be born again." To a father filled with grief he gently said, "Don't be afraid; just believe and she will be healed." He looked a self-reliant young man in the face and said, "Sell all you have and give it to the poor." And to the large crowd of Lookie Lous who followed on his heels, eager for his next big trick, he said, "Any one of you who does not give up everything he has cannot be my disciple."

This was the difference between the true prophets and the false prophets in the Old Testament: the willingness to speak the whole of God's truth, not just the easy part. Many are faithful to portions of God's truth, but how many bring the whole counsel of God home to the hearts of the world today? Remember what God said to the Israelites through Jeremiah?

> "Do not listen to what the prophets are prophesying to you; they fill you with false hopes. They speak visions from their own minds, not from the mouth of the LORD. They keep saying to those who despise me, 'The LORD says: You will have peace.' And to all who follow the stubbornness of their hearts they say, 'No harm will come to you.' But which of them has stood in the council of the LORD to see or hear his word? . . . If they had stood in my council, they would have proclaimed my words to my people and would have turned them from their evil ways and from their evil deeds. . . . Is not my word like fire," declares the LORD, "and like a hammer that breaks a rock in pieces?"
>
> Jeremiah 23:16–18, 22, 29

43

In a church that wants to make it as easy as possible for people to come to Christ, Jeremiah's words hit home.

Dr. Roy Clements is among Britain's finest preachers. I'll never forget these words of his: "Prophetic preaching is speaking God's truth to a specific place and time, digging in to where people are and applying the Bible in specific ways to their circumstances. It's risky. But it is a risk we need to take. We can't play it safe."[2]

Every time we open the Bible, there is an inherent conflict in the lives of those who hear its words. If we filter out those words that confront, and speak only those words that comfort, we deflect the lightning strike and dissipate its power. Humanity awaits a bolt from heaven and receives only the smallest of static electricity shocks.

As Christ followers, we can hold to God's Word with great confidence, standing on its adequacy and truthfulness. But try as we might, we can never perfectly believe or live what it teaches. We always fall outside of the circle it carefully proscribes. For that reason it must always be given room to call us to account. Always, always, we must let truth stand against us, not merely under our feet.

As P. T. Forsyth put it, "We must all preach *to* our age, but woe to us if it is our age we preach, and only hold up the mirror to our time. . . . We must, of course, go some way to meet the world, but when we do we must do more than greet. A crisis has from time to time to be forced, a crisis of the will."[3]

God's Word comes from outside our sphere of existence—the unexpected word of grace, the piercing word of truth, crashing in from outside. That word reminds us that God meets people right where they are. But the transforming power of Jesus Christ is released only when we point people where God would have them be, and then point to Jesus Christ as the only way to get there.

God's Word is for today's world. It is a bolt of lightning sizzling with the promise of new life. And when we, standing on the narrow ledge, faithfully bring Word and world together, the Word courses through us with power and hits home. And the world stops in its tracks, more than ready to listen.

About Chapters 1 and 2

Concepts Worth Remembering

relevance: relating to the matter at hand, pertinent, bearing upon one's life circumstances *actual relevance:* a term to describe communication the content of which is inherently meaningful and significant to the hearer

functional relevance: a term to describe communication in which the hearer is able to grasp the meaning and significance of the message

biblical: in keeping with what the Bible as a whole is about (as opposed to being merely taken from the Bible)

accommodate: change the content of a message to make it acceptable to one's hearers

translate: change the language of a message in such a way that it can be heard clearly and understood

Recommended Reading

On Contemporary Culture

Anderson, Leith. *Dying for Change.* Minneapolis: Bethany House, 1990. An engaging survey of some of the changes taking place in the Western world, including implications for the role of the church in response. *A Church for the Twenty-First Century* (Minneapolis: Bethany House, 1992) elaborates on his vision for a culture-sensitive church.

Dyrness, William. *How Does America Hear the Gospel?* Grand Rapids: Eerdmans, 1989. Dyrness describes some of the main bents of our culture and how those impact the way the gospel is heard. Thorough and insightful.

Myers, Ken. The Mars Hill Tape series. Developed by a former National Public Radio host, these wonderful bimonthly, ninety-minute tapes provide insightful, reflective Christian commentary on today's art, literature, music, and cultural trends. $36 a year (P.O. Box 1527, Charlottesville, VA 22902; 800-984-0400).

Strobel, Lee. *Inside the Mind of Unchurched Harry and Mary.* Grand Rapids: Zondervan, 1993. One of the best short overviews of the cultural currents shaping the men and women we are trying to reach, with practical suggestions for preaching and evangelism.

On the Clash between Church and Culture

Horton, Michael. *Made in America.* Grand Rapids: Baker, 1991. A pointed look at the way our culture has rewritten the gospel, replacing the Bible's message with society's.

Webster, Douglas. *Selling Jesus: What's Wrong with Marketing the Church.* Downers Grove, Ill.: InterVarsity, 1992. Webster eloquently calls for a church that refuses to accommodate to the world's consumeristic ways of thinking.

Wells, David. *No Place for Truth*. Grand Rapids: Eerdmans, 1993. A piercing critique of American culture and the evangelical church. His subsequent books, *God in the Wasteland* (Grand Rapids: Eerdmans, 1994) and *Losing Our Virtue* (Grand Rapids: Eerdmans, 1998), represent a two-volume theology in which he presents his solutions, first addressing the nature of God and then the nature of the person.

Witten, Marsha. *All Is Forgiven: The Secular Message in American Protestantism*. Princeton: Princeton University, 1993. Witten's critique of the self-centered, secular message that comes through in sermons today will give you pause to think.

On Preaching and Communication

Hume, James C. *The Sir Winston Method: The Five Secrets of Speaking the Language of Leadership*. New York: William Morrow, 1991. Hume uses the speeches of Churchill to highlight timeless speaking tips. A joy to read.

Nichols, Sue. *Words on Target: For Better Christian Communication*. Atlanta: John Knox, 1963. Her suggestions for speaking with economy, energy, and subtlety are practical and right on target.

Robinson, Haddon. *Biblical Preaching*. Grand Rapids: Baker, 1980. A masterful book by one of the best biblical communicators today. In the book he spells out his helpful process for moving from text to sermon; his discussion of the "big idea" in chapter two is helpful for any speaker. Beyond its many practical suggestions, this book is simply a treat to read: crisp, fresh, and to the point.

On Evangelism

Hunter, George. *How to Reach Secular People*. Nashville: Abingdon, 1992. A broad historical survey with a host of practical strategies and suggestions about sharing faith.

Hybels, Bill, and Mark Mittelberg. *Becoming a Contagious Christian*. Grand Rapids: Zondervan, 1994. Filled with practical, encouraging ideas—especially the sections on discovering your evangelism style and on starting spiritual conversations.

Petersen, Jim. *Living Proof: Sharing the Gospel Naturally*. Colorado Springs: NavPress, 1989. Petersen's thrust is evangelism as a way of life. Clear, perceptive, challenging.

Part 2

WHO **WE ARE**

Consumers

Mallory Keaton: "I don't go to the mall that much."
Alex Keaton: "Mallory, the mannequins wave at you!"

Family Ties television show

Indulge. It's time to put pleasure back in living. Satisfy your appetite. Leave guilt behind. Become a hedonist. Seek bliss at every turn. Succumb to temptation and revel in the feeling it gives you. A certain gratification, accompanied by a cushion of contentment.

Nieman-Marcus ad

3

Manufacturing the Consumer

We are the object of a heated pursuit: advertisers on Madison Avenue and business people on Main Street are doing their darnedest to shape us into a loyal and lavish buying public. And that concerted effort to turn us into consumers has largely worked. Shoppers now through and through, we think about religion like we think about a new sweater. Does it fit? Is it in style? Will it meet my needs? Is it me?

The people with whom we desire to share the gospel have become reluctant buyers of the faith, guarded shoppers casually browsing through the religious options in search of something that fits. We have our work cut out for us, but perhaps not the work that we might think.

A game caught my eye the other day as I walked through a store at the mall. Across the front of the box was a close-up picture of four glamorous girls in their early teens. Blemish-free, painstakingly made-up, expensively dressed, bubbling with excitement, the girls were carefully posed to look as though they'd just landed together in a spontaneous, happy pile. Their glee seemed to spill off the cover. Printed across the box was the reason for their joy. "It talks! Press the button! Insert your credit card! You never know what the voice of the mall has in store for you! Join your friends on a wild shopping spree as you rush from store to store! Hurry! Your friends may beat you to the bargains!"

On the back of the box are more pictures of the girls: laughing as they run arm in arm, walking through the mall loaded down with stuffed shopping bags, and modeling their new clothes for each other at home. When you open the box you find a glitzy, electronic game board: your very own mall. And to make sure you fully enjoy the adventure, you'll also find— "Wow! Cash and credit cards inside!"—four credit cards and a collection of fives, tens, twenties, and fifties, plus an ATM. ("If you need more cash, just make a quick stop at the bank!")

The game, "Mall Madness: The Talking Shopping Spree Game by Milton-Bradley," says something important and sobering about the world we live in and want to reach. In North America, as this game suggests, shopping is not primarily a chore to be tolerated, a necessary evil when the shelves are getting empty or the shoes are getting worn. It has become a game, a social event, a foundation for friendship, a way of passing time, a source of adventure and excitement, a competition between friends, a basis for self-esteem, a way to spend a rainy day.

Mall Madness is simply reflecting the world around us.

America is a land of compulsive shoppers. Malls have bumped out churches as the central architecture in the community, and shopping has squeezed aside all manner of other activities to become one of our favorite leisure pursuits.

Teenage girls say that their number one way to spend free time is to shop.[1] They prefer shopping to going to the movies, exercising, and even dating. Adults are no different, ranking shopping as their favorite thing to do for entertainment outside the home.[2] "Shopaholism" is now an official psychological malady, and thousands of men and women are treated for it each year.

The mall is our home away from home, and shopping is our national pastime.

America's favorite tourist attraction, beating out Disney World and drawing nearly ten times as many people as the Grand Canyon, is the Mall of America outside Minneapolis, Minnesota, a shopping mall complete with more than four hundred stores, an amusement park, and a full-size roller coaster. Thirty-five million people visited there last year.[3]

We shop when we're bored. We shop when we're lonely. We shop when there isn't anything else to do. We shop when there isn't anything else we need. We shop when there isn't any more money to spend. Impulsively, compulsively, we shop.

You've seen the T-shirts and the bumper stickers.

Born to shop.
Veni, Vidi, Visa; I came, I saw, I did a little shopping.
Shop till you drop.
I want it all.

But all of this is so familiar to us, so *normal,* that we seem to have lost sight of how very strange it is. It is taken completely for granted.

Short Road to the Mall

But it hasn't always been this way. Five factors over the last two hundred years have brought us to the place we are now. It is helpful to see how we've gotten to this point, because the road from the open-air market on the village green to the mall in every town tells us a lot about the thinking of the people we are trying to reach.

Free Market Economy

When the United States began in the 1700s, government of and by and for the people was a new idea. Seeing how well that worked, some people wanted to take the idea further. If a nation's political system could be of and by the people, what about its economy? Why not, thought economic philosophers like Adam Smith, let people buy and sell as they saw fit? Enter capitalism and the idea of the free market.

But today's consumer culture is tied to something more than the mere invitation to buy and sell freely. Underlying and built right into the idea of a free market economy is another root conviction, an evil twin: the virtue of selfishness. The idea is that it is beneficial to spend, to accumulate, to buy primarily with thought of one's own needs. In fact, Smith's "invisible hand" theory about the economy depends on individuals pursuing their selfish desires.[4]

For the first American century, selfishness didn't pose much of a problem. Greed was held in check by an even stronger value: the biblical admonition to give more thought to one's neighbor than to oneself. But over time the urge to spend and indulge was freed from that constraint, and the way was thrown open to consumerism-run-amok. Like kudzu, the ornamental vine that was brought into the South to fight erosion and eventually overran more than two million acres of land, unchecked selfishness has spawned in our society a gnarly, destructive, uncontrollable mess.[5]

The road to the mall begins with a bulldozer called the virtue of selfishness.

The Industrial Revolution

Steam, light bulbs, and rails turned our world upside down a century ago.[6] Until the mid-1800s, everything was handmade. Cloth was woven, lumber was hewn, horseshoes were forged, and beds and chairs were crafted—all by hand. But then the steam engine was refined and put to use, and it was suddenly possible to mass-produce a lot of what was once the work of busy hands. First cloth, then all manner of goods began to be cranked out by steam-driven factories. Manufacturing plants began to pop up wherever rivers and rail lines converged. And people popped up as well, moving from the country into cities to find steady income.

Then, in 1880, Thomas Edison linked the steam engine to a power plant, making electricity available for entire cities. When that electrical power was coupled to the assembly line, even more could be made in even less time for even less money. The tedious process of one person manufacturing one item was broken into a series of steps, each performed by a different person on a long production line. Within a year of introducing the assembly line, Ford Motor Company was able to cut the time it took to put together the chassis of a car from twelve and a half hours to ninety-three minutes.

Around the same time, a national railway network was completed and the manufacturing industry hit full stride. Access to markets was no longer limited by the poky stride of a donkey or the meandering course of a river. Products could go from point A to point B, regardless of how distant point B happened to be.

Nothing stood between the maker and the buyer. The supply of consumer goods that appeared in stores and markets—long a slow and steady trickle—turned into a river and then a flood of things to buy and own and enjoy. With that flood came something new to the American people: choice. No longer would a customer go to the dry goods store and find only one brand of hair brush or disc plow or wool coat. Now there were options, different prices and different styles.

The ground leveled by selfishness, the road to the mall was then paved with this simple idea of choice and the primacy of personal preference.

Rise of the Consumer Market

How did all these busy manufacturers get this mass of new products within reach of the hands (and wallets) of the American public?

Marketing.

Before the Civil War, marketing—catering to customers to get them to buy a product—was virtually nonexistent, limited to occasional notices of farm sales in the back of town newspapers. When Sears, Roebuck, and Company began mailing its catalog to America at the end of the 1800s, it changed the business of buying and selling. Americans began to refer to the Sears, Roebuck catalog as their second Bible—not an insignificant metaphor. Today every home in America receives ninety-one catalogs every year. That amounts to twelve billion catalogs a year in our country alone.[7]

At the same time there came a new kind of store: the department store. Small street-corner dry goods and specialty shops quickly were overshadowed by these swank and snazzy downtown stores. Merchandise wasn't stuffed into crowded shelves along narrow aisles but elaborately spread out for the customer to see and touch and try on and take home. Marshall Fields, Macy's, and the others spawned a new style of shopping—browsing, the leisurely and unhurried wandering of the person who is "just looking, thank you."

In quick succession the child and then the grandchild of the department store arrived: the shopping center in 1916, and then, in 1956, the mall. Today the United States has thirty-seven thousand malls[8] in which Americans spend a billion and a half dollars every day.[9] Each foot of these buildings is dedicated to one thing: enticing the customer to buy. Spacious marble walkways, artificial trees always in bloom, upbeat music, and the smell of Mrs. Field's cookies greet us as we stroll in. Benches and walkways are strategically placed to keep our eyes on the merchandise at all times. Wide entrances open into well-lit, inviting stores with color-coordinated displays meticulously planned down to the smallest of details. Windows are carefully "lifestyled,"[10] filled not only with products but with antiques, outdoor equipment, or other objects that have positive associations for the customers the store is trying to reach. "Guests" (not customers) are warmly greeted, offered assistance, and invited to take their time as they meander along the strategically indirect paths through the store. Returns and exchanges are always welcomed; after all, the customer is always right.

And to make sure that a little detail like being short on cash doesn't get in the way of anyone's shopping, consumer credit is offered. "Buy now, pay later. No money down. Put it on plastic." Charge accounts, installment buying plans, small loans, and credit cards—the first of which was the Diner's Club in 1957[11]—mean that acquiring can push way ahead of savings and common sense. Today forty-three million credit card purchases are made every day in the United States.[12]

The Power of "New and Improved"

What if people are buying—even buying a lot—but manufacturers keep making more and more? Why, don't wait till the old product falls apart and can't be used anymore. Find a way to get the customer to buy a new one in place of the perfectly good one he bought last year. Roll out the new and improved product.

Have you noticed how few of the clothes you buy end up in the trash? Old clothes don't die, they just go to Goodwill Industries, the land of last year's fashion statements. What is style and fashion but the decision of a few designers who are trying to sell new clothes?

New and improved means yet more choice. Economical family-size, handy economy-size, convenient pocket-size, bite-size, low sodium, lite, fat-free, sugar-free, dye-free, additive-free, recycled packaging, environmentally friendly—you can get it however you want it. The other day while I was waiting for a prescription to be filled at our grocery store, I decided to count the number of choices in the salad dressing section. There were 123. And when you combine so many choices with all the sales techniques used by stores—free samples, coupons, discounts, eye-level facings, floor stacks, on-shelf promotional pieces, end-aisles displays, even on-cart ads—it gets tough to resist the urge to buy.

Consumer culture is anything but a casual encounter. The customer is pursued, bombarded, wooed, entertained, and catered to in every way. And that is particularly the case because of one final feature—advertising.

Make Way for Advertising

Every day in the United States, businesses shell out $200 million on advertising, almost one dollar for every person in the country.[13] People who study such things tell us that we are exposed to 1,600 advertising messages a day.[14] One out of every six minutes of television air time is advertising.[15] America's "consumers in training," our children, see 20,000 TV commercials a year.[16] Over the course of an average lifetime we will spend two years watching commercials.[17]

Advertising is one of the most carefully researched, tightly choreographed, and heavily supported ventures in the country. Every ad is designed to "cut through the clutter" for the maximum effect.[18] To make sure they stand out, print ads use scratch and sniff, fold-outs, tear-outs, free samples, and toll-free telephone numbers. Direct-mail advertising goes to great lengths to get the reader to open the mailing, making envelopes appear to hold official government correspondence, checks, or even a handwritten letter from a friend. And television commercials are run past consumer behavior experts, run through time compressors, and then run again and again under the noses of potential customers—just to make sure they stand out from the other twenty to thirty ads shown every hour. Minute for minute, TV commercials are as costly and carefully crafted as major motion pictures. In 1988 the average cost for developing a thirty-second commercial was over $200,000, about what it cost to produce ninety minutes of prime-time television programming.[19]

Advertisements before the turn of the century merely called attention to a product, highlighting its sellable features. Then, in the early part of this century, a shift began to take place. The customer (and his dandruff or body odor or ring around the collar) became the main focus, and the goal of the ad changed from information to persuasion. We find ourselves today on the other side of yet another shift in advertising. Now the focus is on an image, and what began as information and evolved into persuasion has slid into sheer emotional manipulation.

Today, image rules; a visual, nonrational approach dominates everything. With few exceptions, ads portray nothing more than an image, a feel, an emotional sound bite, an implied promise of what life could be. We see ads in which the product is never shown or even mentioned. A brand name simply appears at the end of a thirty-second minimovie that just happens to be filled with the kind of people we want to be like (and be liked by) and with the kinds of experiences we want to enjoy.

People don't buy products anymore. They buy the promise of friends and sex and fun and wealth and youthful beauty and sophistication and physical vitality that seeps through the ad. "Today advertising *is* the product," writes advertising expert Eric Clark, author of *The Want Makers*. "What people are buying, whether it's drink, jeans, medicine, or electronic gadgets, is the perception of the product they have absorbed from advertising."[20]

Advertising aggressively plays on the discontent and futility of the American public. Bored and world-weary men and women are romanced with a picture of a better life. Then they are told that it can be bought at the corner store. "Consumption," as Christopher Lasch has said, "promises to fill the aching void."[21] But it never can.

So here are two final features of our consumer heritage. First, Americans are bombarded by more and more competing messages, only a few to which they can really give any attention. We are wooed, hounded, and ultimately buried with words. We don't want to hear any more.

Second, the shower of advertising we soak in teaches us that we are what we own and that we can be what we buy. Mere things are invested with meaning and hope out of all proportion to their real value.

The Consumer Mindset

The consumer culture shapes so much more than the way we spend our money. Consumer attitudes have crept into virtually every aspect of life, influencing the way we live, relate, and spend our time. Think about the language we use.

- You say your ferret ate your homework? Sorry, but I don't buy it.
- Oh, this realtor is great. I'm really sold on her.
- Andy asked you to go with him to the game? Such a deal!
- I spent four hours with him yesterday. I couldn't afford to do that!

We no longer shop only for blow-dryers, bomber jackets, and bobby pins; now we shop for doctors, a new look, a good school district, a new marriage partner.

Here are some of the guiding principles in a consumer society.

- *Mix and match.* We don't feel bound to stay with one brand, or even one store. We'll buy a skirt at the department store, accessories at a mall kiosk that specializes in African jewelry, shoes across town at the outlet store, and a blouse through the mail from L. L. Bean. We'll pick and choose until we find the combination that suits us best. We readily carry that same mentality over into the realm of religion; there's nothing the least bit odd about blending a Christian view of God with a New Age view of the earth and a dab of Tai Chi and Zen meditation on the side.

- *Hunt for the bargain.* We don't want to pay a cent more than necessary, so we skimp, snoop, scrape, and bargain, all in an effort to give as little as we can to get as much as possible. What that often means is that the people we talk with are eager to consider the benefits of Christianity but reluctant to talk about the cost.

- *Comparison shopping.* We'll go in one store and check out its prices and service, then walk down the street to see if we can get a better deal. We have no allegiance to any store. We are inveterate comparison shoppers. That, too, carries over into consideration of religious issues. People expect us to know about various religious options, and they want to know about them too. What, exactly, makes Christianity different from the other choices? And why should I choose Christianity?

- *Does it fit me?* We don't have patience for the one-size-fits-all approach. We want—expect, even—what we buy to be just the right fit for us, whether it be a coat, a car, or a cat. Most people think about religion in the same way, not in terms of seeking what is true but of "finding a right fit," landing on something that is "me." It's about meeting my needs, not about submitting myself to God's call. That makes for some real challenges when talking about a faith in which the Master says to the MasterCard generation, "Following me starts with dying to yourself."

- *Return policy.* If it doesn't fit or if it doesn't work or if we simply get tired of it after a while, we take it back. I want what I want, and I expect to get what I pay for, and if it isn't exactly what I wanted, I'll return it. That means we'll be impatient with surprises, just as much in a search for religion as in the purchase of a CD player. Don't make the faith out to be easy and then let me find out later that it ain't so.

Paying the Price

Consumerism affects the way we think. But even more deeply, it shapes the way we live. Our attitudes reveal the way a marketing mentality influences us at the foundational level of who we are.

- *Life, liberty, and the purchase of happiness.* Aggressive marketing targets each of us with a hedonistic approach to life. Consumerism breeds selfishness. Our efforts and energy and resources are best directed toward things that give us pleasure, make us happy—or so says the message that our consumer culture continually reinforces. Giving and sharing are out of the question. Advertisers plant and feed the notion that the best person to spend my money on is myself.

  Remember Verruca Salt in *Charlie and the Chocolate Factory,* the snooty, whiny, demanding little girl who insisted on having it all? Discontented with the many fine things she owned, she constantly grabbed for more. Some of us aren't much different. Madison Avenue has spawned a population of me-first Verruca clones.

- *You are what you wear.* Another attitude flourishing in a world of things is that appearances matter most. The kind of car I drive gives me substance; the shoes I wear show I'm a quality person; the label on my jeans says I'm on top of things; the sunglasses I sport prove I have class. Externals matter in our culture; what's on the inside doesn't.

  I remember standing in a checkout line in a grocery store when my wife, Sharon (who is, by the way, a very attractive woman), picked up a glamour magazine and looked at the model on the cover. I grabbed the magazine, put it back on the shelf, and said, "Don't look at that— you'll only get discouraged." Sharon gave me a look of something between hurt and shock. "What?" Then the cashier reared up from checking our purchases, looked at me in disbelief, and said, "Did you just say what I think you just said?"

  Oops. What I meant to say was that magazines foster an unhelpful emphasis on externals, holding out as the norm for beauty an impossible standard of huge eyes, high cheek bones, long lashes, full-bodied hair, sleek curves, tanned skin, and ridiculously thin bodies. Any woman could look at one of those cover shots and be left feeling less than attractive.

- *The Roadrunner syndrome.* Advertising and the consumer culture it supports also communicate the idea that boredom, anguish, grief, emptiness, and anxiety can all be relieved by whipping out a Visa Gold. My worth as a person, my sense of well-being, my meaning in life, my personal health, my personality all can be bought. But it isn't so. Wile E. Coyote comes to mind, that obsessive critter who is forever sending away for some new device from Acme to help him catch the Road-runner. But the coyote never manages to snag his nemesis. Instead, he ends up again and again in a cloud of dust on the canyon floor, his tail scorched from his Acme Pursuit Rocket Thruster.

We end up in a similar place, victims of what Paul Wachtel in *The Poverty of Affluence* calls the "fallacy of individual commodity."[22] That is the idea that this new thing I'm about to buy—*this* thing as opposed to the mounds of other things I've hopefully bought and dejectedly discarded—will be the answer to all that is missing in my life. But Saks Fifth Avenue is as incomplete a supplier as Acme. Like the coyote, we'll keep on chasing but always manage to come up empty-handed and a bit burned.

American consumers are being pushed more and more to look to things for what things can never deliver. But they are catching on to the fact that these things don't seem to come through, and they are beginning to won-der if there might be somewhere else to look.

God's **Word**
to a Discontented World

hat does it mean for us as biblical communicators that the men and women we seek to reach are shoppers to the core, people who want to know the options, understand the benefits, and have the freedom of choice?

Consumers or Seekers?

At first glance, "marketing the faith" seems to be a valid approach in a consumer culture. It is true that Christianity involves a choice. Regardless of how one views the biblical idea of election, God does not impose a response on us. Even as he chooses us and draws us to himself, he does not take away the full involvement of our minds, emotions, and wills. Rather, God gives us the freedom and responsibility of choosing him.

It also is true that Christianity brings us benefits. Christianity delivers. It meets our needs. It is, in a sense, a good deal.

People we talk with are also well aware that there are religious options out there. They have been exposed to—and possibly drawn to—the single-mindedness of Islam, the simplicity of Zen, the respect for creation found in traditional Buddhism, and the friendliness and family orientation of Mormonism. It is only natural that they would want to see how the options compare.

So from one perspective it would seem that seekers are consumers shopping for a fulfilling religion and that we should meet them on those terms. But should we? Are people really shoppers when they enter into the area of making religious or spiritual decisions? And do we want to foster that way of thinking? The seeker's choice is not between competing brands of religions but between submitting to God or denying him, between taking God at his word or rejecting him.

We should invite questions about comparative religions and take them seriously, ready to answer them. But we fail if we leave the seeker thinking the decision comes down to opting for a personal favorite. We're talking about choosing between a way that is God's way and another that isn't, not about weighing a good fit versus a better one.

Although benefits result from following Christ—tangible ways in which our heart's deepest longing is answered—we need to discourage our listeners from thinking that the decision to follow Christ comes down to having our needs met. That is only a fraction of what Christianity means. A decision to follow Christ is about God first, about his intentions more than our needs.

Christianity is not something we can pick up after a little browsing, wear for a thirty-day trial period, and then, dissatisfied, drop off slightly used at Goodwill. A Christian life is God's intention for us, and we should talk about it that way.

For us to "sell" Christianity is to make it something far different and far less than it is. It is not an option; it is a claim. It is not a way to have needs met; it is a way of life. When we market the faith by reducing its claims to a set of comforting and nonthreatening benefits that make it easy to come to Christ, we strip it of its substance and warp its intentions. It becomes nothing more than a cut-rate item on the self-help shelf.

The Customer May Not Be Right

When we present the Christian message—this impossible tale of a king who laid down his life for us, then called us to lay down our lives for him—we shouldn't present it as one brand of religious myth alongside many. It is truth. It is not a religious option, a matter of personal preference, a great blue-light special. It is the only door that God has opened for humankind to live in the way he intended, in right relationship with him.

God calls everyone to approach him not as consumers but as creatures standing before their Creator. As broken, messed-up sinners in need of a gracious restorer. As people on whom he already has a prior claim.

And that is the rub with a consumer mentality, the heart of the tension. A consumer stands over, with the freedom to pick and choose, mix and match, return or exchange at will. But a follower of Christ stands under, having relinquished the freedom to pick and choose. He or she is submitted, committed, under the sway of another. The disciple is no longer a buyer but a person bought at a price. Products don't call their buyers to obedience; Jesus does. Shoppers don't submit to their purchases in any sense of the word; followers of Christ are nothing if not submitted.

So here's the challenge of gaining a hearing in a world defined by buying and selling: We can and should be sensitive to the consumer mindset people bring with them as they look over the claims and promises of Christianity. But we dare not leave the autonomy of the consumer intact. We have to make sure people know that to choose Christ is to relinquish the very thing they are probably most eager to retain: their control.

Counting the Cost

In this land of shoppers, two parables of Jesus bear repeating. The first is the simple word picture Jesus tells in Matthew 13:45–46. "The kingdom of God is like a merchant looking for fine pearls. When he found one of great value, he went away and sold everything he had and bought it."

Jesus is the fulfillment of our every longing. That nagging discontentment that propels us to the mall on a rainy day, the unsettled itchiness for *something*—he is the answer for it. And he is ours to have.

But there is a cost. Commitment to Christ is an expensive proposition. It costs us everything we have. Not just relinquishing the savings accounts and turning over the title to the car but giving up, signing over, trading in ourselves.

Here is one way we might introduce this parable into a conversation or message. "Have you ever noticed there's a pattern when we buy something? A new CD, a new pair of hiking boots, a new car—it doesn't matter. It always happens. When we first get whatever it is, there's an energy we have, an excitement. It wakes us up, makes us alive.

"But then, after a while—usually a pretty short while—there's a kind of a sleepy dissatisfaction that comes over us. This new thing doesn't feel new anymore, and it doesn't bring that energy anymore. It becomes familiar, normal, ordinary, and soon it blends in with everything else we own. Now we're restless for something else.

"Have you ever stopped to think about what's going on here? There's something in us that yearns for something outside of us that will settle our hearts, that will give us peace, satisfaction, fulfillment. Back in the 1600s a thinker named Blaise Pascal wrote something I think really explains what's going on here. He said, 'There is a God-shaped vacuum in every heart that only God can fill.'

"Have you noticed that when a salesperson asks if we need help, we often say, 'No thanks. Just looking.' Looking? For what? Obviously, if my light bulb burns out and I run down to the store to get a new one, I'm just looking for a new light bulb. But what about when we go to the mall just because we're out of sorts or restless? What are we looking for then? Wouldn't it be fair to say that whenever a man goes into a clothing store to browse, or a woman goes to the pro shop just to poke around, or a kid runs into a music store on the way home from school, that person is looking for the peace and purpose and settledness that only God can bring to us? I think that is what Pascal was getting at.

"And that fits with something really interesting Jesus said once. He said that what he offers to people is like a really expensive pearl. And when people see it, and see how special it is, they run off and sell everything they have to buy it. Because that's what a new and right relationship with God is worth—everything.

"Jesus says, 'I'm what your heart is longing for, but the cost is everything you have. Give yourself to me. Set aside all those other things you go dashing after and put me first.' When we do that, we will suddenly find we have everything we've been looking for."

Another Scripture of great importance to a generation of mall rats is the parable of the rich fool in Luke 12:16–21. Jesus tells the story of a wealthy man getting wealthier. Suddenly his life ends, his wealth and possessions slip through his fingers, and he stands before the one who owns *him*. "Not a very wise way to spend your time, was it now?" God asks the man. "You should have been investing your life in things that matter, not merely spending it on things that don't." To God, this world's way, the way of accumulation and self-interest and having it your way, is not the way to make much of yourself but to make little of yourself. Jesus' introduction to the parable sums up its between-the-eyes point. "A man's life does not consist in the abundance of his possessions" (Luke 12:15). We are lost, not found, in our sea of purchases.

Breaking Through the Clutter

Here are some other practical ways we might think about speaking sensitively to people who think like shoppers without catering to their marketing mindset.

How We Preach and Teach

Be practical. Our listeners are accustomed to the idea of take-away value. That is, if they invest their time or energy or money, they expect to have something to show for it. That is a listener's fair expectation of a speaker, and one we should honor. Beginning a message in a way that makes a clear connection with the concerns and experiences of our audience, showing over the course of the message how it relates to various types of people who are present, and ending with practical, specific applications are three ways to give a sense of take-away value to our listeners.

This doesn't mean, of course, that we should preach or teach only "how-tos." Some of our most important work is simply to help people think clearly and rightly about something. But we can still be sensitive, even as we go about teaching and preaching the whole counsel of God, to the desire of our listeners to come away with something that will benefit them not only for eternity but also at 3:30 next Tuesday afternoon.

Be personal. People are tired of phone calls asking for "the man of the house." Anything that has the ring of a canned spiel is suspect. Personal delivery with lots of eye contact and warmth, along with honest illustrations that let your hearers into your world and show that you are familiar with theirs, will go a long way to ensure that your message doesn't come across like one more impersonal sales pitch.

It is true that Paul calls those in positions of church leadership to be "above reproach" (1 Tim. 3:2). But he does not call us to be "beyond approach." Honest sharing from the podium is important, giving room in our struggles and failure for God's power to find expression (2 Cor. 12:9–10). In a message on forgiving those who hurt us, I developed the idea that it is especially difficult to forgive someone a second or third time. It feels so personal, and you cannot help but feel missed, disrespected, and deeply disappointed with the other person. "I know," I then said. "There are some places in my relationship with Sharon where I repeatedly miss her heart and cause her hurt—even as recently as last night. And every time I blow it in the same area, it adds to her pain and makes it harder and harder for her to move past the hurt." Candor about our shortcomings can easily spill over into a sort of spiritual self-exposure, compromising our credibility and undermining our message. Rightly done, however, it adds to our integrity and trustworthiness as communicators.

Be fresh. When you prepare to speak, be sensitive to the fact that your message is just one more among thousands that compete for your hearer's attention. Without resorting to slickness or showmanship, how can you cut through the clutter? Delivering your message in an engaging conversational style, using creative introductions and unpredictable illustrations, and occasionally including slides, music, or a video clip can all help. Retelling the biblical story, especially through the eyes of an onlooker who has a unique vantage point, reenacting a conversation or event, or even interviewing one of the people involved in the story are other approaches that will help your message penetrate and stick.

One Sunday I was preaching the prologue to John's Gospel and felt a need for a fresh approach, one that would allow us to hear in a new way the audacious claims John makes about Jesus in his first eighteen verses. It seemed to me that John's aim was to explain why Jesus was no ordinary man and to answer the question, How on earth do we account for someone who said and did the things that Jesus said and did?

What better way than to contrast it with a "normal" biography? So I wrote a story about John submitting his manuscript to a New York publisher. The editor launches into a critique of John's unacceptable opening and compares it with the opening lines of several recent biographies. "See? Biographies don't start with this sort of Shirley MacLaine metaphysical nonsense; they start with parents, hometown, date of birth, that sort of thing." And the point was made.

Foster identification. An elder in our church stood up one Sunday morning and explained that Jesus had been confronting his materialism and challenging him to answer the question, How much is enough? That brief account has remained in the minds of the congregation far longer than anything else that was said that morning.

Hearing someone else's story is one of the best ways to visualize how *our* lives might be changed. Never is this more true than when people describe the way Christ has bid them to redirect their priorities away from money and possessions to the things that really matter. Regularly ask church members to stand before your congregation and describe the difference Jesus has made in their lives.

Offer options. Customers like options. Offering two or three adult classes that appeal to different age groups or interests or meet at different times may generate a real show of interest. The only caution is to do this without reinforcing the idea that the customer is in charge. Providing a few options is great. But an extensive, Mall-of-Americas-like bunch of offerings that compete for "customers," cater to the whims of the audience, and further the idea that Christianity is about me getting what I want, while it may be a fine way to get numbers, is not a good way to develop disciples.

63

How We Share Faith

Expose existing priorities. One of the most helpful approaches to sharing faith is to cause people to see the inadequacy of their way of life or worldview. If Madison Avenue is to be believed, our happiness and identity can both stem from our possessions. Christians can draw people to the faith by helping them see that it is simply not possible to buy one's way to happiness. Neither is it possible to construct a new sense of self out of the things we own. In honest moments, most people will own up to the fact that they are really not any happier, more attractive, more popular, or more content now A.D. (after disposal) than they were B.C. (before consumption).

Regardless of how many things people manage to accumulate, they still feel confused about themselves, alienated from others, and distant from God. That is the human condition apart from Christ, and recognition of that opens doors to share him. (I develop this idea more fully in the appendix, where you'll find an approach to sharing faith that is built around seven characteristics of the person who is outside a relationship with Christ: alienation from others, bad life experiences, confusion between intention and action, absence of direction, lack of esteem, uncertainty about the future, and a sense that God is absent.)

Encourage the weighing of benefits. Another approach to faith sharing is Pascal's wager.[1] Pascal says that in this life there is neither absolute proof that there is a God nor any way of proving that there is no God. Many clues suggest that the Christian view is true, while other things suggest that it might not be. So, Pascal says, which option will you buy? A cost and a package of benefits come with either option. The person who pursues the faith endures the rather substantial cost of right living for God but has the infinite benefit of eternity in God's presence if he is right. The atheist, on the other hand, gains the benefit of freedom to live as he desires and faces very little cost—unless Christianity happens to be true, in which case the cost is great. So, asks Pascal, how will you wager? The smart bet, he says, is to put your money on God.

Provide informed comparison. Taking the time to sit down and talk through the beliefs of different religions can also be a helpful way to share why Christianity is the best explanation of life and the best hope for the seeker. We should invite comparison of Christianity with other religions, provided we're well versed in the similarities and differences between the faiths, and are able to give some account for the options. Are they really all roads to the same mountaintop? If not, why not? How do we explain why there are so many choices if only one is true? And which one seems to square most with reality and with my heart's longings?

I sat down for lunch with a friend from India in a restaurant where butcher paper is used for tablecloths and each table has a bucket of crayons. We got to talking about questions of religion, and soon I was contrasting Christian and Hindu views of the person, time, and the goal of human life. As we talked I drew. By the time we got up to leave a couple of hours later, I had used almost the whole tabletop to sketch out the differences between the two faiths. My friend started scooting plates to the side of the table and pulling out the piece of paper. "Do you mind if I take it with me?" he asked.

What We Communicate

Christianity thrusts us into an alternative perspective. Every facet of life, every way of thinking and doing business, is viewed differently through the lens of Scripture. Here are some of the areas in which Scripture stands at odds with the consumer mentality, terrain that will be helpful for us to go over again and again with our hearers.

Character. God doesn't care one whit for the thing consumers often care about the most: the externals of appearance. "The LORD does not look at the things man looks at. Man looks at the outward appearance, but the LORD looks at the heart" (1 Sam. 16:7). What brand of jeans we wear or whether we have Maybelline lashes—who cares? What matters to the Lord is the substance of who we are, the content of our character. Beauty, Peter reminds us, comes from the inside (1 Peter 3:4).

Esteem. In God's jurisdiction, esteem and identity are not bought but imbued. We are twice loved and twice owned. God made us, and then bought us at a price. It is from those events, creation and redemption, that a sense of our enormous value and distinctiveness as Christians is derived. In Christ, our fallen nature is restored and our fragile identity is reestablished. We are declared "God's chosen people, holy and dearly loved" (Col. 3:12).

Needs. God promises to meet our physical and financial needs. Paul tells us that God "richly provides us with everything for our enjoyment" (1 Tim. 6:17). Having said that, it would be wrong to conclude that God's desire for us is physical or financial prosperity. The health-and-wealth gospel—the idea that faith should result in more and more money and less and less sickness—is wrong and flies in the face of everything the Bible teaches. The call to follow Christ is an invitation to submission, obedience, service, suffering, and glorifying God, not to a fat wallet and an easy life. God's concern is to make us rich in the things that matter to him: trust, humility, integrity, thoughtfulness. Paul warns those who are well off not to put their hope in wealth. Instead, he tells Timothy to direct them "to do good, to be rich in good deeds and to be generous and willing to share" (1 Tim. 6:17–18). Enjoyment of what we have takes on a whole new meaning in God's economy. Money is a community asset, not a purely personal one.

Money. We tend to think of our paychecks as the reward for our hard work, money that we are then free to spend as we see fit. According to the Bible, our money is not ours. It is God's, and we are his stewards, his managers, of that which he has entrusted to us. Our responsibility is to faithfully use, invest, share, and give money as he directs us, consistent with his purposes. As the parable of the talents reminds us in Matthew 25:14–30, everything we have is his.

Concern for others. The Christian view of money spills out of the Christian view of people. The free market is grounded on the idea of selfishness, greed, thinking first of self. God calls us to "otherishness," benevolence, thinking first of others and their needs. "In humility consider others better than yourselves," writes Paul. "Each of you should look not only to your own interests, but also to the interests of others" (Phil. 2:3–4). The Christian call is into a caring community, not out into a solo orbit. As Jesus says, "It is more blessed to give than to receive" (Acts 20:35).

Service. From God's vantage point, people are not things to be had but individuals created in his image for us to respect and honor. To view friends or marriage partners as existing to meet our needs lowers them to the level of a commodity to be used or discarded. A biblical perspective calls us to serve those God has placed in our midst and to honor our marriage vows. Paul's letters brim with this idea. It is particularly evident in Ephesians 5:21, where he heads up an entire section on relationships with the admonition to "submit to one another out of reverence for Christ." People are not products for consumption.

Joy. We tend to see happiness and joy as one and the same, but they are not, in God's view. Happiness is a fleeting moment of ease when circumstances, feelings, and good fortune all manage to line up. But it can never be tamed or predicted. It comes, then—*zip*—it's gone. Joy, on the other hand, remains through all manner of bumpy and painful circumstances. It is a settled confidence in the goodness of God that is not tied to how we feel, how things are going, or how much we have. Happiness is tied to things, joy to a person. "The LORD has done great things for us," writes the psalmist, "and we are filled with joy" (Ps. 126:3).

66

Freedom. An important distinction should be made between freedom and accumulation. Freedom comes not in an endless chase to obtain more but in a contentment with what one has. The Bible's invitation to step out of the press of upward mobility and accumulation into a life of simplicity is an invitation to step out of a trap into freedom. The writer of Proverbs advocates the freedom of moderation and simplicity. "Give me neither poverty nor riches, but give me only my daily bread. Otherwise, I may have too much and disown you and say, 'Who is the LORD?' Or I may become poor and steal, and so dishonor the name of my God" (Prov. 30:8–9).

Right focus. The Bible challenges the idea of accumulation. Things often stand in the way of single-minded devotion to the Lord. They threaten to upend our readiness to look first to him when we feel need, face insecurity, struggle through pain, or lose our way. Because of that, Jesus often warned about the danger of relying on things and more than once told people that their accumulations prevented them from faithfully following him. "No one can serve two masters," he said. "You cannot serve both God and Money" (Matt. 6:24).

Contentment. Finally, according to the Bible, contentment does not come from what we have, and discontentment is not the automatic result of failing to get what we want. Rather, contentment—that confident quietness of the spirit in the face of what life brings upon us—comes from being rightly related to God. "I have learned the secret of being content in any and every situation," writes Paul, "whether well fed or hungry, whether living in plenty or in want. I can do everything through him who gives me strength" (Phil. 4:12–13).

About Chapters 3 and 4

Concepts Worth Remembering

free market economy: Adam Smith's innovative approach to a country's economy, based on the idea of unrestricted buying and selling and built on the virtue of self-interest

Industrial Revolution: the sudden growth of factory production resulting from the harnessing of steam power at the end of the 1800s

marketing: getting one's product within reach of a potential customer and catering to customers' needs and feelings in an effort to induce customers to buy the product

consumer society: a society in which the central position of the mall, of shopping, and of advertising is taken for granted

consumer mindset: a way of thinking that becomes natural in a consumer society that asks questions like, Does it fit? Is it in style? Will it meet my needs? Is it a good deal? Is it me?

Recommended Reading

Clark, Eric. *The Want Makers.* New York: Penguin, 1988. A thorough study of the advertising industry, covering everything from the initial concepts through production and market testing all the way to the completed ad campaign.

Kavanaugh, John F. *Following Christ in a Consumer Culture.* Maryknoll, N.Y.: Orbis, 1991. Presents a Catholic Christian philosophical perspective on consumerism, exposing what Kavanaugh calls the commodity gospel as being at odds in numerous ways with a Christian worldview. Thought provoking.

Lux, Kenneth. *Adam Smith's Mistake: How a Moral Philosopher Invented Economics and Ended Morality.* Boston: Shambhala, 1990. Exploring capitalism's underlying premise of selfishness, Lux considers what would happen to society if we were to elevate benevolence as a value alongside self-interest.

Schmookler, Andrew. *Fool's Gold: The Fate of Values in a World of Goods.* San Francisco: HarperCollins, 1993. A spirited and personal reflection about the way an economic view of life has crept into and devalued other parts of life.

Shames, Laurence. *The Hunger for More: Searching for Values in an Age of Greed.* New York: Vintage, 1991. An easy to read series of reflections on the scramble for accumulation and the shopping lifestyle that seemed to take over in the '80s.

Part 3

WHO **WE ARE**

Spectators

We find rest is unbearable because of the boredom it generates. We have to get away from it all, and so we go around begging for new excitement. We can't imagine a condition that is pleasant without fun and noise. We assume every condition is agreeable in which we enjoy some sort of distraction. But think what kind of happiness it is that consists merely in being diverted from thinking about ourselves!

Blaise Pascal, 1656

Television: chewing gum for the eyes.

Frank Lloyd Wright

5

Bringing the Spectator into Focus

One morning I looked out in our front yard and saw my kids had rustled up a huge box from somewhere in the neighborhood. They were climbing in and out of it, flipping it over, hiding inside it, turning it this way and that. Some sort of appliance had once occupied it, but now it had been liberated from its boring job of housing a mechanical contraption and set free to be whatever the kids wanted it to be.

I thought of the many hours I'd spent playing in boxes like that, cutting them up, painting them, and turning them into pirate vessels, spaceships, time machines, forts, playhouses . . . even a steel cabinet bound with locks and chains from which Houdini Henderson would—to the amazement of all—inevitably make his escape.

I grinned while watching the kids, three of them now in the box. I turned to Sharon to ask if she knew what they were playing. She anticipated my question and, with a rather stony face, said, "They're playing Nintendo with the box." Nintendo! We don't even have Nintendo! Ours is a home where the kids didn't even know the TV had channels till they were four or five! What do you mean they're playing Nintendo?

Entertainment has oozed its way into every inch of our lives. Even into our front yards.

In a world of couch potatoes, spuds glued to the tube, how do we break through with biblical truth? Christians who want to communicate to this world run headlong into a formidable obstacle. The challenge of the world of entertainment is just the opposite of the world of the consumer. Where consumerism is troublesome because of the way it makes us think, entertainment is challenging in the way it *keeps* us from thinking.

Which Way Is Up?

For centuries civilization took its bearings from the Bible, which provided a spiritual perspective on the rest of life. That outlook gave a sense of where humankind was, as well as of what waited over the next rise.

Then as the scientific worldview began to emerge in Europe four hundred years ago, the perspective shifted. People saw themselves living not in a spiritual world but in a purely physical one, a world of matter, of things, and that view was the compass to which life was oriented.

Today we take our bearings from yet another source. Not from the Bible nor from the physical world but from luminescent boxes perched in the corners of our family rooms. Television, radio, and other media have become our source of perspective, providing a safe and convenient window onto our jumbled world. They decide for us who is important, what to think about, even how to dress each day. We orient ourselves to the world through what we see and experience on the tube. Two-thirds of Americans tell researchers that they get "most of their information" about the world from television.[1]

The trouble is that the channels of entertainment—and television is the chief culprit—disorient more than they orient. Promising to make sense of the world for us, they merely multiply the collage of disconnected images and sounds and experiences that come at us.

Don DeLillo's novel *White Noise* is a superb, warped study of contemporary culture, its shallow consumerism and its preoccupation with the media in particular. DeLillo relates a conversation between Prof. Jack Gladney and his fourteen-year-old son, Heinrich, as they drive to school one morning.[2] Heinrich breaks the silence with a comment about the weather.

"It's going to rain tonight."

"It's raining now."

"The radio said tonight."

"Look at the windshield. Is that rain or isn't it?"

"I'm only telling you what they said."

Look how pervasive our dependence on the media is. Today virtually every home in the country has a stereo and a television set, and about two-thirds of American homes have multiple stereo systems, at least two TV sets, cable television service, and a VCR.[3] New homes reflect our preoccupation with entertainment. Living rooms are disappearing, and most family rooms have become nothing more than entertainment rooms, with a multimedia entertainment center their central piece of furniture. High-end homes often come with complete built-in movie theaters and can house as many as seven televisions. Even in the average homes, $8,000 entertainment centers with six-speaker surround sound are becoming more common.[4]

The average person in the U.S. watches more than four hours of television a day. That's twenty-eight hours—more than one full day—every week plunked in front of the tube, 1,500 hours a year spent staring at the screen.[5] We spend more time watching television than doing anything else, except sleeping and working. On any given night, as much as half of the population of our country can be found in front of the television.[6]

And that's not to say anything about Nintendo, video rentals, drive-time radio, the weekend pro football game, Sea World, or any of the other sources of amusement and entertainment we enjoy. Every day, for example, two-thirds of a million people visit amusement parks,[7] three million go to the movies, and six million rent a video.[8] I've already pointed out that America's favorite place to visit is Mall of America. Know what's a close second? Walt Disney World, with twenty-nine million visitors a year.[9] What does it say that, in this nation filled with hundreds of spots of breathtaking beauty and dozens of great cities, our favorite destinations by far are a place to buy socks and a place to meet Mickey?

Making a Nation of Spuds

The entertainment industry popped up, it seems, out of thin air. Just over a hundred years ago there were no movies or movie theaters, no radios or televisions, no record players or compact discs. How did so much change come about in such a short time? Three factors ushered in the age of fun and games.

The Telegraph and the Camera

Two bits of technology pried open the door that would be knocked off its hinges later by the entertainment machine. These inventions—the telegraph and the camera—were pivotal in the shift from words to images that transformed our culture.[10]

Samuel F. B. Morse's telegraph first was used publicly in 1844. What made the telegraph so significant was its unprecedented ability to carry communication across long distances (*tele* means "far"). That development, as Neil Postman points out so effectively in his excellent book *Amusing Ourselves to Death,* meant society had to deal for the first time with information that had no context, no setting.[11] And as Postman points out, there isn't much you can do with information that has no context except use it for entertainment. "The only use for information that has no genuine connection to our lives," he says, "is to amuse."[12]

The first message to run across the wires between Baltimore and Washington, D.C., suggested Morse had at least an inkling that he was opening a door to something huge and unknown and perhaps not fully positive. The message asked simply: "What hath God wrought?"

Joseph Niepce might have asked a similar question when, in 1826, he made the first photograph in a light-sensitive asphalt compound. For out of his sticky solution emerged the whole world of reproducible images and, in a few short years, a little nowhere place in Southern California called Hollywood.

The telegraph ultimately provided the means of removing information from its context. Photography did the same thing with images, uprooting them from their original surroundings and dropping them, like Dorothy's Kansas house, into strange new settings.

Today we live in a world overrun with images and short on words. We are flooded with pictures, but we have lost the script that goes with them. There is no narration, no meaningful thread that connects them, only one image after another. Our visual world is a world of what is, not of why it is, or how it is, or what it could be.

The Workplace Blues

The most important product that came out of the Industrial Revolution, from the perspective of the entertainment industry, was not the phonograph, the transistor, or even the movie projector.

It was something that proceeded from all three: boredom.[13]

The arrival of the factory meant the creation of the factory job. A steady wage in exchange for twelve-hour workdays filled with drudgery and emptiness. An impersonal, fill-in-the-blank occupation in which personality, family roots, and life experience mattered not a whit.

A new rhythm began to take over in the workplace. For centuries it had been work and relax, work and relax. Now it was boredom and escape, boredom and escape. This put new demands on America's free time. Once life was experienced all day long; now it needed to be squeezed in between shifts at work and sleep at night.[14]

It is no coincidence that America's entertainment industry blossomed in the soil of the Industrial Revolution. With the growth of industry at the turn of the century, leisure time took on an urgency for significance. The spectator society was birthed out of a desperate need for distraction.

The Entertainment Machine

As the years rolled over from the 1800s to the 1900s, America entered headlong into the era of entertainment. In rapid succession, advances in technology plunked down a number of new entertainment devices before the listless American public.[15]

First came the cinema. The first American film was called *Fred Ott's Sneeze*. It was a brief clip of one of the workers in Thomas Edison's labs sneezing into the camera, filmed in 1889 on the new Edison Kinetograph. A mere six years later, the Nickelodeon Theater, America's first public movie house, opened its doors to a brisk business in Pittsburgh. Fred Ott's sneeze, it turns out, was contagious.

The new century also began with news of Marconi sending a radio signal across the Atlantic in 1901. Within two decades, in 1920, KDKA in Pittsburgh began broadcasting music and drama programs, and the radio craze took off. Soon life in the home and even in some factories was structured around air time for radio greats like *Amos 'n' Andy, Little Orphan Annie, Buck Rogers,* and *The Shadow.*

The development of television was inevitable, marrying radio's broadcasting technology with film's ability to capture and reproduce an image. Philo Farnsworth was the twenty-one-year-old whiz kid who made the first successful test of a television in 1927.[16] Perhaps he was hinting at an answer to Morse's telegraphed question when he chose the image he would broadcast. Or maybe he was just doing some wishful thinking. Either way, it certainly showed a lot of foresight. The image was a dollar sign. Just twelve years later, NBC began its first regular broadcasts, and today the television industry makes billions of dollars each year.

Movies, radio, and television—the three essential nutrients for cultivating couch potatoes—all were in place and were full-fledged businesses before the start of World War II. The entertainment age had hit its stride.

Other technologies hit the scene within a few decades: the record player, color film, sound synchronization for movies, stereo radio, reel-to-reel tape recording, color television, televised sportscasting, cable television, videotape recording, and video games, to name just a few.

Only one thing remained to be invented for the entertainment era to enter into its own. Digital technology? No. High-resolution television? Nah. How about MTV? Satellite? Direct TV? Nope.

The perfect chair.

Something cushy, wide, comfy, reclinable, with elevated foot support and a soft but firm headrest—all fully adjustable at the flick of a lever. Enter the La-Z-Boy chair, the definitive piece of furniture for a nation of budding spectators, arriving in the 1940s.[17] As the entertainment industry hit its stride, America pulled up a seat and made itself comfortable. We plopped down and settled in, passive, alone, and wanting to be amused.

No Man's Land

Movies, radio, and television have three important features in common. First, they all provide, before anything else, ways to entertain. Their primary purpose is not to teach, to remind, to challenge, to propose, or even to record; it is to happily distract us.

The word *entertain* comes from two French words that mean "to hold between." With good reason. When we watch something, whether it be a game on TV or the newest release at Cinema Sixteen, we often find ourselves with the awkward feeling of being trapped between active engagement and complete uninvolvement. We're thinking, but we're not. We may try to wrestle with the ideas that come to us from the screen, but more often we are quickly pinned by them. We get "held between," caught in a land of mere amusement.

The second thing in common is that all three media provide essentially private things to do. True, we're twice as likely to go to the movies or watch television with someone else than to do it alone.[18] But the nature of the experience makes it essentially a solo venture. Not exactly the kind of thing that invites chatting. We may be in the same room together, breathing roughly the same bit of air, but the room is dim and all the seats are facing forward. Imagine what we would do if we were sitting watching the tube and someone piped up, "So, how was everyone's day?" "What? Are you nuts? Couldn't you find a better time to have a meaningful conversation? They're just about to kick the field goal (or announce the Academy Award winner, or give the weather, or reveal who she's having an affair with, or . . .)."

And the pace of television certainly doesn't invite idle conversation either. When's the last time you saw an actor in midmovie step toward the camera and say, "Listen, we're just gonna take a break up here for a few minutes. You know, stop the action. Take five. So why don't you guys just turn your chairs, face each other, and talk among yourselves?"

"Television!" exclaims Stu Erwin, on *The Trouble with Father*. "I'm against it in principle! People huddle around in the dark, straining their eyes while their vocal chords dry up. The very art of conversation is becoming extinct!"

75

So entertainment is neither good company nor good quiet. It holds us between company and solitude, suspending us in a peopled but oddly lonesome place.

Third, all three of these central cogs in the entertainment engine grind our minds and bodies into low gear. They push us into a passive mode. They think for us, anticipate for us, set the pace for us, make decisions for us. All we need to do is be spectators (literally "people who watch without getting involved, without taking part"). It's been shown that the only things that require less concentration than television, the only activities in which we are more passive, are resting and doing nothing.[19]

Chewing Gum for the Eyes

Most critiques of the entertainment media, particularly those from a Christian perspective, focus on the trashy content that seems to be served up regularly by Hollywood. And with good reason. An awful lot of what oozes out of L.A. is offensive, shallow, unnecessarily graphic, and pre-occupied with sex and violence.

But not all of it. From time to time some really worthwhile shows come on, and it can be a pleasant break, even for the committed follower of Christ, to flop in front of the TV for a while. We may choose *Home Improvement* or *Touched by an Angel* instead of *Married . . . with Children* or *NYPD Blue,* but we're still watching, still being impacted by the entertainment industry.

For that reason, my focus here is not on the content on the screen but on the impact of the entertainment medium itself.

Television serves as a helpful case study for all entertainment. It shares much in common with the other media, and we have more exposure to it than anything else. So although the next section talks specifically about television, the things I am saying about television's impact carry over to virtually every other kind of entertainment.

The impact of television is enormous. Here are three of the primary ways in which TV adversely affects all of us, including the people we are trying to reach with biblical truth. While I've already suggested some of these, let's dig into them a little deeper.

Television Distracts Us from Deeper Considerations

Moment by moment, television wrestles to get and keep our attention. With many tricks, obvious and subtle, the movers and shakers of television scramble to stay ahead of our declining interest and keep us tuned in. The boredom curve, as it's called in the industry, comes when our interest in what we're watching begins to drop and our curiosity about what is on other networks begins to rise. When those two factors meet—*click*—we're off to a new channel. And that, from the perspective of the TV producer, is a fate worse than technical difficulties. Channel surfers, or grazers, as they're sometimes called, are the accursed lot in television circles, and producers are willing to do most anything to keep them from punching their remote controls. When viewers stay tuned, the television station or network can present them as devoted watchers to an advertiser, who will pay huge wads of money to parade his ads in front of a loyal audience. See why our friend Philo showed so much foresight when he first showed the dollar sign? It's all tied together.

A local station manager told me about some of the tricks of the trade for keeping an audience's attention.[20] Running multiple plots is one trick, with half-hour shows having as many as three plot lines unfolding at the same time. In a sense, the show is changing the channel for you, moving you on to another show within a show before you have time to get bored. In some rip-roaring, hour-long shows, like *ER,* you can see as many as six, eight, or even ten parallel plot lines.

Even within a given plot segment, producers will jump the viewer around, changing the camera angle every couple of seconds (or even more often, in some cases) just to keep the viewer from getting fidgety. *Boom.* It's a sweeping shot of four people sprinting frantically. *Boom.* A close-up, slow motion shot of the one in front, her teeth clenched, neck muscles taut, eyes intent as she runs. *Boom.* A shot from behind, showing they are running toward a man silhouetted against an open window. *Boom.* A shot from the side, the four of them running at full tilt. *Boom.* A close-up shot of the one they are running toward. Frantic, sweating, he holds a gun against a child's forehead. *Boom. Boom. Boom.*

And with nearly every change of scene comes a dramatic change in the sound track. It is common, for instance, to leap from the quiet rustling of branches and chirping of birds during a stroll in a park to the roar of a jet fighter's engine as it blasts off an aircraft carrier. The bombardment of change is constant, flooding every one of our senses.

Sometimes even these techniques are not enough; each shot must have movement. Enter liquid television, or what has come to be known as the MTV look. Now it is not only people and cars that move; the camera moves, too. A lot. Off angle. Zooming in. Off center. Bouncing. Quick spinning. A constant stream of motion hits the viewer. When that kind of perpetual action is put together with multiple cuts and vibrating letters, the effect is a bit like surfing in a blender.

77

For all the griping about shows being unnecessarily graphic, producers are no dummies. They know what viewers want, and they deliver it. For example, shows will be criticized in the industry for not having enough blue-sky shots, scenes in which characters are outside in the sun, giving an excuse to show some barely covered, bikini-clad skin. Refined and subtle forms of entertainment require better writing and higher production costs. Violence and sex are easier and cheaper and keep viewers glued to their seats.

Producers also have figured out that commercial breaks, particularly at the end of shows, are when channel surfers are most likely to grab their surfboards and search for better fun. Because of that, they've begun seamless programming—squeezing credits to one side of the screen and using the other side to conclude the show, run bloopers or other funny clips, or make a cold start of the next show without a commercial break.

Another secret is setting the hook at the start of a show. Begin an episode with some explosive predicament that grabs viewers and keeps them hanging. The thought is that if you can get them to stay with you for the first part of the show, you've probably got them till the end. And if early on you can find some person or situation or setting that the viewer can identify with, all the better. People watch shows to which they can relate.

Even news programs are driven by entertainment more than anything else. What else accounts for anchors who look more like models than investigative reporters, forty-five-second news stories heavy on sound bites, teasers at commercial breaks to keep the audience watching, and the dramatic buildup to the weather report at the end of the show? Entertainment. Hooking the audience.

Excitement drives entertainment. And what creates excitement is the characteristic Ken Myers describes as television's "frenetic intensity,"[21] the constant activity and change carrying the viewer through one unexpected turn after another. Television is a restless distraction, a perpetual motion machine, relentless in its assault on the senses. It is fidgety even at its slowest times and becomes downright frantic at its most tense.

And the average American gets more than four hours of this every day.

Think what that means. Television doesn't give us a chance to get ahead of it. It grabs our heart and dashes off, leaving the brain behind. Its only goal is to keep us fixed on the screen, and it will do anything to accomplish that.

I remember riding with my sisters one time on a subway in Tokyo at rush hour. Subways in Tokyo are so full that workers sometimes use a pole to shove the mob of passengers into the car so the doors can close and the train can leave the station. As we began to pull away from the station my older sister looked up at me—she was shoved up against my side—and said, "I'm not sure my feet are touching the ground." Television is like that crowded subway. There is no elbow room for reflecting, no place to stand to consider another perspective, no pocket of space for critical thinking about what is being heard or seen.

Not only does television not allow much in the way of deeper reflection, it doesn't invite it. Much of what appears on TV is like the foam on top of a root beer float: so much space filled with so little substance. Television is filled predictably with things that don't require any thought at all: sarcastic heads of household and crazed kidnappers and stunning women and rapscallions on most wanted lists and grumpy bosses and whiny children and political scandals and wild chase scenes and pushy talk-show hosts and ever-smiling anchor people. As Fred Allen said, "Television is called a medium because it is so seldom rare or well done."

Even if it were to give us the space, television rarely presents much worth chewing on. It studiously avoids consideration of life's harder questions: The issue of meaning and direction, the person and purposes of God, our limits and struggles as finite human beings, humanity's moral boundaries and anchoring points, and any number of other matters of real consequence. It is as though we are on a cruise liner traveling across life's ocean, and we spend all our time in the pool on the ship instead of in the deeper and scarier waters below.

As a result, I think we have let slip our ability to think clearly, deeply, intentionally, daringly. We have lost the courage to ask hard, probing, dogged questions. And we have lost the knack of personal reflection, no longer knowing how to get in touch with, much less come to grips with, our discontentment, disappointment, failure, and loss. And our deep spiritual rumblings, our most probing doubts and hopes, those thoughts and feelings so substantial that they sometimes elude words—they are lost in the deep bass throb of our surround sound systems.

Television Makes Us Expect Entertainment

After we've been barraged with hyperstimulation for four hours a night, ordinary life comes to feel a bit like a faded black and white photo. We come to like that stiff-wind-in-your-hair feeling that comes with being hit by one stimulus after another. We seek a rush, a sustained level of excitement. We want to lose ourselves in an unfolding story, to get caught up in a plot that sweeps us along. We have come to like and to want the unceasing motion, the relentless noise, the nonstop, heart-stopping twists and turns.

We carry that expectation over into other parts of life. We want to be entertained most everywhere we go: standing in line at the grocery, driving to work, waiting on hold on the phone, eating dinner out with the family, waiting for a movie to start. The expectation of stimulation has become a given.

Not surprisingly, one of the places we see this is in the pew on Sunday morning. As Haddon Robinson has said, "I think people sit there with clickers in their heads. They turn you on, they'll turn you off. People will decide in the first thirty seconds if you're going to be interesting or boring."[22]

We have forgotten how to slow down, how to experience life in real time.

And sometimes that is because we don't want to. We're afraid to slow down, afraid of what might bubble to the surface in the silence, so we try our best to stay a step ahead of the quiet. We welcome distraction from life and its struggles.

We want the comfort of plunking down in front of something that won't challenge us, hound us, or expose us for who we really are. We're tired of sitting down across the desk from a boss who points out we are failing to make our sales quota, or across the breakfast table from a spouse who tells us we are failing to meet his or her needs, or across the rug from a pet who reminds us that we are failing to make any friends. We like dropping in front of a nonthreatening device that does nothing more than assuage us, reassure us, and quiet those nagging voices.

Remember the TV show *All in the Family?* One time Edith turned to Archie and said, "Do you like being alone with me?" Archie grunted back, "Certainly I like being alone with you. What's on television?"

Television is a great set of earplugs, blocking out at once the whines of the surrounding world and the cries of the heart. After the O. J. Simpson trial came to a close, mental health experts cautioned the watching American public that it should be prepared for depression and a sense of loss as TV coverage of the trial ended. "When a distraction evaporates, you have to come face to face with your own troubles," psychiatrist Carole Lieberman warned. "People are not going to like what they're going to have to face."[23]

Sometimes we turn on the TV to watch a worthwhile show or enjoy a game with a friend or watch a video with the kids. But research shows that we often flip on the tube when we have nothing else to do, when we're bored, when we're lonely, or when we're depressed, in spite of the fact that we inevitably feel worse after we've watched TV.[24] But while it's on, it is an enjoyable, easy escape. Little wonder so much of our free time can be filled with it, and small surprise that it is such a struggle to get up out of the chair and turn the television off.

Television Fosters Artificial Views of Life

We look to television to give us a sense of what life is all about and how it should be lived.

And that is a bit of a scary notion because life according to television is artificial. It does not square well with life from God's perspective. For instance, the world that is delivered on screen is largely secular. God is like Jack Benny: a slightly eccentric, amusing old man who used to show up on TV from time to time, but no longer, because he passed away a few years back.

The world according to television is also one in which we are accountable to no one. It is a world with no thought of sin (only failure), of commitment (only getting needs met), of death (only the present), of duty (only opportunity). It is a world in which the self with its needs and desires looms large and in which little else—including God—exists.

Television gives a picture of happiness that is far removed from any biblical understanding. Finding fulfillment in our gracious acceptance by God through Christ is immaterial; life is about material accumulation. The electronic view of fulfillment can be summed up in two words: prestige and products. Happiness comes when we have fame and fortune, throngs and things. Flashing cameras and full closets convince us of our worth and value as people.

But for the typical person who is settled in front of the tube, those things are unattainable. So TV invites us to find happiness secondhand through the people who seem to have it all. We begin to live virtual lives through these two-dimensional personalities we call celebrities. We find vicarious meaning for our lives as we look in on theirs; we borrow our significance from them. We talk of them—these people who know nothing of our existence—on a first-name basis, chatting about their goings-on as though we've just had them over for a bite to eat. And because of the artificial intimacy of television, which so easily blurs the lines between reality and fantasy, we feel as though we have.

Television also muddies the water when it comes to relationships. Interactions in the world of Beevis, Al Bundy, and *Seinfeld* are nothing like the relationships of quiet humility and mutual submission to which God calls us through his Word. Instead, they are all about staying in control through manipulation, sarcasm, put-downs, and disrespect. People are to be mastered, not served. They are to be used, not honored. And they are certainly not to be thought of more highly than ourselves.

Another startling distortion is television's implication that life can be lived meaningfully and its challenges dealt with decisively in twenty-two minute segments. Life-threatening diseases can be halted, alcoholic parents can be confronted and rehabilitated, jobs can be lost and found, and dangerous criminals can kill, be hunted down, and be brought to justice, all in a half hour, minus commercials. TV is an environment of instant resolution in which all of life's struggles can be solved quickly. How unlike real life. Ours is a world in which God extends to us hope, not a quick fix or easy answers. Sometimes problems last a lifetime; sometimes pain never fully goes away. Nonetheless, God invites us to trust his hand on the course of future events and to find our rest in him.

The world according to television stands, in nearly every respect, in stark contrast to the way of life put forward in the pages of the Bible.

God's Word
to a Distracted World

So what do we say to today's watching, expectant world, cocooned in front of the television? And how do we speak in such a way as to be heard, competing as we are with a highly efficient distraction machine?

Breaking Through the Static

There are two biblical ideas that I think demand to be spoken to a population of media fries.

First, people need to be challenged to allow God, not Bart Simpson or Blockbuster, to define life. In his letter to the Colossian church, Paul cautions believers about how easy it is to allow those around them to influence what they think. Then he challenges them to stay unentangled with the world, to keep the proper perspective. "Set your hearts on things above, where Christ is seated at the right hand of God. Set your minds on things above, not on earthly things" (Col. 3:1–2).

One of the most valuable things we can do as we talk with seekers is help them see that there is more than one way to make sense of the world and that the Bible does a better job of putting together some of the hard pieces than any other explanation of existence. We need to offer fresh perspective through the Scriptures, reminding people what is real and what is important.

Television pushes us into setting our hearts and minds on things around, not things above. But according to the Bible, God looms large at the center of the universe. How he views us and how we view him are the only things that matter. All of the rest of life spills out from those two things. In our conversations with people fixed on the tube, we do well to suggest a new focal point: God.

Second, people need to be prodded out of passive distraction from reality into a passionate pursuit of the full-color, three-dimensional life that God has offered. "I have come that they may have life," Jesus says in John 10:10, "and have it to the full." Other translations say "abundant life," "life in all its fullness," and "more and better life than they have ever dreamed of." God calls us to embrace reality, not shrink from it. It is life, not escape from life, that Jesus offers.

Let me share with you how I developed some of these ideas in a PrimeTime message about television. It may spark some thinking about how you might approach the subject. After saying that television has impacted our daily lives more than anything else in the past forty years and briefly talking about what that impact involved, I stepped back and began to compare what Christianity promises with what television does.

"Ultimately, TV distracts us from real life, it disconnects us from real life, it makes us discontent with real life, and it devalues real life. How different that is from the life that Jesus offers us. TV says, 'I have come to take you out of life.' Jesus says, 'I have come to *give* you full life, to redeem your life, not to pull you out of the emptiness of ordinary life but to invest your daily life with meaning and purpose.'

"How? The message of Christianity is this: Life is only genuinely satisfying and fulfilling when it is lived for God, because he made us to live for him, and doing anything short of that means we are not doing the very thing we were made to do. But when God is not at the center, when he is not the defining reality of our lives, we are. And that is a recipe for the discontentment, shallowness, and disconnectedness that characterize life for most of us. The salvation that television offers from that emptiness is a devaluing of life in the ordinary, a false promise of happiness coming through the things we buy and the people we know. In the end it is no salvation at all; it is only distraction and escape, stepping out of life and into an endless barrage of things and people and images so relentless, so hounding, that we have no time to feel the pain. Television's hope is just an escape, a fantasy, a fairy tale.

"The life Jesus offers us couldn't be more different. According to the New Testament documents, Jesus was no ordinary man. He was God with

84

Us, God himself in our midst. And his solution was to restore for us life as it was intended to be lived, with himself—God—at the center.

"He doesn't remove us from life. He redeems life. He doesn't offer us a life free from hardship, but he promises to bring good to us out of the difficulties we face. He doesn't offer us a life of success and happiness and self-fulfillment but one of deep contentment, unwavering purpose, solid joy, and fulfillment in him. He doesn't offer us glamour or fame, the bright lights and big bucks of celebrity life; he extends to us the bright promise of forgiveness, healing, and new life.

"And that's not a fairy tale. It's true."

We then ended the program with a song by Amy Grant called "Fairy-tale."

> I know there's more to life than a fantasy
> There's so much that my life was meant to be
> So much more than make believe
>
> Fairytale, it seems just like a fairytale
> But there's something in my heart that says this time the story's real
> Fairytale, extra-ordinary tale
> Of a King who offers love so far beyond what I can feel.[1]

In a television world that cranks out all kinds of counterfeit versions of life, we hold out the real thing.

Stay Tuned

Here are some other approaches that may prove helpful as we seek to gain a hearing from a world glued to the tube.

How We Preach and Teach

Seek excellence. Hundreds of thousands of dollars are thrown into virtually everything that appears on the TV or movie screen. As a result, people have come to expect excellence whenever they sit down as an audience. Is the speaker prepared, sensitive to the value of their time, giving them his or her best shot? If not, today's men and women would have to come up with a good reason to give a person their attention. Things poorly done are poorly heard. "Winging it" doesn't fly with a TV audience. We do well to set high standards of excellence for ourselves whenever we stand up to speak.

Use a conversational style. Who are we compared with (even if only unconsciously) when we stand up to speak? For the most part, it is not John Stott or Haddon Robinson who comes to mind for audiences today. It is the likes of Jay Leno, Oprah Winfrey, David Letterman, and Dan Rather. While most people wouldn't necessarily be aware of it, they cannot help but compare us to the TV anchorpeople and talk-show hosts who spend hours in their homes each day. And how do those people speak? By and large, they are warm, informal, free-moving, accessible, up close, with no notes or podium coming between them and the viewers. The only time people see formal, emotionless communicators on TV is when a president dies or when Sam from Sam's Carpet Warehouse comes on and robotically says, "Hi, I'm Sam, from Sam's Carpet Warehouse. Have I got a deal for you." While being sensitive to both the degree of informality in our part of the country and the appropriate decorum of a worship setting, we will find it advantageous to take some risks with a more informal, warm, podiumless style of communication.

Find common ground. The world of entertainment fills the lives of our hearers. Its special effects grab their imaginations, its plots fill their conversations, and its jingles get stuck in their heads. Because of that, we will engage our hearers more effectively if we are conversant with the world of the screen. Anymore, a suspenseful season finale on *ER* or the arrival of a blockbuster like *Titanic* will stir up as much interest and conversation as real news—or more. Mentioning something you saw on TV or quoting from a movie just out at the theaters can create a point of identification for people whose frame of reference is the land of the screen.

Speak with vitality and from a fresh perspective. Viewers bred on the pace and stimulation of the media have developed an appetite for communications that captivate. There's a tension here for us as communicators, and it is found along the fine line between engaging communication and entertainment. To engage is to draw in, to make a connection, to actively involve. To entertain is to perform, to amuse, to give the audience what it wants.

There is much we can and should do to be engaging speakers. Communicating informally, speaking with vivid, well-chosen words, moving around, using carefully selected illustrations and personal anecdotes, keeping a steady pace, involving not just the intellect but the emotions, asking rhetorical questions that pull in the listener, and using a variety of speaking forms are all helpful ways to keep the attention of the audience. Showing a clip from a current movie or MTV, stopping partway through a message to play a Top 40 song, or setting up a talk with a short slide show are other ways to create variety and interest.

As an example of one way to bring new energy to a message, I recently preached a sermon on the Old Testament tabernacle. To draw in the listeners and help them get a glimpse of what the tent of meeting was like, I removed our podium, set up two huge platforms in the front of the sanctuary, and draped them with woven cloths. Then I laid out a fresh-baked loaf of bread, a *menorah,* and a ceramic censer. At the start of the service we lit the incense and the candles, sounded the *shofar* (the traditional ram's horn trumpet used at the temple), and then recited together the *shema,* the Israelite call to worship from Deuteronomy 6. And during the message I walked around the sanctuary, describing where each part of the tabernacle would have stood, what it looked like, and what was significant about it. The number of comments I received that morning made it clear that people were involved.

First-person narrative also can be effective. One advent season I dressed in a three-piece suit and sunglasses and walked in talking on a cellular phone. I was the Bethlehem innkeeper whose Holiday Inn sign said "No Vacancy." Another time I wore a tunic and a leather apron and told Joseph's story. I have also acted the part of the blind man in John 9, the shepherds in Luke 2, and Ananias in Acts 9. Each time, my sense was that the audience had been engaged and moved. If we give ourselves the freedom to think a bit unconventionally, we can find many appropriate and sensitive ways to engage our listeners without compromising the integrity of what we are trying to say.

Engaging the audience is crucial. But we should guard against slipping over into entertainment. When speaking becomes a performance, the speaker becomes a showman, his content becomes negotiable, and the applause of the audience becomes all-important. Those are big compromises for the Christian communicator, who from the perspective of the Bible is called to be more an arrow pointing past himself than a neon sign calling attention to himself. Let's leave entertainment to David Letterman.

Build dramatic tension. Any good speech, message, or sermon has an element of drama. The flow of drama grips an audience, first setting the stage, then introducing complications or an antagonist, and finally seeing the characters and the story through to a satisfying resolution. Those are the components of an engaging plot line, and they should be the elements of an effective message as well.

In particular, inductive communication, which starts with the details and ends with the big-picture conclusions, is a great way to maintain a healthy suspenseful tension throughout a message. The introduction sets the stage for the unfolding drama, raising a problem for which we need an answer. Then we turn to the passage and, asking one question after another, begin to track the clues toward an answer, connecting ideas until they come together in some satisfactory solution to the struggle.

For example, a message based on Psalm 73 might begin with the injustice of virtuous people repeatedly capsizing in life while sinful people have smooth sailing. Why does that happen? And where do we go with the anger and hurt we feel over that kind of unfairness in life? A talk on James 1:2–4 might start by saying, "According to Romans 8:28, God works all things together for good to those who love him and are called according to his purposes. We've all heard it a hundred times. But what does that mean when I am called into my boss's office early Friday afternoon and told I am being let go because the company is experiencing some financial pressures? Or when I get a phone call at two in the morning and find out that my mother has had a severe stroke? Or when a routine set of tests for my baby girl reveals that she may have leukemia? How can God possibly work those things together for good?" We are now poised to leap into James' words.

Give clear roadmarks. An audience accustomed to the rhythms and turns of television drama is a bit out of practice at following the close logic and development of a spoken message. Because of that, it is helpful for us to speak in such a way that we can be clearly followed. A message that communicates one main point in an oral style with lots of restatement, review, and clear-as-a-road-sign transitions, will greatly help. You might even think about sharing some ideas about how to listen to a message, such as taking notes, identifying the topic and its main idea, following the flow and anticipating where the speaker is going, reading the passage in its context, weighing the speaker's analysis of it, and working to find areas of personal application in life.

Encourage active participation. Anything that might push a listener out of the role of audience member and into being a participant is to our advantage as communicators. You might think about breaking the passivity barrier by asking a question at the beginning of a message and inviting people to write down a response or give answers out loud. Or you could ask for written questions to be submitted and answered during the message. Interacting with specific audience members by name during the message or having someone come forward to serve as an example in an illustration—if appropriate in your setting—can also be valuable. You might consider having members of your congregation share personal experiences, interviewing people in the audience about the issues at hand, or having a question and answer period after you've finished speaking. Another way to involve the audience might be to provide some sort of outline or a brief series of questions in the bulletin: "What was the issue being addressed in this message? What was the main idea of the passage? How would God have you apply this idea in your life in the days ahead?"

How We Share Faith

Tell your story. Because of the impact of the entertainment media, stories are the windows through which people look out onto the world. The news is in story form; ballads tell a story; sportscasters are always looking for the story line. And that is not to mention every movie, sitcom, mystery, drama, or adventure show that hits the screen. Story is everywhere, and it can be one of our most important means of sharing faith today.

We have two intersecting stories to tell. The first is our own, the story of coming to faith or, more accurately, of faith coming to us. It takes shape along the lines of questions like these: What things most influenced you before you came to Christ? What were you like? And how did you first come to hear the great news about Jesus? What did you come to realize? Do you remember the light bulb going on? Do you remember taking that first step of faith? And now that you have been a Christian for a while, how has it impacted you? How are you different?

All of us should be ready and eager to tell the story of God laying hold of us. Our account of God's involvement in our lives is one of the least threatening and most informative ways to share the gospel. It cannot be disputed, because it is our experience. And if our faith makes a noticeable difference in our lives, people will be more than ready to listen.

I remember Shawn coming to visit me at the church. Not knowing me, he was reluctant, but a friend brought him and put him at least somewhat at ease. Shawn was in a wheelchair, and as we got talking, he told me why. He was paralyzed when a carload of drunk teenagers ran him off the road and then shot him in the neck. He nearly died. Hospitalized for months, he went through nearly a dozen surgeries. One time a group of well-meaning Christians came in, prayed for him, and promised him that he would be fully healed. He wasn't. When he went home from the hospital, his wife announced that she was leaving him and his infant child to fend for themselves, a feeling much too familiar to a man who had been abandoned as a child. With good reason Shawn was skittish about me and "this Christianity stuff." But he had reached the end of his rope, and he wanted to know if there was somewhere beyond himself to look for hope.

As we sat downstairs in the toddler room at the church, his son playing among the Little Tykes toys, I shared my story with Shawn. I told how I had become a grumpy atheist by the time I was in high school, how I had run my life with thought only of myself, and how I ultimately had come up proud, self-reliant, and empty. I shared about my trip around the world while in college, the death of my parents in a plane crash, and how I first heard about who Jesus was and what he offered me: life lived not for me but for him, as he had intended it from the start. I told about how God's Word came alive to me and how I came to realize there was no choice to be made. The God of the universe summoned me, and I yielded my life to him. Not long after we talked, Shawn became a Christian, and now he has a story of his own—an amazing one—to tell.

Let's be ready at a moment's notice to give an account of how joy came home to our hearts.

Tell God's story. We have another story to tell, one that connects with our own and puts it in context. It is the sweeping story of redemption, of God working out his purposes in human history. In a world of jumbled images and disconnected experiences, there is something startling and winsome about a coherent picture of why things are the way they are and what that has to do with us. This is a world that longs to hear the truth that accounts for life as it is. We need to be able to give a quick and clear summary of the unfolding of history from a biblical perspective, of the way God "works out everything in conformity with the purpose of his will" (Eph. 1:1). The ability to walk a person from creation to fall to kingdom to fulfillment—from living for God to living for ourselves to living again for God—is an evangelistic tool of enormous value. People today want to recover the missing narration, to recapture a sense of the plot. We have a story to tell.

Use drama as a door. The other evangelistic tool of real value in the world of the screen is drama. When properly used, drama invites involvement, engages the whole person, and fosters identification. That is why it has been an outreach tool in the church ever since the mystery plays of the late Middle Ages.

One effective use of drama is to get people thinking. In the movies *Chariots of Fire, The Mission, Dead Man Walking, Saving Grace,* and *A Man for All Seasons,* drama very effectively hints at what the gospel is and what kind of impact it might have on a person's life. If it is employed to spark reflection and in that way pave the way for a coming message, drama can work quite well. Challenging scenes, whether light or serious, raise an issue and stimulate reflection. They can be put to good use as an introduction to a message, readying people to hear. Like the ministry of John the Baptist, drama can push people off center enough that they are ready to listen to what comes next.

Drama also can be enormously effective when used to retell the grand, sweeping story of redemption in fresh terms. *Godspell* and *Tetelestai* do that wonderfully in musical form, while C. S. Lewis's *The Chronicles of Narnia,* Calvin Miller's *Singer* trilogy, and Nussbaum and Weaver's *Ezebulebb and the Poison Scepter* use fiction and fantasy with great results.[2]

A word of caution: Don't let drama begin to scoot God's Word out of its crucial central place. Christianity is decidedly word centered and, because of that, rather confrontational. Allowing drama to replace preaching and using drama in the church merely for its entertainment value is not just unwise, it is wrongheaded. Each time Jesus told a story—which was often—it wasn't because he wanted an audience. He did it not to amuse or entertain but to move people to a deeper level of reflection. His stories were like mirrors held up in front of his listeners so they could see themselves more clearly. He introduced a crisis, a confrontation between the world as is and the world that could be. If in our efforts to present something palatable and enjoyable we wash out the radical, confrontational encounter between God's Word and our world, then we have lost. All we have done is water a bunch of budding potatoes.

What We Communicate

Reality. The Bible pushes us into life rather than pulling us out of it. This is the arena in which God desires to work, redeeming us in all the ordinariness of our lives. Christianity is not pie in the sky by and by; it is an earthy fistful of life in the here and now. To embrace Christ is to embrace life—"life to the full," as it was intended to be (John 10:10). And he redeems all of life—our boredom, our fears, our pain, our loss, our work, our struggles. Like a divine alchemist, he turns our rocks into something precious.

Self-denial and self-examination. Remaining in reality means all that is hard about life is to be faced, not avoided. Couch potatoes flee the frying pan. But God's promise is to redeem our hardships, using them to do two things: deepen our trust in God and strengthen our character. "Consider it pure joy, my brothers, whenever you face trials of many kinds, because you know the testing of your faith produces perseverance," writes James (James 1:2–3). Similarly, Peter writes that we can rejoice when we're struggling, because God uses challenges to produce a faith "proved genuine" that results in "praise, glory, and honor" (1 Peter 1:6–7). In God's economy, pain is redeemed, making us women and men fit for the kingdom.

It also means that all that is ugly within us is to be declared, not denied. It is simply not possible to be a faithful follower of Christ and remain bobbing on the surface. God's Word pushes us down, probing our motives, challenging our self-concern, bringing our secret sins into the light. We are called to examine ourselves (1 Cor. 11:28) and to confess our sins (1 John 1:9). Here too, God's goal is nothing less than making us like Christ and leading us to cling in dependence on him.

The disciplines of self-denial and self-examination fly squarely in the face of the siren songs of the screen that promise distance and distraction from all that hurts.

The active adventure of life. The life of a spud is passive, removed, a cautious sampling of 144 channels filled with the same bland fare. The life of a Christian is active, a great-guns leap into the real adventure God puts before us. Anybody who thinks that Christianity is boring has not seen much of real Christianity. It is active, engaged, a laying hold of the life God offers. There can be no spectators in the kingdom. When Christ comes to us, we come alive. "Because of his great love for us, God, who is rich in mercy, made us alive with Christ even when we were dead" (Eph. 2:4–5).

The call into community. We are called out of isolation into community. While God deals with each of us individually, he does not allow us to walk alone. The call to Christ, as we'll see more in the next chapter, is a call to abandon our La-Z-Boys and our remotes and step out of the dim light of our dens into the bright light of life together. When we come to Christ, we are transplanted into a body, "joined and held together" in Christ (Eph. 4:16).

The lure of entertainment. Finally, while it may be obvious, we would do well to speak directly to the problems that come from getting sucked too much into being spectators of entertainment. This is not a call for abstinence so much as for moderation. Taking in a movie or sitting down to watch a favorite show from time to time is not a concern and often can be a pleasure. But long hours of uncritical TV viewing, movie going, or video game playing cannot help but be counterproductive to forming the image of Christ in us. Paul instructs us to fill our minds with "whatever is noble, whatever is right, whatever is pure, whatever is lovely" (Phil. 4:8). That's a bit tough when, for four hours a day, we fill our minds with whatever is suggestive, whatever is graphic, whatever is distracting, whatever is on.

About Chapters 5 and 6

Concepts Worth Remembering

entertainment: any of a number of pursuits that have as their main purpose amusement, diversion, distraction

entertainment culture: a society in which entertainment is central, both in the time and money invested and in its impact on the culture

Industrial Revolution: the sudden growth of factory production resulting from the harnessing of steam power at the end of the 1800s

medium: any one of the many vehicles through which sound or images
are communicated; print, film, television, and radio are examples

entertain: amuse, distract, literally "to hold between"

spectator: a person who watches without getting involved, without
taking part

Recommended Reading

Galli, Mark, and Craig Brian Larson. *Preaching That Connects.* Grand
Rapids: Zondervan, 1994. Borrowing insights from the world of jour-
nalism, the authors offer a number of helpful suggestions to increase
the impact of spoken messages.

Ford, Leighton. *The Power of Story.* Colorado Springs: NavPress, 1994.
This book tells how to use the appeal of stories to reach people with
the gospel today. Ford shares some of the insights into contemporary people that have made him one of the most effective evangelists today. Well worth reading.

McKibben, Bill. *The Age of Missing Information.* New York: Plume,
1993. McKibben contrasts what he learns from watching a single
day's programming on ninety-three cable TV channels with the
insights that came to him during a twenty-four-hour period spent
camping in the Adirondacks. One of my favorite books—enormously readable, well researched, and profound.

Myers, Ken. *All God's Children and Blue Suede Shoes.* Westchester, Ill.:
Crossway, 1989. An introduction to entertainment, television, and
music from a Christian perspective, this book is thoughtful and
clearly written, a valuable map as we wade into the various streams
of popular culture.

Pederson, Steve, ed. *Sunday Morning Live.* Grand Rapids: Zondervan,
1993. These top-quality, ready-to-go skits developed by the folks
at Willow Creek Community Church could be used effectively to
engage the attention of an audience in the entertainment age. Scripts
and videos are available.

Postman, Neil. *Amusing Ourselves to Death: Public Discourse in the
Age of Show Business.* New York: Penguin, 1985. Provides an informative, reflective stroll through the last 150 years of American history, recording the shift from what Postman calls the typographic
age to the television age.

Part 4

WHO **WE ARE**

Self-Absorbed Individuals

> Be your own rock.
>
> ad for Prudential

> Individualism lies at the very core of American culture. . . . Anything that would violate our right to think for ourselves, judge for ourselves, make our own decisions, live our lives as we see fit, is not only morally wrong, it is sacrilegious.
>
> sociologist Robert Bellah, *Habits of the Heart*

Isolating the Individual

While flipping through the Sunday paper, I saw something that got me thinking about some of the crosscurrents in our culture. Bold across the front page of the Sunday magazine was this question: "Whom should we admire?"

Behind the words was a photo of the sky at twilight, pink and purple from low sunlight, to me an analogy of a culture losing its light and heading into darkness. What will divert us from our moral decline? Who will point the way? To whom should we turn?

Inside the magazine, eight prominent Americans talked about their heroes. Among the admired were Thomas Jefferson, Abraham Lincoln, Rosa Parks, and Eleanor Roosevelt, men and women of substance, courage, integrity, and resolve. Implicit throughout the article was this conviction: We benefit by learning as much as we can from those who have traveled ahead of us, and our lives are better when shaped by the example of honorable men and women.

Musing on the article, I gathered the sections of the Sunday paper to put it away. Out of the stack fell an insert, a clothing ad from one of the department stores in town. The cover showed a bunch of T-shirts. Emblazoned across the front of one of the shirts was this statement: "I'm my OWN role model."

Me, Myself, and I

Our brazen preoccupation with self ripples through every tributary of our culture. It shapes how we do business, how we teach, how we parent, how we vote, how we marry. Not surprisingly, our individualism and self-concern wash over into the way we approach matters of faith. In a supreme act of self-reliance, we decide for God what is true about him and his intentions for us.

We drive alone, make life's hardest decisions alone, raise our children to stand alone, and lay down to die alone. Boil any one of us down and what remains stuck to the sides of the pot is simply this: my concern for me.

"Self-" has become the modifier of choice as we approach the year 2000: self-image, self-esteem, self-actualization, self-concept, and self-help are all newcomers to the English language, products of a culture that has the individual as its primary concern.

Think over some of the big hit movies in recent years: *Star Wars, Dances with Wolves, Raiders of the Lost Ark, Rambo, True Lies, The Fugitive, Robin Hood, Batman, Braveheart, Working Girl*. What is the plot? One person stands up against the corrupt town of Nottingham, all of Nazi Germany, a multimillion dollar Middle Eastern terrorist group, or Darth and his Dark Force denizens throughout the universe. The entire story line comes down to this: lone individual relies on self and single-handedly saves the day. It is the myth that shapes our dreams and defines our hopes. Whom do we admire? James Bond, Arnold Schwarzenegger, Sylvester Stallone, Indiana Jones, myself.

Flying Solo: American Individualism

Self-concern is so much a part of Americans that I don't think we fully realize how novel this condition is. We have not always been this way. About seven hundred years ago a chunk of snow began rolling, a little piece of independent spirit that has tumbled and grown into the avalanche of fierce self-reliance we now think of as normal. Here's how it snowballed.

The Renaissance and the Rise of Humanism

For many years God, not the individual, loomed largest in the Western world. Human identity was seen as derivative, coming from outside

97

oneself. Within the biblical perspective of the Middle Ages, personal value and uniqueness came not from some sense of self-importance but rather from a right relationship to the one who made the world, owns it, and is over all as Lord.

That began to change in the fourteenth century, the beginning of the Renaissance. God began to recede from the cultural foreground and the individual began to scoot to the front and center. Beginning in Italy and quickly spreading through the rest of Europe, this cultural rebirth marked the start of the shift from a biblical outlook to a modern one.

Two developments kicked the Renaissance into motion. First, Europeans rediscovered the ancient humanist writings of the Greeks and Romans. For the centuries leading to the Renaissance, education in Europe centered around theology and belief in a personal God. Everything—the arts, political thought, philosophical reflection, medicine, the study of nature—was grounded in this biblical worldview. The arts and philosophy and political theory of the ancients, by contrast, had centered on the individual, with few reference points outside the self. This way of making sense of the world, once revived, began to wash away the God-centered view of life on which Christianity stood—and Western culture with it.

The second important trend in the Renaissance was the disconnection of theology from art, the creation of art for art's sake. To this point in Christian Europe, art serviced a higher cause. Medieval art was not always what we might call good art. Its rigid composition often lacked perspective, distorted space, misrepresented light, and portrayed people who seemed to float in the air. But it was great art in this sense: It was about the great themes of life, and thus full of meaning. It brought biblical stories and themes to life, making God real and faith viable for those who viewed it. Mary and her infant son Jesus, Adam and Eve, David, and Moses figured prominently.

Toward the end of the Renaissance, it was clear that a shift was taking place. The human figure and the natural world became more and more the real subjects. The Christian story became a backdrop, a setting against which to showcase the human being and his world. You can see aspects of this, for example, in Michelangelo's famous painting on the ceiling of the Sistine Chapel in St. Peter's Cathedral in Rome. While the main thrust of the painting is formed by nine striking scenes from Genesis, those pictures are framed by twenty painted male nudes who have nothing to do with the rest of the work. The seated figures are posed like artist's models. They bend, gesture, twist, and strain—chiseled celebrations of the human form. Man had become the measure of all things.

The Renaissance gave birth in the years following to a new view of humanity: not humanity connected and collected but individual women and men, good in and of themselves, dignified, independent of the one who had made them. Since the Renaissance, it is the individual, more than God, more than the community, that matters most.

Democracy and Individual Rights

Three hundred years after the start of the Renaissance, in a period called the Enlightenment, the humanism that was born during the Renaissance came of age. Humanity's belief in humanity—expressed in the ideals of optimism, progress, skepticism, reason, and freedom—flourished. A contagious, heady view had captured the Western imagination: We are now out from under the oppressive thumb of God, free to do as we see fit. Released from living for the sake of God, we can now live for ourselves.

At just the time when these optimistic ideas about the nature of humanity were finding their full expression, the American colonies successfully broke away from their British rulers and struck out on their own. In the process, they revived another ancient concept called democracy. It was a way of governing built not around the idea of God and his due but around the individual and his rights—a government run not by a king but of, by, and for the people.

The English philosopher John Locke was a leading advocate of this political system. He argued that, left to themselves, men and women would not be destructive or antagonistic toward each other. They would get along just fine, relating with "peace, goodwill, and mutual assistance."[1] Even more, they would and should respect each other's rights: "No one ought to harm another in his life, health, liberty, or possessions." Those solid and certain privileges no one could take away. Less than a century after Locke published his views, those rights were proclaimed inalienable and incontestable when they were ensconced in the Constitution of the United States.

The Renaissance said the individual matters. The foundational idea that rippled through Locke's system was that the individual matters and the individual has *rights* that matter. Where once *responsibilities* mattered most, now rights were to rule.

Romanticism and Individuality

On the heels of the Enlightenment, in the last half of the nineteenth century, a head-turning clatter arose on the Continent. It was a rumbling called romanticism, a protest of sorts. At its root was a tremor of discontent with the stern rationalism of the Enlightenment. Growing numbers of men and women were frustrated by the way the modern world had stripped the core out of humanity. In a world that exalted the intellect, the system, and the machine, some felt robbed of their imagination, their feelings, their intuition, their spirituality. It was time to restore the balance.

But in spite of the fact that the Renaissance and Enlightenment had stripped humanity of its dignity by stripping humanity of its God, the rumblings never became calls to restore the biblical worldview. Romantics actually shared many Enlightenment beliefs: optimistic confidence in human progress, skepticism toward the church, and assurance that humans were good and had within them all they needed to live meaningfully. The romantics merely disagreed with modernists about what meaningful living entailed.

This group of writers, artists, and thinkers felt the answer was to be found in self-expression and self-reliance. Ralph Waldo Emerson, Henry David Thoreau, and Walt Whitman set the course for romanticism in the United States. Together they would take the growing individualism of the previous five centuries and accelerate it into warp speed. Their message: I have no need of others. I have within me everything I need. My heart is my final authority. What is true for me is what is true. I am self-sufficient, free to do whatever I'd like. The individual—proud, self-reliant, alone—comes first.

Listen to some of their writings.

"The Individual is the world."
"Every man for himself."
"Trust thyself: every heart vibrates to that iron string."

Emerson[2]

"If one advances confidently in the direction of his dreams, and endeavors to live the life which he has imagined, he will meet with a success unexpected."
"If a man does not keep pace with his companions, perhaps it is because he hears a different drummer."

Thoreau[3]

"Nothing, not God, is greater to one than one's self is."
"I celebrate myself, and sing myself."
"I need no assurances. I am a man who is preoccupied of his own soul."

Whitman[4]

The "have it your way" and "sometimes ya gotta break the rules" world of Emerson, Whitman, and Thoreau is here to stay. It isn't hard to recognize their voice in this portion of a contemporary poem titled "I Am Myself" by Mark Mikal.

> Do not try to mold me to suit your needs or standards,
> Nor try to impress your feelings and opinions upon me.
> Do not condemn me, or degrade me,
>   For not matching up to your design.
> To do so would mean the loss of my identity.
>   And I would no longer be me . . .
>
> I know who I am,
>   I like who I am,
>   I am at peace with myself,
>   And I am happy.
> Simply,
>   I am myself, a person, a being, an individual.
>   I am myself![5]

The earlier movements of the Renaissance and the Enlightenment gave us the individual and the notion of personal rights. Now, from romanticism, we have inherited individuality.

The Therapeutic World

A final factor that helped cement the growing self-absorption of the Western world is the rise of the self-esteem movement in the twentieth century. Riding the national optimism that followed World War II, four psychologists—Abraham Maslow, Carl Rogers, Erich Fromm, and Rollo May—developed a new approach to counseling. This style of therapy, concerned above all with building up the self-esteem of the person counseled, was based on four supreme values.

- *self-understanding:* getting in touch with what I'm feeling
- *self-acceptance:* having a positive view of myself regardless of what I say or do
- *self-expression:* being myself—even defining myself—without regard to others
- *self-fulfillment:* getting my needs met; being happy

Pivotal to the four psychologists' thinking was the belief that we are essentially good and have within ourselves all that we need for growth

Culture Shift

and healing. Accordingly, Rogers developed a style of counseling in which nothing confrontational or even remotely critical is ever said. He called it "reflective listening," a what-I-hear-you-saying-is approach in which "the client experiences himself as being fully received . . . whatever his feelings . . . whatever his mode of expression . . . just as he is."[6] I am special, wonderful, unique, worthy of your respect—just for being me. Out the window goes any standard of character, integrity, or responsibility against which I might be measured. Acceptance is the name of the game.

Maslow developed the landmark "hierarchy of needs." Unfortunately, Maslow's hierarchy was quickly co-opted by the prevailing cultural trend toward self-concern, and soon opened the way for a nation to define its problems purely in selfish individualistic terms. In this approach, more than our rights—and certainly more than our responsibilities—it is our needs that define us.

Sharing the self-esteem movement's optimism about humanity and swimming in the same cultural current, Norman Vincent Peale began preaching the gospel of personal well-being: salvation from poor self-esteem through the power of positive thinking. In this gospel, God—once the Lord of the individual before he was squeezed out of the picture by Renaissance optimism and Enlightenment skepticism—returns as the servant of the individual, existing for our happiness. The unfortunate legacy of this teaching is a package of need-centered discipleship, feel-good sermons, easy-answer evangelism, and be-happy attitudes.

In the "therapeutic culture of feel-good-ism,"[7] what defines me are my needs, and what drives me is getting my needs met. Only when my needs are met will I be happy, and happiness, after all, is what life is all about. Finding myself. Making peace with myself. Expressing myself. Feeling good about myself. What else is there?

Here, then, is the legacy of the past seven hundred years, a shift of focus

from God to humanity,
from the group to the individual,
from responsibilities to rights,
from others to self,
from service to self-expression,
from blessings to needs.

Be all you can be. Go for it. Look out for number one. Ours is a world turned in upon itself. Severing the self from the anchor of being under God, we have exalted the individual, drawn personal rights to the fore, and turned in upon ourselves in glorious and horrible freedom.

102

The Lone Ranger Syndrome

The self-absorbed individualism we have inherited expresses itself in a variety of ways.

I'm All the Company I Need

We experience little meaningful contact with others. In our too-busy-to-chat, mobile world, in which homeowners move every ten years and apartment dwellers every three, it is increasingly difficult to be meaningfully connected to those around us.

I once spent a Saturday morning doing a survey in our community. One of the questions we asked was, What are the greatest needs that you and others in this neighborhood face? The responses surprised me. More than any other, the answer most often given was, "I don't even know my neighbors." Researchers say that three out of four Americans don't know the people who live next door to them, and one in seven doesn't even know the neighbor's name.[8]

We think we can live life meaningfully in isolation and independence from others. We teach our children that asking for help is a sign of failure, and we raise them to be independent. We run errands on our own, do yard work on our own, drive to work on our own. We tackle our problems alone, wade through loss alone, face the future alone. Flying solo is the American way.

During my freshman year at Miami University, while still an atheist, I was asked by my English professor to write a paper about the most important person in my life. In a move reflective of the warped way in which our culture increasingly thinks, I wrote an autobiography. We think about ourselves first; our highest regard is reserved for ourselves.

Contrary to what you might see on a map of the United States, America is a land of islands. Disconnected and alone, we have forgotten the benefits of mutuality and life shared.

Safety in Virtual Community

Once we do land in the company of each other, we are like strangers on an elevator, relating awkwardly, unsure how to act. The time-consuming and painstaking business of simply getting to know each other—let alone lay down our lives in service to one another—is a bit beyond what we feel able to do.

103

Some see a turn back toward community among those born after 1964.[9] But even among members of generation x, as that group is sometimes called, "hanging together" seems to be more common than genuine community. More and more people today don't want to be alone but aren't sure how to be together.

Because of this relational awkwardness, we live in networks more than communities. Churches and neighborhoods are more often locations through which we pass than places where we live and forge deep, meaningful relationships. Instead, the workplace and the Internet give many of us our main sense of community.[10] Both offer the companionship without obligation that we welcome today. Work's appeal is its distraction. We work side by side, but our focus is not on each other. We are acquainted, but we don't really know each other. The attraction of interacting on-line, of course, is tied to the user's anonymity and autonomy. We can log on and off at will and reveal about ourselves only what we choose. Many on the Internet weave together fact and fiction, presenting themselves as people who don't even exist. We are in complete control. None of this messy getting-to-know-you stuff.

Even in our families we often experience less than gratifying relationships. Given our whirlwind of activities, the time available for family members to connect gets whittled down to a few minutes each day. Those brief pockets of time get crowded even further by the hubbub of chatty TVs, cranked-up stereos, and other entertainment devices. Surveyors report that half of Americans regularly watch TV during dinner, and we spend most of our time in the evenings glued to the tube.[11] Sure, we're together—unless, as is increasingly the case, each family member has a personal TV—but conversations limited to "Who's got the remote?" and "Oh, I've seen this one a million times" are not exactly dialogues destined to deepen relationships.

It's the day of virtual communities with all the "benefits" and none of the mess. We are reluctant to enter into the real thing.

A Man's Home Is His Bunker

The world seems more and more to be a threatening, scary place that we should avoid whenever possible. It is too much to take in and too hard to deal with. What are we to make of burgeoning national debt in the U.S., increased racism in central Europe, escalating poverty in Haiti, and the rising cost of grain in Sioux City, Iowa—all of which seem totally beyond our control? Between the world's troubles—which seem unsolvable—and the tenacious assaults on our homes by aggressive marketers—which seem unstoppable—we find it becomes much easier to focus on what is right around us. We wrap ourselves up in the little things: what

104

color to paint the living room tomorrow or which game to watch this afternoon. We retreat into our homes—our world-within-a-world—locking the doors, screening all calls, and warning our children not to talk to strangers. We become private, guarded, intolerant of anything that might threaten our peace or ring our doorbell.

When I was in seminary, I spent some time making home visits for the Massachusetts Association for the Blind. With few exceptions, I found that people who lost their sight narrowed their focus to what was right around them. Having been bumped out of a world filled by God and governed by his purposes, we too have lost our vision. Overwhelmed by a world we cannot make sense of, we have narrowed our focus to what appears within six inches of either side of us. As for the rest—out of sight, out of mind.

Mind Your Own Business

High on our expanded list of inalienable rights, right up there with acceptance and tolerance, is the right to personal autonomy. I don't want others telling me what to do or how to do it. I want to do it my way, and I don't need to ask your permission, thank you very much.

In a world of individualists, giving advice is a no-no. Sticking one's nose uninvited into the lives and choices of others is even worse, one of the seven deadly sins (deadly for those who do it). We just don't want to hear it. We believe we are perfectly able to make good choices. So keep your nose on your face, not in mine.

I had the privilege of leading to the Lord a young man I enjoyed a lot. He had a sharp probing mind and a big Cheshire-cat grin, and he wasn't afraid to say what he thought. He was eager to wrestle with the tough issues and welcomed the hard questions I put back to him.

But not long after he came to Christ, something painful happened. He began to cross the line in a relationship with a married woman in our church—nothing blatantly wrong, just a little too cozy a relationship. But when I and some others in the church challenged him about it, he would hear none of it. He resented what he saw as our inappropriate intrusiveness and meddling, and he left the church. Here was a man who had a clear understanding of the gospel but who was opposed to anybody setting foot on what he considered private territory. This was a man who wanted to stay in charge. So do the rest of us.

Here Today, Gone Tomorrow

Another feature of individualism is the idea that who we are is negotiable, up for grabs. We select a lifestyle as though we're picking out a pair of shoes. We go shopping for a look, a style, that suits us and even makes a statement. Individuality is what counts. I heard a radio commercial for a cosmetic surgery center that promoted "Surgical technology for a better you." This is the land of fresh starts, new beginnings. If we can up and leave our family, our job, or our spouse, why not ourselves? We can leave the old self behind and adopt a new and improved one.

In a country in which roles are always negotiable—with twelve-year-old entrepreneurs running statewide businesses out of their garages like adults, and fifty-year-olds wearing ponytails, jeans, and in-line skates like teens—we pick and choose the "me" we want to be. We've become a nation of chameleons, remaking ourselves more often than Betty Crocker. As one writer has put it, we have gone from the "self-made man" to the "man-made self."[12]

I Want What I Want When I Want It

Individualism breeds a preoccupation with pleasure. What makes us happy is by definition right and worthwhile; it is the individual's greatest good. The pursuit of happiness is not only one of our inalienable rights; it is also our favorite freetime activity. One of Socrates' students, a philosopher named Aristippus, summed up 2,500 years ago the way many of us have come to think today: "The highest good is pleasure; the greatest evil is pain."

Avoid pain and seek pleasure. If it feels good, do it. That is hedonism—and that is our M.O., the normal and acceptable way of doing business for most of us. If it feels good. Not if it *is* good or right or sensitive or appropriate. Just if it *feels* good. Little wonder we are a people in hot pursuit of feel-good moments to punctuate our gnawing boredom. We've come to a place where there is almost an obligation to do what we want to do.[13]

Coupled with our preoccupation with pleasure is our concern with getting our needs met. We don't view the good things of life as things we are fortunate to have. They are things we *must* have. Alone in the universe, with nothing else to live for, we allow needs to become the focus of our lives.[14] For who, besides yours truly, really matters? We think first of ourselves. Always.

I'm Not My Brother's Keeper

Absorbed with our own needs, we lose sight of our responsibilities to each other. For most of us, there is no concept more foreign or incomprehensible than loyalty, service, or duty. We are beholden to no one.

There was a day, back when the Bible occupied the thought world of society, in which others were seen as the deserving recipients of faithful service. Today it is just the opposite. A relationship is not for the other person's sake, it is for mine. This is equally true whether it be a friendship, a marriage, an extended family, or a working relationship.

When I began to look seriously at Christianity during my senior year in college, I began to meet occasionally with a campus ministry staff worker named John Whitehouse. One day he looked across the table at me in the student union and asked, "David, what is your purpose in life?" I stalled. Then I finally answered: "To make the world a better place for other people." Sounded virtuous to me, a worthy goal. The only problem was, it was a complete lie. I was disgusted when I realized the real answer was that my purpose in life was to get ahead, to do whatever I wanted to do, and to meet my own needs, regardless of what that might cost someone else.

A slogan on a T-shirt sums up quite well where we've come: "Galileo was wrong. The universe *does* revolve around me."

Apart from God, what else *can* it revolve around?

God's Word
to a Disconnected World

How do we gain a hearing in a world of Lone Rangers who are isolated, guarded, and self-concerned—and having gained it, what do we say?

Bridging the Islands

God's intentions for life rarely square with the way men and women live when left to their own devices. Nowhere is this truer than in the confrontation between the loving heart of God and the self-absorption of our day. A life of isolation and self-reliance is, from God's vantage point, no life at all.

In a world in which men and women experience about as much meaningful interaction as a pair of Barbies side by side on the shelf at Wal-Mart, two messages beg to be communicated. First, men and women need to be called away from a life of self-sufficiency into a life of dependence. The pride that stands behind our independence is at odds with God's calling. No one can be subject to two kings at the same time.

Coming to Christ means we relinquish control. Jesus says it bluntly: "If anyone would come after me, he must deny himself and take up his cross daily and follow me. For whoever wants to save his life will lose it, but whoever loses his life for me will save it" (Luke 9:23–24).

Nothing flies more in the face of the American bent than this. All of our lives we wrestle to gain control, and now we're being asked to give it up.

This was one of the hardest things for me to face when I came to Christ, and it continues to be one of the biggest stumbling blocks for others as well. We don't want to let go.

I knew a high school student whom I'll call Jesse—a pleasant guy, but tough. I found out later that he was one of several who had repeatedly vandalized our church building during construction. Smooth, controlled, self-reliant, Jesse learned early that he couldn't rely on anyone else. He was on his own.

I had several chances to talk with him about the gospel, and each time he listened politely. But after I got done spelling out some of the responsibilities that fall on believers, he said it just wasn't for him. He finally was making something of his life, and he wasn't willing to turn it all over to someone else. Sure, he believed in God, but he wanted to worship God in his own way. He didn't want God or anybody else telling him what to do.

When Jesse graduated from high school and enlisted with the Marines, I wrote him a letter in which I challenged his thinking one last time.

"Jesse, there's a story in Mark's Gospel, in chapter 10, about a confident young man who reminds me of you. One day this young man encounters Jesus and asks him how he can inherit eternal life. Jesus knows the man's heart, but he wants the young man to see his heart for himself. So he walks through the list of the Ten Commandments and then says, 'These are your measures of a religious person, aren't they? So how have you done with them?'

"The young man answers, 'Hey, no problem. I've done great. I've been religious all my life. Is that all there is to it?'

"Now listen to Jesus' answer. He looks at the man and says, 'No, as a matter of fact, that's not all there is. This is what you lack, and it is no small thing. You are bound by your desire to serve yourself, to meet your own needs. Your preoccupation with your wealth shows that. If you were willing to part with all that you own and to follow me for the rest of your life, that would be evidence you no longer are living for yourself and you have the faith in me that brings eternal life. But as long as you continue to live for yourself, no dice. It is all or nothing. Which will it be?' Sadly, the young man left, unwilling to let go of his life and live for someone else.

"My sense is that you're a well-liked guy, Jesse. Others enjoy you and think highly of you. But can I be honest? It seems to me that your life is pretty much lived just for yourself, with your own interests in mind. That's just the way my life was before I became a Christian. All through high school and college I'd mastered the art of looking like I was concerned

109

for others, but in the end I really only cared about myself. My sense is that that could describe you as well. Am I very far off?

"The real problem comes when that kind of thinking seeps over into your relationship with God. I keep up appearances. I pray. I read the Bible. But all of those things are more to appease God than they are genuine attempts to know him and grow in my relationship with him. I nod to God from time to time, but I really live my life for myself, not for him.

"If I had really looked into it seriously, I'd have learned that this God who made me is not open to whatever form of religious expression I may choose to offer. He doesn't just smile and pat me on the head regardless of what I believe. His Word tells me that God created me to live for *him,* to bring *him* glory. I have rebelled against and deeply offended the one who made me and who alone has a claim on my life, and he takes that rebellion so seriously that he sentenced me to death. But he loves me so much that he sent his son to die in my place, and there is no other way to be made right with him. He wants my life—all of it. He wants me to live for him.

"Talk about an adventure! This is something that will make all other adventures pale—becoming the person *God* made you to be by becoming a fully devoted follower of Jesus Christ. It is only then that we really live.

"What do you think, Jesse? As you head off into the military, you face a lot of new challenges, and potentially risk your life. Do you have that kind of unshakable contentment and purpose in your life that comes from turning over your life to Christ? Have you experienced the eternal life through Jesus Christ that takes the fear out of death? Could it be time?"

I heard nothing from Jesse for a year. Then one day, to my surprise, I got a six-page letter back from him. Boot camp had broken him. One night he hit a wall. He was out on a grueling all-night hike with an eighty-pound pack, and he realized he couldn't do it on his own anymore. He turned over his life to Christ.

In a world of Indiana Joneses, it needs to be said as clearly as possible that self-reliance is counter to what God knows is best for us. It has no place in the kingdom. Coming to Christ means reining in our self-sufficiency, hog-tying it, and laying it at Christ's feet.

The second thing people need to hear is the call into community. Christianity and community are inseparable.

As he neared his death, Jesus looked down from the cross and saw his mother in front of him. Then he looked over and noticed John, one of the disciples, standing nearby. He turned his eyes back to his mother and said, "Dear woman, here is your son." Then turning to John, he said, "Here is your mother" (John 19:26–27). When we come to the cross, Jesus folds us into a family of faith with others who love him.

It is not possible to be a Christian in the way God intends and remain a loner. We can't stay in orbit around each other. Isolation is not an option. We are called to honest and caring relationships with those who share the bond of faith with us. When we come to Christ, self-forgetfulness, gracious encouragement, and sacrificial service move out of the optional category and into the one marked "required." This becomes our duty: to lay down our lives for each other, just as Jesus Christ laid down his life for us (1 John 3:16).

It doesn't take long to realize what a privilege that particular duty is.

While I was writing this book in Colorado Springs, Sharon and I were stretched thin. I was in ministry, we had four kids under age seven, and I was trying to write a book. Fortunately, we were in a home fellowship group with Mike and Beth Royal, and Rick and Kathleen Both, faithful friends who saw us through some very tough days.

To show you how interlaced our lives were in those days, I jotted down what one fairly typical week was like. On Sunday all three families went to church together and had lunch together, including some time to pray together with an international student who is a friend of the Boths. Then we went with the Boths' kids and the Royals for a hike at the Air Force Academy, giving Kathleen a break from parenting duty while Rick was away on a mission trip to Turkmenistan. Tuesday Kathleen picked up our son Sean and took him with her daughter to art lessons. Wednesday evening found us at the Boths' house for a birthday party for their son and a welcome home for Rick. Thursday morning Beth came over—as she did each week—and covered the home front all morning so Sharon could serve as a parent volunteer in Brandon's class. She changed diapers, put the girls down for their naps, cleaned up the kitchen, and made dinner for us. Then, when afternoon came, Sharon watched Beth's son Jonathan so Beth could get ready for teaching on Friday. At the end of the day Mike and the rest of the Royal family came over for dinner, enjoying the meal Beth had made for us that day, and then we all went over to the soccer fields, where I coached a team that included my sons and Emily, the Royals' middle daughter. And Saturday afternoon we piled our four kids in the van and went with Mike, Beth, and their kids to a pumpkin farm, and then to a nearby nature center for a hike. What a happy way to spend a week!

Luke gives a picture of life together for the early disciples. "They devoted themselves to the apostles' teaching and to the fellowship, to the breaking of bread and to prayer. All the believers were together and had everything in common. They gave to anyone as he had need. They broke bread in their homes and ate together with glad and sincere hearts" (Acts 2:42–46). Coming to Christ is an opportunity not only to lay down our self-sufficiency but also to lower our guard and risk life in community. This is God's desire, that the separate strands of our lives would be woven together into a single beautiful whole. Having experienced it, I understand why.

Breaking Through the Walls

People today have their guards up, their walls built high. But most every wall has a door, and this one is no exception. Here are some other thoughts about how to communicate biblical truth in a leave-me-alone world.

How We Preach and Teach

Be specific. People who are used to thinking first of themselves, their circumstances, and their needs will have trouble hearing speech that is vague, general, or universal in scope. Mail addressed to "Occupant" gets tossed in the trash—as do sermons. Let's avoid as much as we can messages that use convenient catchwords to describe whole segments of our population. Lumped-together labels such as "secular humanists," "religious right," "pagans," or "liberals" slide past the hearing of individual-minded folk. Let's try instead to describe what (or who) we are talking about. The more specific and descriptive we can be in our examples, the more likely we are to help the audience identify with what we are saying.

This is going to be especially important in the introduction and application areas of our messages. I began one message with six "you might be" scenarios which gave examples of struggles some in the audience might be experiencing: a high-school student on the first day at school, a childless couple dealing with infertility, a businessperson laid off from a longtime job, a single mom scrambling to take care of her kids, a volunteer teaching unruly children at the church, and a woman alienated from a best friend. I went on to open the text and explain it. At the close of the message I came back to those scenarios and showed how the text spoke to each situation. While not everyone in the church was included in those descriptions, few walked away that morning without a good sense of how the passage related to the specifics of their circumstances.

The more specifically we speak, the more we will keep our listeners with us.

Include corporate application. It is tempting to over-personalize everything in our speaking: How does this apply to *you?* What should you do in response? What will this do in your relationship with the Lord? What is God saying to you? It is crucial that we move beyond talking only to the individual. Think back on messages you've given or heard recently. How often did the application relate only to individual issues of "you" and "your," instead of having to do with "we" and "us"?

Problems arise when we neglect this. First, it dangerously reinforces the message that, when I come to Christ, I can come with my self-concern intact. Self-denial is optional. Jesus really is concerned first with meeting my needs. Heaven and earth are again inverted, and I end up on top. That's no small problem.

Second, when we boil the Bible's ideas down to a bunch of individual points of application, we can miss a lot of what the Bible says. Most of the Bible's language is corporate, not individual. It speaks to two broad groups, the church and the world. We need to follow suit in our messages.

From God's point of view, the sky of humanity is not filled with North Stars, six billion cynosures, each standing alone. He has put us together with others into constellations: families, small groups, churches, neighborhoods, cities, regions, nations, language groups, the world, the kingdom. Our messages need to reflect the corporate character of the Word.

How We Share Faith

Put friendship first. A guarded, get-lost society requires that we approach people with the gospel in the context of a relationship. In the middle of the twentieth century, when America was still warm toward the Christian message and reasonably friendly toward strangers, there was little problem with strolling up to an unknown person unannounced, a stack of tracts in hand.

No more. Today, walking up cold to the door of a suburban home or to a stranger on a city street nearly always sets the conversation off on the wrong foot even before it starts. With few exceptions, an uninvited visitor is as unwelcome as a door-to-door vacuum salesman—and gets about the same swift treatment. Cold calls lead to chilly responses.

Just after I became a Christian in the early eighties, I went with an Intervarsity Christian Fellowship group to the beaches of Fort Lauderdale to share Christ with the throngs of college students who descended on Florida during spring break. We would walk along the beach in pairs praying like mad, and then just stroll up to somebody lying there on a beach towel and engage that person in conversation. I had a few conversations that turned out to be pretty significant during that week. But even then, fifteen years before this writing, I saw the hesitation with which these college students would talk with us. That reluctance has turned into what seems to be full-blown skittishness. It doesn't serve us well today to rely on stranger-to-stranger evangelism.

Instead, it is crucial that we befriend non-Christians, winning our way into their distracted hearts and busy schedules. That means spending the kind of time with them that lets us get to know each other: having them over for a cookout, watching their kids play in a high school football game, feeding their fish and collecting their mail while they're on vacation, all the while waiting and praying for the opportunity to comfortably and naturally talk about our faith.

One day at the church in Colorado Springs where I served as associate pastor, I told Bill Tibert, our senior pastor, that I thought we should cancel church on Labor Day weekend and tell our people to spend the day with non-Christians. His eyes got pretty wide, but he thought about it, prayed about it, and the following Labor Day we had our first Outreach Sunday. We still held a small service, but we encouraged the congregation to spend the morning, the day, or the weekend with people who they had reason to believe were outside of a relationship with Christ or the church. A block party, a Rockies game, a family reunion, a summer T-ball team get-together, the zoo—how they chose to spend the time didn't matter. The time together did.

Four years ago I began a friendship with my neighbor Gary. At the time he was a stubborn New Ager. Today he is a Christian. "And as far as I can figure," he told me recently, "it was your friendship with me that God used more than anything else to make me a Christian. You've been really faithful as a friend, and I never once had the feeling that our friendship depended on whether I agreed with you about your faith. I trusted you, so when I started struggling with some stuff in my life and needed to talk, I knew I could turn to you." If you don't get to know people, they won't get to know God. It's that simple.

Expose the failures of self-reliance. Another valuable approach to evangelism is to help people realize the inadequacy of self-reliance. Truth is, regardless of appearances to the contrary, every one of us will eventually hit the same wall Jesse did. We cannot do it on our own—in spite of the testimony of mounds of self-help books to the contrary. We are finite and fallen, a rather lethal combination for men and women who are trying to go it alone. We will always bump up against our limits, and we will forever make wrong choices. We simply cannot do it on our own. Conversations that help people stop long enough to see what they already suspect are some of the most important pre-evangelism talks we can have.

In spite of all his boasting, Walt Whitman later circled back on himself and expressed some very different sentiments from those I quoted earlier. You can hear the emptiness when, at one point, he penned this stark admission:

O baffled, balk'd, bent to the very earth,
Oppress'd with myself that I have dared to open my mouth,
Aware now that amid all that blab whose echoes recoil upon me I have
    not once had the slightest idea who or what I am,
. . . the real me stands yet untouch'd, untold, altogether unreach'd.[1]

My non-Christian friend Michael is a picture of candor and confidence. But the minute he answered the phone one day, I knew something was wrong. "It is a really interesting thing that you happened to call this morning," he said. "You'll never believe what happened to me last night. You know I've had a lot of things on my mind lately. Well, last night when I went to bed I couldn't stop worrying, and before I knew it I was sweating and breathing hard—I couldn't get a grip. It was like a panic attack. Well, finally, around two in the morning I got down on my knees by the side of the bed and said, 'Okay, Jesus, *you* deal with this.' And guess what? Nothing happened! I was awake all night. Lotta good that did!"

Michael and I had been friends for several years, and I'd won his trust, so I was able to shoot straight with him. But even I was surprised at how direct I was. "You know why I think God let you have that experience? Because he wanted you to see what life is really like when you are in charge. No matter how hard you try to control things, you can't. And do you know why I think he ignored your prayer? Because he doesn't want you to come running to him only when you're desperate. He doesn't want to fix your problems and then have you go on your way without him; he wants all of you. He wants you to turn over your life to him, not just your worries."

There was a long silence. Then Michael said, "You know what? I think you are absolutely right. Control is such a big issue in my life, but things aren't exactly going the way I want them to go with me in charge, are they?"

Give an honest portrayal of the Christian life. There is nothing worse than giving a false picture of what it means to be in a relationship with Christ. How we talk about that is crucial to the expectations women and men carry with them into a new life with Christ. It is directly connected to how long and how well they will last in the faith.

I've been thinking quite a bit about the inadequacy of the images we typically use when we talk about what it means to come into a relationship with Christ through faith. The most common of the metaphors we use is entering into a friendship with him. That certainly is a biblical metaphor. Jesus told his disciples, "I have called you my friends" (John 15:15), and James wrote that Abraham was, because of his faith, a friend of God (James 2:23).

But the problem is that we tend to think of friendships in terms of how they meet our selfish expectations. So when we think of our relationship with God in the "buddy" category, it's easy to turn things around. It is no longer I who exists for the sake of God, but God who exists for me. In that setting, holiness is tough to grasp, obedience is a touchy subject, accountability becomes awkward, and claims of ownership are a little hard to handle. Companionship eclipses confrontation when we think of God as a peer.

I'd like to suggest three other metaphors that more adequately flesh out the kind of relationship God intends to have with us. If we were to take time in our conversations with seekers to explain the Christian life in word pictures like these, we might see fewer come to Christ, but those who do will come prepared, having counted the cost, and will be far more committed as a result (see Luke 14:25–33).

Three biblical images that we need to reclaim are those of a subject in the Lord's service (Luke 17:7–10), a pupil under the master's instruction (Luke 6:40), and kin in a father's extended family (Matt. 12:46–50). These could be helpfully expressed in three metaphors familiar to most of us: The faithful knight submitted to his king, the apprentice learning a trade by watching and emulating the master, and the member of a multi-generational farm family, enjoying the head of the family's presence and provision, while working with other family members toward a common end.

What good does it do for us to fold into the family of faith a man whose pride and self-reliance remain intact or a woman who insists on staying in control? Is that person really a follower of Christ?

What We Communicate

The Bible spills over with passages that address the independent of spirit. Let me highlight a few of the most important.

The reason for our existence. Christianity is not about getting our needs met. Now, it is true that God does meet our needs. When we are made right with God through Christ, we experience a measure of fulfillment and satisfaction never known to us before.

But that is not why God exists, and that is not why we exist. We live for the one who made us, to bring him glory and honor in our every word and thought and action. "Whatever you do, do it all in the name of the Lord Jesus" (Col. 3:17).

The place of rights. Coming to Christ also means coming to a place where we lay down our rights. "You are not your own," Paul writes. "You were bought at a price" (1 Cor. 6:19–20). When one of the crowd said to Jesus that he would follow him but needed some time to go say good-bye to his family—a request that was certainly within his "rights"—Jesus' response was stern. "No one who puts his hand to the plow and looks back is fit for service in the kingdom of God" (Luke 9:62).

God calls us to stand humbly before him, gladly receiving all that he brings to us, rather than insistent, self-assertive, ready to sue the Almighty the moment things don't go our way. Remember God's rebuke of Job when he began to insist that God respond in a certain way? "Brace yourself like a man," God thundered. "I will question you, and you shall answer me. Where were you when I laid the earth's foundation?" (Job 38:3–4). God gives us much, but owes us nothing. In the kingdom of God, *right* is an adjective, not a noun.

The importance of others. People are not means to our ends. The depth of our need for affirmation and acceptance—a need that seems to run deeper than the Marianas Trench—pushes us scrambling toward others. But the greater depth of God's love for us, when rightly understood, delivers us from the need to use others to meet our needs.

In God's economy we don't need to look to others for a sense of our worth. We don't have to rely on those around us for love, acceptance, and security. All these come from above, not from the person next door. The enormousness of God's love for us is shown in his having made us and in his having died for us. Those actions confirm our uniqueness, openly displaying our great worth in God's eyes. As Paul writes, "God demonstrates his own love for us in this: While we were still sinners, Christ died for us" (Rom. 5:8). And daily that love is confirmed by ten thousand tangible bits of evidence: among them, the warmth of his presence, his overflowing provision, and his superintendence of the events of our lives.

Once we have found our well-being in Christ's love for us, we have the freedom to love and serve others openly. Only then is it possible to "do nothing out of selfish ambition or vain conceit, but in humility consider others better than yourselves" (Phil. 2:3). One Christmas, William Booth, the head of the Salvation Army, sent a one-word telegram to his partners in ministry. It said simply, "Others." We love because we have been loved.

Lives of mutual dependence. Our society values privacy, honors competency, and shuns input from others. But relationships between believers are to be different, with lives interwoven and mutually supportive. According to the Bible, our responsibility as Christians is to "spur one another on toward love and good deeds" (Heb. 10:24). Formally, that takes the shape of church discipline. Informally, that means an invitation to get close to each other and "meddle" a bit. I'm not talking about needle-nosing our way

117

into matters that are best left private or gossiping about one another under the guise of sharing prayer requests. But it is our place to meddle in the best sense of the word: to give encouragement that nudges others toward maturity in their relationship with Christ. This kind of meddling is a lost art, but a necessary one in the family of faith.

But mutuality means not only giving but also receiving suggestions. From a biblical perspective, people who are open to corrective input from others are prudent; those who resist such advice are "stupid" (Prov. 15:32; 12:1). We cannot come to Christ and isolate ourselves from the observation and concern of the church family. We cannot hang "Do Not Disturb" signs on our noses. Life in Christ is life together.

An accurate view of humanity. The self-esteem movement and its Rogerian approach to therapy are built on a positive, optimistic view of men and women, but this view is a misplaced confidence.

There *is* something absolutely amazing about people, a captivating dignity and majesty and resourcefulness that eludes words. As we know from the biblical record, that uniqueness comes from being God's image-bearers (Gen. 1:26–27). But we land in a big old kettle of hot water when we forget the other half of the creation story: that man and woman rebelled against God and—like a flooded basement carpet—all are now stained and smelly from sin. No part of us is unaffected. "All have sinned and fall short of the glory of God" (Rom. 3:23). This side of the fall, each of us is at once dignified and dank, a majestic mess.

The result is that, much as we may want to, we don't have it within us to lift ourselves out of the muck that, in our independence, we have shoveled ourselves into. The therapeutic culture unhelpfully pushes us inward. Christianity, aware of the bankruptcy of our inner resources, pushes us outward. It is the Lord who redeems our lives from the pit (Ps. 103:4).

Pleasure and pain. Finally, pleasure-seeking individualists need to hear something that makes no sense to their ears: Not all pleasure is good, and not all pain is bad.

Much that gives us pleasure is bad, a self-destructive and self-serving reflex deserving of God's harsh denunciation (see Eph. 2:1–3). Neither the pleasure we find in vengeance for raw wounds of the heart, nor the fulfillment we find in sexual expression divorced from love or commitment—nor any of the thousand other destructive pleasures into which we so readily fall—is good. Because of our fallen nature we often find pleasure down the dark alleys of sin instead of in the bright boulevards of God's grace.

At the same time, much that gives us pain is actually for our own good. Like the growing "Youch!" that comes screaming up our arm as a warning when we touch a stove, pain can be used by God for our benefit.

The very things we most want to run from are often the things he has a way of turning to our good. He uses our struggles with sin, our losses, and our hardships in two main ways: to deepen our faith and develop our character. "We also rejoice in our sufferings," writes Paul, "because we know that suffering produces perseverance; perseverance, character; and character, hope. And hope does not disappoint us, because God has poured out his love into our hearts by the Holy Spirit, whom he has given us" (Rom. 5:3–5).

With pleasure and pain, as with everything else, God redefines the categories. Seeking pleasure is not necessarily wrong; it all comes down to where we seek it. And avoiding pain is a normal response; what matters is why we are avoiding it. Ultimately, real pleasure is found in doing what God calls us to, pain in ignoring his constraints and doing only what we want to do. "Make me walk along the path of your commands," prays the psalmist, "for that is where my happiness is found" (Ps. 119:35 NLT).

About Chapters 7 and 8

Concepts Worth Remembering

individualism: an approach to life that places primary emphasis on the individual as the center of focus and the core societal building block

Renaissance: a period of new artistic expression and humanistic thinking that followed the rediscovery of ancient classics, marking the close of the Middle Ages and the start of the modern era (1300s–1500s)

humanism: a way of thinking that emphasizes the dignity, potential, and primacy of the human, generally with a worldview in which God is minimized or absent

Enlightenment: a period of rational and humanistic thinking in the 1600s and 1700s, marked by optimism, progress, skepticism, reason, and freedom

individual rights: initially, within democracy, the rights of an individual to own land and fully participate in the democratic process; today, the rights to income, health care, privacy, choice, free expression, and most anything else

romanticism: a reaction against Enlightenment rationalism, surfacing in the 1800s, that encouraged creative self-expression and sensitivity to intuition and imagination

therapeutic culture: a culture in which secular therapy's assumptions dominate, such as the virtue of self-acceptance, the value of self-expression, and the priority of self-fulfillment

self-esteem movement: a popular psychological approach based on self-understanding, self-acceptance, self-expression, and self-fulfillment

Recommended Reading

Bellah, Robert. *Habits of the Heart: Individualism and Commitment in American Life*. Berkeley: University of California, 1985. Written by a group of sociologists headed by Robert Bellah, this classic is chock-full of insights about our self-minded culture, including extensive interviews and a helpful history of the rise of individualistic thinking in our country.

Friedman, Lawrence. *The Republic of Choice: Law, Authority, and Culture*. Cambridge: Harvard University, 1990. Friedman does a beautiful job of painting the rise of the individualistic bent in America, carefully exploring the implications of freedom, choice, and self-expression.

Vitz, Paul. *Psychology as Religion: The Cult of Self-Worship*. Grand Rapids: Eerdmans, 1977. A thoughtful Christian critique of the self-esteem psychology movement.

Walters, Tony. *Need: The New Religion*. Downers Grove, Ill.: InterVarsity, 1985. Walters takes a close look at how we have drifted into a way of thinking that elevates needs as the highest good. The opening chapter, "A New Morality," in which Walter contrasts the present view to a biblical one, is particularly valuable.

Witten, Marsha G. *All Is Forgiven: The Secular Message in American Protestantism*. Princeton: Princeton University, 1993. In a study of forty-seven recent sermons on the parable of the prodigal son, Witten shows how subtly the me-first worldview has crept into, and even come to dominate, much biblical exposition.

Part 5

HOW **WE THINK**

Beyond God

Our nada who art in nada, nada be thy name thy kingdom nada thy will be nada in nada as it is in nada. Give us this nada our daily nada and nada us our nada as we nada our nadas and nada us not into nada but deliver us from nada; pues nada.

Ernest Hemingway, "A Clean, Well-Lighted Place"

God created dinosaurs. God destroyed dinosaurs. God created man. Man destroyed God.

Jeff Goldblum's charater in the movie *Jurassic Park*

Shoving God Aside

Russ was using a radial arm saw to cut a piece of lumber in his shop one morning. Suddenly, the saw caught the glove on his right hand. It jerked his hand under the blade, and the next moment his thumb was lying at the back of the saw, cut off at the base. Russ was rushed to the Limb Preservation Institute in Denver, where a team of specialists operated for ten hours to reattach his thumb. When they returned later to inspect their work, they weren't confident that they had done the best job possible, so they disconnected the thumb and began all over again.

Reattaching a severed limb is an incredibly intricate task. It's not a matter of simply lining up skin to skin and stitching it back together. Each blood vessel, nerve, muscle, ligament, tendon, and bone must be reconnected where it was cut. In Russ's case, as a radial arm saw doesn't exactly make a surgical cut, the specialists had to put a steel pin through the thumb to stabilize it, shave down the severed bone, and take nerves and blood vessels from other parts of Russ's body to replace ones too damaged to repair. This is medicine pushed to its outer edge.

Six months later, Russ had regained nearly full use of his thumb. You'd never guess it had been severed from his hand.

I'm shaking my head as I write this. Amazing. Absolutely amazing. That God would have crafted our bodies in such a way that this is even possible. That God would actively heal us in such dramatic ways. And that God has given to some men and women the experience and skill to take part in such a miracle. Amazing.

Russ would be the first to agree. A committed Christian, Russ sees the use of his thumb today as an "absolute blessing from God." He believes that, in every respect, God had his hand in restoring its use.

The doctors seemed to think it was pretty amazing, too. On a follow-up visit, the surgeons were grinning from ear to ear, pleased with the results. "Isn't this great? I can't believe how well it has healed."

But it was clear to Russ that what amazed him was not what amazed them. Their wonder was not over the work of God, but over the results of their own skill and hard work. "This came out much better than we would normally expect," they announced. "The surgery really worked well. You sure were lucky."

Therapists looking at Russ's thumb on follow-up visits reflected the same nearsightedness, "Wow, isn't it amazing what modern medicine can do! Those surgeons, they are great!"

No mention of God at all. To Russ, for whom this was an intensely spiritual experience, the response of the medical staff was hollow. To the team, miracles are the routine work of medical specialists, not the gracious intervention of God.

We live in a world where God is irrelevant. God is not so much dead as he is superfluous. We manage quite well without him, thank you very much.

The word *secular* describes our culture well. To be secular is to be concerned only with the flesh-and-blood life on this planet. Secularism means dismissing God and disregarding a spiritual dimension of any sort.

But what about statistics like the polls of George Gallup and George Barna that show 94 percent of Americans believe in God[1] and 89 percent agree that "there is a God who watches over you and answers your prayers"?[2]

Two things need to be said. First, while most people in the United States believe in God, far fewer live in a way that shows they take God seriously. They are self-reliant and independent. For them, God is not a factor; they are secular.

Biblical faith and secularism stand sharply at odds with each other, while nominal faith—the bare-minimum faith that makes no real demands and causes no noticeable impact on the believer—is quite at home in a secular culture. Unfortunately, according to George Gallup, there is a lot more of the latter than the former. "There is an 'ethics gap' between Americans' expressed beliefs and the state of the society they shape. While religion is highly popular in America, it is to a large extent superficial; it does not change people's lives to a degree that one would expect from their level of professed faith."[3]

Second, our culture as a whole also fails to take God seriously. Stephen Carter, in his book *The Culture of Disbelief,* argues that American culture fails to provide a place either for God or for those who ardently believe in him. This is the message that comes through in the public sphere: "Pray if you like, worship if you must, but whatever you do, don't on any account take your religion seriously."[4]

In our world, it isn't that God is dead so much as that he is simply not, as they say in the business world, "a player." We have shoved God aside.

Pulling Back the Curtain

A familiar scene in the movie *The Wizard of Oz* serves as a picture of the way God's place has been diminished in our culture.

As Dorothy and her friends stand in the Great Hall, a green face glowers through a wall of fiery flames and bellowing smoke. "Do not arouse the wrath of the great and powerful Oz!" it shouts. Scarecrow winces, Lion cowers, and Tin Man's legs rattle like a can of spray paint. But just then, Toto, Dorothy's little dog, begins tugging at a curtain off to the side. The curtain slides back to reveal a little mustached man turning dials, shoving levers, and shouting into a microphone.

The great and powerful Oz, it seems, is not so great and powerful after all.

The last five centuries have pulled back the curtain on God. For countless generations men and women lived in a world made by God, filled with God, under God's sway. He was all-powerful, all-knowing, awe-inspiring, and worthy of our deepest reverence. Now, as *we* loom so large, God seems to be only a little old man of small consequence. This transformation resulted not so much from a single swift yank on the curtain as from a series of fateful tugs over time.

During the Renaissance, when man became preoccupied with man, God was not actively rejected but eclipsed, nudged aside. From that point, four other key influences effectively shoved God outside and locked the door on him altogether. Let's consider each in turn.

Descartes and the Autonomous Person

The Western world was in the habit for fifteen hundred years of turning to the Bible for answers whenever questions of substance arose. What is true about God's character? Why does the world exist? Who am I? Why am I here? What happens when I die? For a millennium and a half, those questions and a thousand others like them brought people into the pages of a Bible for answers.

Then along came René Descartes, and all of that began to change. Descartes, a Christian mathematician and philosopher at the start of the

1600s, set out to make a list of the things people could know with absolute certainty. He started with things he thought could be said with confidence. God exists. I exist. I have a body. I am not dreaming. My senses are accurate. There is an outside world. Then Descartes started asking some hard questions. He adopted a posture of radical skepticism, calling everything into question and throwing each cherished belief overboard unless he could prove it beyond doubt. His list got shorter and shorter until finally all that was left was this: *cogito, ergo sum,* "I think, therefore I am." The only thing I know for sure is that I exist. My experience tells me that's true—if I am thinking, there must be an "I" in there somewhere doing the thinking.

But everything else is suspect. God, the outside world, tradition, the evidence coming to me through my senses. I can't know any of that for sure. This conclusion was an ax blow to the authority of the Scriptures— one that Descartes never intended. In fact, part of what he was trying to do was to show how humankind could have confidence in the existence of God.

So here is his unwitting legacy. First, his skeptical probing raised suspicions about the Bible. Can we be confident of its accuracy, its truthfulness? The world began to raise an eyebrow, wondering. Second, Descartes' example said a person didn't need to think under the umbrella of Christian thought but could step out and look at the sky for himself. "Why should I believe what the Bible says? And who are you to tell me what's true? I can think for myself."

Sound familiar? It should. That's the turbulence left in the wake of Descartes' thought experiments, and it's the way most people around us think today. One summer I went on a whale watch off the coast of Cape Ann north of Boston. On the way back, as I huddled against the cold ocean air, I listened to two teenagers, a boy and a girl probably fourteen years old, as they talked. They complained about the exclusivism of Christianity, corruption in the church, and fighting between Christians and other religions, before ending on this note.

Boy: "All because these people believe stuff that was written a thousand years ago."

Girl: "All this s—— because of a novel, a bunch of novels."

Boy: "Yeah! It's probably just a sitcom from two thousand years ago!" They both laughed.

Is the Bible simply the script for an ancient Middle Eastern version of *Touched by an Angel,* a collection of purely human reflections? Or is God its ultimate author, filling its pages with his revealed truth? The authority for the faith is at issue here: the source of our information about what is true about God, reality, humanity, and Jesus Christ. Christianity stands on confidence in the inspiration, reliability, trustworthiness, and sufficiency of the Bible. Descartes' radical thought experiments began unintentionally to pull back the curtain.

The Scientific Revolution

The second unwitting factor adding to the mounting drift of secular thinking was the rise of what was called the New Science. For centuries, Christian students of nature depended on divine revelation to answer their questions about what makes the world tick.

Then came Copernicus, Kepler, Galileo, Bacon, and Newton, who introduced a new way of making sense of the natural world. Unlike their predecessors, they relied not on reason or revelation but on firsthand observation and empirical, measurable evidence. Microscopes, telescopes, prisms, and test tubes replaced copies of the Scripture as the tools of choice.

Virtually all the early scientists were Christians of deep devotion. For them, science and religion were not at odds. Rather, science naturally spilled out of faith. Understanding how creation worked and taking an interest in the physical world were meaningful ways of expressing devotion to the Lord.

But the result of the early scientists' work was to push people away from God and make people lose even more confidence in the Scriptures. This happened in three ways.

First, Francis Bacon and his colleagues insisted theology is not capable of answering all one's questions about existence; there are certain questions only science can answer. How do the planets course through the heavens? How is disease passed on? How does light refract? How does gravity work? Those questions fell in the domain of science. It didn't ask why God created the planets and ordered them as he did. Nor did it ask why God allowed disease to spread or what purpose in God's world was served by light being broken into colors. Those were questions for theology—questions, certainly, that mattered a great deal to those early scientists, but not the questions with which they wrestled. Science's business was not purpose but process, not questions of why but how. Basing its work on observation and measurement, science showed an independence from the Bible as a source of traditions and authority. It created a growing confidence in the reliability of hard facts while fostering a creeping distrust of unverifiable tradition handed down from above. It wasn't long before humanity's convictions were divided between facts, in which people could have complete confidence, and opinions or beliefs, about which there was considerable uncertainty. The Bible clearly fell into the second category.

Second, scientists used a closed-system model; that is, for the sake of their experiments they ruled out God's intervention as a factor in their work and looked at the world with a purely mechanical emphasis on cause and effect. Soon the elliptical orbit of the planets around the sun, the spread of disease through bacteria, and all sorts of other natural phenomena were adequately accounted for without recourse to God. The scientists weren't saying God was uninvolved altogether, but gradually, with more and more of the universe "explained" by science, the closed system became a logical way to think about the world. In a universe so efficient and self-contained, why resort to supernatural explanations?

Third, by making such thorough sense of the surrounding world—and even mastering it in many ways—science fostered an optimistic confidence in humanity's ability to tame nature and solve the problems of people. God, as a result, didn't seem particularly necessary to individuals whose needs were met quite adequately through the fruits of science. What is God's place in a world where I take medicine if I get sick, make superior weapons if I want to win a war, or dig irrigation ditches if my land is parched? God became the ever-shrinking God-of-the-gaps, having a place only in those areas science had not yet come to understand.

Thus, the Bible was viewed with increasing reservation as a source of authority. And in a world demystified by purely natural explanations, God seemed to be increasingly irrelevant. During the Enlightenment, the growing rumblings about God and the Bible let loose, and the avalanche of secularism crashed through Europe with a fury.

The Birth of Secularism

The thinkers who gave shape to the Enlightenment—Rousseau, Voltaire, Hume, Locke—in many respects articulated nothing new. Their tenets were little more than the logical extension of the individualism, humanism, and optimism that began with the Renaissance.

Where the Enlightenment broke from all that came before it was in pushing the ideas of the Renaissance to their extreme. The growing awareness of humanity's resourcefulness and artistry quickly accelerated into a swaggering confidence in humanity, a boastful optimism about scientific progress, an unchallenged trust in reason, and an equally dogmatic affirmation of the fair-minded goodness of the individual. The era also was marked by an aggressive skepticism toward God and the debunking of all things religious.

Prideful humankind at the center, reason as final authority, God nowhere to be found. This was secularism, the modern way of understanding the world that untied the Christian worldview from its moorings and sent it spinning downstream.

127

In particular, it was the dismissal of the divine that set secularism apart from thinking that had come before. Three ways of curtailing God's place in the universe spilled out of Enlightenment secularism, all of which are still very much with us today.

1. God Is Distant

The first way of thinking about God to emerge in the modern era was deism, the theology of the gap-filling God. Deists believe that God exists but that his place in the universe is merely that of the architect of the machine. He fashioned the universe, put its inviolable natural laws in place, set it running, and then essentially left, never again intervening in the system. Yes, he exists, but he may as well be on vacation in another solar system, for he is not involved in the world in any meaningful way: no answers to prayer, miracles, or wonderful plans for a person's life, and certainly no incarnation, substitutionary death, or resurrection. This meant that men and women occupied a world in which—for all practical purposes—they were free to do as they saw fit.

For the deist, the Bible is a small cake of truth frosted with many layers of myth. Thomas Jefferson produced his own version of the New Testament, edited from a deist's point of view. It eliminated every miracle, every hint of Jesus' divinity, every reference to the supernatural. What remained after Jefferson's snipping was a paper-thin volume containing only the barest of "actual" events.

Agnostics, nominal Christians, Jesus Seminar scholars, and twelve-steppers submitting to their higher power are all present-day heirs of the deist view of a distant, uninvolved God. "(God Is Watching Us) From a Distance" could have been the deists' theme song.

2. God Is Absent

A second way of making sense of God that emerged during the Enlightenment was naturalism. Naturalism is the WYSIWYG worldview of the modern scientist: what you see is what you get. Matter, energy, and the natural laws that govern them are all that exist. This view, the closed-system model of science, doesn't leave any room for God at all. It also makes quick business of the Bible, dismissing it as a purely human bit of work. It is not God's Word but a record of the way a certain group of people came to think about the supernatural. A curiosity, yes, but certainly not an authority.

Pierre-Simon Laplace was a famous French mathematician and astronomer in the late 1700s and early 1800s. He gave a copy of his book *Celestial Mechanics* to Napoleon Bonaparte. After Napoleon read it, he sent for Laplace and said, "You have written a large book about the universe without once mentioning the author of the universe." "Sir," Laplace answered, "I have no need for that hypothesis."[5] That is naturalism.

As with deism, naturalism is a popular way of thinking today, particularly among well-educated folks with a scientific bent. My friend Bart, a brilliant computer programmer, laughed at the idea of trying to reconcile the Bible and its view of God with current scientific findings about the universe. He felt the Genesis account of creation was impossible to fit with the facts, and miracles simply couldn't happen in a world of fixed physical laws. The whole idea of God seemed most improbable to him.

Marv had similar concerns. He not only had problems with miracles and the Genesis creation accounts, he also found the idea of a personal God ludicrous in the light of the vastness of the universe. The whole spiritual realm seemed like a bunch of superstitious hogwash because there was no measurable evidence of it. Ours is a material world.

3. God Is Compartmentalized

The third concept of God in the Enlightenment could be called the two-worlds approach. This view, which traces back to the writings of Immanuel Kant, says there are two spheres of life that are tough to reconcile. One is public, the realm of hard facts, hard tabletops, and hard currency. It is the world of math, science, politics, and economics, governed by facts upon which we can all agree. God, for all intents and purposes, has no place in this arena.

The other sphere—the private—is governed by beliefs and values. This is where God is active and involved. But in this world nothing can be known for sure; there are only opinions. Whether God exists, what happens when we die, how we experience salvation: it's all conjecture, at best. We cannot know for sure, not in the sense we know that two plus two is always four.

People still compartmentalize God, acknowledging his presence freely in their private devotional worlds, but refusing him recognition in the broader world of public life. God matters a great deal to two-worlds people—but he only holds sway on the inside. He gives me peace and hope, he answers my prayers, he is always with me, but he has nothing to do with my life "out there." He is the Lord of my heart, but not of High Street. While I am sitting in my cubicle at work, casting my vote at the ballot, chatting with my friends over coffee, or pulling out my MasterCard at the mall, God is nowhere to be found. This public world is not his world. It is mine.

This is consistent with the message that comes to us all the time. As Stephen Carter puts it, "The message of contemporary culture seems to be that it is perfectly all right to believe that stuff—we have freedom of conscience, people can believe what they like—but you really ought to keep it to yourself."[6]

In this way of thinking, the Bible becomes a mere handbook for personal well-being, filled not with shouted affirmations of lordship but only with whispered messages of love and acceptance.

Whether distant, absent, or compartmentalized, God was shoved aside during the Enlightenment. All that remained was a swift kick to send him sprawling altogether out the door of the modern world. It came in 1859 in the form of a book called *Origin of Species by Means of Natural Selection.*

Charles Darwin and Evolution

Though the Bible was viewed with increased suspicion as a source of authority, there still had been no real challenge from science about what the Bible claimed to be true. No accepted scientific assertion stood in direct contradiction to the Bible's teachings.

Then along came Charles Darwin. Based on his studies of animal life in South America, and on the Galapagos Islands in particular, Darwin said that he had found evidence for a process called evolution. According to his conclusions, every species of plant and animal could be explained by two wholly natural mechanisms: mutation and natural selection. Species changed, and then some of those species, by virtue of improved ability to survive and thrive, became new species.

With one blow, Darwin sent God and the Bible flying out the door. First, he seemed to have provided convincing proof that all life had come into being without any superintending from God. Second, the whole notion of evolution taking place over millions of years seemed to disprove the Genesis account of creation.

Boom. The Bible is wrong, and God is unnecessary.

Of course, Darwin actually proved neither point. More than a hundred years later, the evolutionary model is still only a shaky theory, in spite of being accepted as fact by virtually the entire scientific community. The theory of evolution rests on two bits of evidence: a fossil record that shows species becoming gradually more complex, and evidence of small adaptations over time within specific species, such as change in wing color, neck length, or beak size. However, no one has ever come up with proof of a leap from one species to another, what we call macroevolution. Darwin and his successors have not even come up with a convincing explanation for the origin of single complex bits of anatomy on a single creature—features such as eyes or wings—let alone for an entire species. Further, in all the millions of fossils that have been unearthed, there is not a single undisputed example of a transitional species. In fact, in an embarrassing layer of fossils considered to be about 540 million years old, scientists have discovered virtually every animal family (phylum) whole, intact, ready to go. Evolutionary theory is hard pressed to give an explanation for something that looks so much like creation out of nothing. (For more on this, see Philip Johnson's exceptional look at the evidence, *Darwin on Trial.*)

In spite of the many pieces missing from his theory, Darwin seemed scientifically to disprove the Bible and dispense with God, all in one swift kick.

The humiliation of William Jennings Bryan and his biblical views during the Scopes "monkey trials" in the 1920s merely sealed the fate of a worldview that had been largely discredited by Darwin seventy years earlier.

In a span of five hundred years, the secular forces of our culture have declawed the Lion and made him little more than a house cat.

Missing Person

God is simply not a part of our daily world. He is not mentioned, not included, not consulted.

Think of some of the arenas in life: business, leisure, politics, television. God is not a central feature of any of them. We can read the paper in the morning, listen to the radio on the way to work, spend the day at the office, go out for dinner, attend a PTA meeting, come home and watch some TV—all without hearing God mentioned once.

I worked at Procter and Gamble for a year in marketing and brand management. I cannot think of one time when anybody even referred to God, except for the times when I was the one who raised the subject (or when someone was swearing). One time I suggested that an ad for one of our shampoo products would be displeasing to God because it prominently featured a married woman flirting with a man and thereby devalued the family. The room, filled with advertising executives and brand management people, went silent. On another occasion, when I asked if I could reserve a conference room for a weekly Bible study during the lunch hour, I was met with the blankest of stares. And when I told my bosses I believed that, at some point in the future, God was calling me into ministry, they were stumped and tongue tied. When they finally found their voices again, they asked me to leave the company. "Listen, David, you're doing great work here. But if you know you're going to go into ministry, there's no reason for us to continue to invest in you as a future leader here at P&G. Now, if, uh, that wasn't really, um, *God's* voice that you heard, if you get to a place where you change your mind, we'd love to have you stay. But otherwise, we need to ask you to leave." Taking God seriously in the hallways of Procter and Gamble was considered about as strange as if we had taken off our shoes and socks and played hopscotch between office cubicles.

Talking about God in the public forum is just about as odd. I once wrote an op-ed article about the culture wars that have divided Colorado Springs and sent it to our local paper. I pointed out that neither condemnation nor tolerance were particularly satisfying solutions. I suggested we could benefit from looking to Jesus' example of relating across lines of difference with compassion *and* conviction.

The editor of the paper called. Long pause. "I, uh, I have your article here in front of me. Now, I just skimmed it, but . . ." Another long pause. "Would you call this a religious article? Do you see this as advocating a particular theological point of view? Because if it is, I don't think I can run it." I explained that it was not a religious article. It was not an article in which I suggested that everybody became a Christian. If he were to read it a bit more carefully, he would see that it was an article about cultivating communication across lines of difference in our community, and it merely used Jesus' way of relating as an example.

Long pause again. "I, uh, I still don't think I can run this. It will just stir up too much flak on the editorial page. Religion always does. Even if you say this is not a religious article, most people won't read it carefully, and they'll think it is." I believed what I wrote needed to be said and was representative of a worldview that was shared by many in the community. Then I mentioned Stephen Carter's book about the way that religion has been marginalized in our culture and said I believed it was important to express a point of view that was often neglected: a Christian one. Very long pause. "All right, I'll run it. I have to admit, I live in the rarefied secular atmosphere of the newsroom where belief in God is viewed as outdated and quaint. I forget that some people really think this way. You're right. What you're saying deserves a hearing." Jesus on the editorial pages. There's a novel idea.

It's true wherever we turn. God is out of place and out of line in today's secular society.

Abhorring the Vacuum

Because God doesn't figure in "the real world," four other things become true, each of which raises enormous challenges for us as biblical communicators. God is whittled down to next to nothing, people replace God as head honcho of the universe, the Bible is thrown overboard as a source of authority, and people who take God seriously are taken far from seriously by our world. Let me explore each of these a bit.

- *God is whittled down.* In our secular world, God—like a cotton shirt left too long in the dryer—has shrunk. For those of a deistic bent, God is reduced to his transcendent qualities—majesty, omnipotence, and eternality—but stripped of his immanent qualities—love, gracious care, and involvement in our daily lives. If God is uninvolved in my life and world, then he is more concept than person, an indifferent lump of divinity tied up in some far corner of the universe. He is only half a God.

  For the "two worlds" person, whose world is divided between public atheism and private theism, just the opposite is true. God has no place in the affairs of humanity or the sweep of history, and no influence in the public arena, so he becomes little more than a household idol. If God is not lord over the affairs of men and nations, what is he left to be lord of but me and my small interior world? Gone are his transcendence, his omnipotence, his sovereignty; all that remains are his grace, his love, his intimate care. Again, he is only half a God.

  And for the naturalist, God is reduced even further, stripped of his very existence. For many today, the idea of a personal God is unwarranted. It doesn't fit the facts. Why believe in him? That is a "theory" of which we have no particular need. Our physical world and we as its occupants find ourselves managing quite well without him. Who needs him?

- *People replace God.* Whenever a culture throws God overboard, its people inevitably rush in to take God's place, even while the throne is warm. With God no longer God, we put ourselves in his place as an object of worship and preoccupation. It is no coincidence that secularism and self-absorbed individualism are both features of our culture; the one is the fruit of the other. Our hearts are made to worship, and when the rightful object of our devotion is taken away, we gladly substitute ourselves.

  A children's poem by Robert Frost about fireflies captures the mutinous spirit of modern man:

  > Here come real stars to fill the upper skies,
  > And here on earth come emulating flies
  > That, though they never equal stars in size
  > (And they were never really stars at heart),
  > Achieve at times a very starlike start.
  > Only, of course, they can't sustain the part.[7]

- *The Bible is thrown overboard.* A third result of the stark secularity of our world is that the Bible is written off as a source of truth and wisdom. With the rise of science and reason and the growing skepticism toward the supernatural and miraculous, people see the Bible far differently from the way it was previously viewed. At best, it's seen as irrelevant. It is a bunch of superstitious stories that are the product of a premodern world, valuable only as a text in a graduate level ancient literature class. At worst, the Bible is regarded as just plain wrong. It is a collection of faulty, misguided myths that we are better off throwing away. The one thing modern men and women feel sure they cannot do is take the Bible seriously as God's reliable word.

- *People of faith are not taken seriously.* A result of living in a world that has written off God is that it also writes off those who take God seriously. When a person's religious devotion goes beyond a "due and proportionate sense of social sensitivity" and plunges over into the area of deep devotion, our world doesn't know what to do. Committed Christians are put in the same category with people who believe a camera is an evil eye that threatens their souls or with those who wear the same lucky (and stinky) pair of socks every game day in the belief that that will influence who wins.

    Not surprisingly, the chilly reception given ardent devotion reinforces the division between a private world God inhabits and a public world from which God is absent. I think Stephen Carter hits it on the button when he says the pervasive intuition is that "religion is like building model airplanes, just another hobby: something quiet, something private, something trivial—not really a fit activity for intelligent, public-spirited adults."[8]

So here is our challenge in a secular age, to bring biblical truth to a world in which men and women are giants, God is dwarfed, the Bible is trivialized, and believers are suspect. No small task.

10

God's **Word**
to a **World Alone**

A half hour into a flight from Atlanta I was kicking myself for not introducing myself to the man seated next to me. I'd been absorbed in editing this book and hadn't paid much attention to him. Now his tray table
and the seat between us were covered with spreadsheets, and striking up
a conversation would be quite awkward ("So, whatcha doing? Balancing
your checkbook?"). But I sensed that I should talk with him, so I prayed
that the Lord would somehow open up an opportunity.

Ten minutes hadn't gone by when he tapped me on the shoulder. "I'm
sorry," he said, "I seem to have grabbed this by mistake off the seat
between us." Then, before he handed me my legal pad, he looked at it
again and said, "What language is this?" It was my handwriting—an editorial I had just written while driving to my pastor's covenant group. Grinning, he said, "I'm usually pretty good at deciphering handwriting, but
I've never seen anything quite like this. Mind if I try?"

He began: "People on the outskirts of the human race have become
negotiable. For them, life has become optional." He looked up from the
page and over his glasses to me. "Whew, this is heavy! What is this?" I
explained to him that it was an editorial about the way our culture has
come to see people in consumer categories; we weigh the worth of a life
on the basis of usefulness rather than with a sense that life is worthwhile
intrinsically, the gift of a creator. I wrote the article to get people think-

ing about whether we may not have been a bit hasty in ejecting God from our modern worldview.

That got the man thinking. "Let me ask you something. Do you think things happen for a reason?" I told him that if there isn't a God, then no, things can't happen for a reason. Everything is random, an accident with no author. "But if there is a God, and God is concerned about us and wants to be involved in our lives, then absolutely yes, things happen for a reason. And in my life, I see all kinds of evidence for that. What about you?"

The man, whose name is Bob, frowned. "My psychiatrist in New York is really pushing me to think about my life in spiritual categories, but I've never done that in my whole life. God has no place in my life. You know what my life is about? The bottom line. Results. Success. It's all up to me. Taking everything personally. I've never let God into any of it. I've got all the money I want, a great wife, beautiful house, incredible job."

He leaned across the seat between us. "But you know what? My life is empty. It's like the myth of Sisyphus. I roll a rock up a hill, it rolls back down; I roll it back up again, and on and on. My life has no point."

He stopped and thought, running his fingers across his chin and staring at the floor. Then he looked back at me and, with eyes both tentative and eager, whispered, "What is God like?"

"For the longest time," I said, "I wondered the same thing." And for the rest of our flight we talked about a man from Galilee who pitched his tent in the midst of humanity and made God known.

How do we gain a hearing in a world that has stopped its ears to the existence of God?

Reanimating a Hollow World

First, I believe we need to begin by holding before the world an alternative way of making sense of existence, one with God at its center. Ever since the first stirrings of secular thought, Christians seem to have fallen into feeling they need to meet scientists on their terms, "proving" God's existence from within a largely naturalistic framework. There certainly is a place for evidence, for apologetics or proofs that the secular mind can grapple with. But I think we need to stand back and unapologetically state the truth that God *is*. He exists, he is real, and he has a claim on the world and on each of us.

God's truth, while unverifiable by science, is true nonetheless. It confirms itself within men and women as God's Spirit impresses it upon their hearts. Tangible evidence can help nudge a heart in that direction, but ultimately, our seeing the truthfulness of God and his Word is God's doing, not our doing.

That being the case, we need to take every opportunity simply to announce the presence of the one the world presumes to be dead and gone. In the newspapers and public schools, in the conference rooms and courts of law, we need to reinvert the world and reintroduce its God. The things we say and do, the integrity of our character, and the quality of our life together should reverberate with this basic truth, announcing in unison: There is a God!

"Do you not know?" shouts Isaiah. "Have you not heard?"

Has it not been told you from the beginning? Have you not understood since the earth was founded? He sits enthroned above the circle of the earth, and its people are like grasshoppers.

"To whom will you compare me? Or who is my equal?" says the Holy One. Lift your eyes and look to the heavens: Who created all these? He who brings out the starry host one by one, and calls them each by name. Because of his great power and mighty strength, not one of them is missing.

Do you not know? Have you not heard? The LORD is the everlasting God, the Creator of the ends of the earth.

Isaiah 40:21–22, 25–26, 28

It is time to invite this secular world again to take God and his Word seriously, to once again factor the person of God into its equations. It is time to reconsider our hasty dismissal of the Almighty.

Beyond this, today's secular person needs to be challenged with the limits of science and its way of making sense of the world. Science is a net whose cords are not fine enough to catch God. But that does not mean God doesn't exist.

Marv and I took a trip together, driving for about four hours late one night. Marv's framework as a mechanical engineering student and amateur astronomer was naturalistic, one that assumed God was outside the pale of real life. After we'd driven for a while I told Marv about my recent conversion to Christ. He was silent. Then, very graciously, he said, "Well, it sounds like you've found something that's meaningful for you, and that's good." He paused, and then he went on. "I guess I just have a hard time believing in stuff like that. I tend to look at the world more as a scientist, and that doesn't leave a lot of room for God. For me to believe in something, I need proof, facts."

"And that rules out God?"

"Well, why should I take the idea of God seriously? There is no way to prove that God exists. There is nothing to hold up in a test tube and say, 'See? Proof!'"

"But science can't prove everything," I said. "All it does is measure the physical world and explain how it works. That leaves a lot out."

"Like what?"

At the time, Marv was in a serious relationship. "Do you love Cindy?" I asked.

He grinned and looked at me, puzzled. "Of course I love Cindy—but what does that have to do with anything?"

"Well, how do you know you love her? Can you measure love? Can you prove it exists? No, but it is still very real. Science just isn't able to measure love. There are lots of aspects of life that don't register with science at all: our feelings, freedom, honesty, purpose in life. Science doesn't even admit any of those things exist.

"All science does is tell us how the physical world works. It doesn't tell us why there is a world or who designed it. It only tells us that every action produces an equal and opposite reaction, and things like that. Just because you can't measure God doesn't mean you can leap to the idea that God doesn't exist.

"To know if there is a God and why the world is the way it is, you can't look to science. You've got to turn somewhere else."

It is important to remember as we relate to secular people like Marv that science began as a way for people to understand only the what and how of the world. The first scientists were aware of science's limits and actively looked to the Bible for answers to the why questions of meaning and purpose, questions long since thrown overboard. But as Lesslie Newbigin thoughtfully puts it, "If purpose is a significant category of explanation, then revelation is an indispensable source of reliable knowledge." The modern world needs to be reminded of the limits of its favored scientific method. It is the source of much, but certainly not all, that there is to know.

The third beginning point with secular people is in the Bible itself. Today's men and women need to be invited to get their noses into the pages of the Bible. It is so easy (and safe) to write off the Bible without ever reading it. In a secular world, our efforts will be better spent if we work to get people simply to read the Bible than if we seek to convince them of its trustworthiness before they ever open its cover. We don't need to prove that the Bible is accurate (though we can draw on some important bits of apologetics). We merely need to get people to read it. God will show the truth of his Word as it is read.

Bart and I were talking at one point, and he was asking another of his great questions, something about reconciling the God of the Old Testament and the God of the New. Bart and I had spoken often, and I could tell this was more a way of avoiding the issue than it was a genuine question. I stopped him and said, "Bart, I think you're asking the wrong questions."

He looked at me, nodded, swallowed hard, and said, "All right. All right. What are the questions I *should* be asking?"

"There are three," I said. "First, is there a God? Is there someone out there who made me and has a claim on me? Second, if there is, what is it that God would have of me? Why do I exist? What *is* his claim on me? And third, how do I know? Where do I go to answer my questions about what is true about God, about me, and about God's purpose for me? What is my source of authority for answering spiritual questions?"

Bart looked at the palm of his hand for a minute. "And how did you answer those questions?"

"Well, when it first occurred to me to ask those questions, I was an atheist. And I saw that I had answered the first two—no, God does not exist and, no, nothing has a claim on my life—without ever really thinking about the third one. As I thought about it, I realized that I had been deciding for myself what was true about God. And I had found it convenient to believe that there was no God. But it never occurred to me till then to ask God what was true about God.

"I had never read the Bible before; I had just dismissed it. Now I went back and looked hard at the Bible for the first time, asking myself, If I was God, how would I communicate to the people I'd made? Well, if the creatures I made had brains, language, and the ability to think clearly (as we presumably do), it would make sense to me to do more than just drop a bunch of hints through sunsets and tornadoes and newborn babies. I would find a way to speak with them directly.

"Maybe, I thought, just maybe that's what the Bible is. Interestingly enough, when I began to look through the pages of the New Testament, I found out that is exactly what the Bible claims to be: God's word to us. For instance, in one place it says that the Bible comes straight from God's mouth and that it gives us everything we need to know God and to become the people God would have us be (2 Tim. 3:16–17). The more I began to read it, the more convinced I became that it is God's word to us.

"Tell you what, Bart, how about if we dig into it a bit and see what the Bible says about who God is and why God made us?"

Much of the secular world around us would put money on two sure statements: God does not exist, and the Bible is unreliable. However, when we announce the supremacy of God at every turn, when we point out the limits of science's ability to answer our questions of purpose, and when we dare secular people to discover for themselves what the Bible says, we press this world's men and women to rethink these "facts" that they have come to believe unquestioningly. For God is most assuredly not dead, and the Bible is anything but a dull and lifeless collection of myths from cultures past.

The Bible in a Secular World

Here are some other thoughts about how to engage our world with biblical truth.

How We Preach and Teach

Focus on the hearer. The hearing we gain will be greatly improved if we are able to stay in the life of the listener from beginning to end. Don Sunukjian put it this way: "A man does not come to church asking about the connection between Romans 8 and 9. He comes saying, 'My daughter's going out with a yo-yo, and I'm afraid he's going to get her pregnant.'"[1] If we talk to secular people about the Bible, we lose them. If we talk to them about themselves from the pages of the Bible, we grab them. Effective communication is not merely telling biblical truth. It is bringing biblical truth to bear in the life of the hearer. Otherwise, the words of the Bible remain dead.

Use the Bible as support rather than proof. The Bible is our final authority in all matters of faith and practice, but the world does not see it in the same way.

In our secular world, "the Bible says" carries about as much weight as "Alfred E. Neumann says." So what? Quoting a passage of Scripture as a proof will raise questions more often than it will carry any kind of authoritative clout.

When we want to bring biblical wisdom to bear in a conversation or evangelistic message, we need to remember that a thing isn't true because it's in the Bible. It's in the Bible because it's true. For instance, the Bible wisely admonishes us not to let the sun go down on our anger (Eph. 4:26). Staying up until we work out our problems forces us to keep short accounts with each other and prevents the destructive stuff of bitterness from festering. And when Jesus says that we cannot serve both God and Money, that we will come to love one master and hate the other (Matt. 6:24), he is saying something that is borne out by experience. Materialism is a jealous god that demands our exclusive devotion. When we draw on the wisdom of the Scriptures, we can take care to show that it is with good reason that we turn to the Bible for answers.

Bringing truth to bear means beginning where our audience stands and making sure that the gap between the modern world and the biblical world is not too broad to cross. "More and more in our culture," says Haddon Robinson, "you can't assume that people will come saying, 'Oh my, I wonder what the Bible says about this?'"[2]

When it comes time in an evangelistic message or conversation to introduce what the Bible says about a topic, we need, as Robinson once put it, to walk the bridge and not jump the river.[3] Here are some ways he suggests we might help our hearers across to the text.[4]

> "It's interesting that this topic we are talking about is talked about in the Bible. But that's not a surprise, because the Bible is about God, and God cares about this."
>
> "The Bible doesn't answer all questions. If you want to make a chocolate cake, I don't know which book of the Bible to send you to. But it deals with the important questions."
>
> "One of the reasons people turn to the Bible in crisis is because it answers the kinds of questions we ask. Let me read to you just one sentence from the Bible."
>
> "The Bible is deeply concerned with this issue. Let's take a look at what it says."
>
> "You know, there's a sentence in the Bible that is really pregnant with meaning."
>
> "At the heart of what we have been talking about so far is the issue of power. But power to do what? As you know, there is a good and right use of power. That kind of power is what the Bible is all about."

Anticipate obstacles and doubts. When addressing women and men who have inherited a secular, skeptical worldview, it is to our benefit to anticipate some of the obstacles that will crop up as we speak. If we talk right past a question that is forming in the minds of our hearers, we will lose the hearing we've worked so hard to gain.

To many people today, the Bible is an untrustworthy source, brimming with exaggeration and faulty information. In an audience of non-Christians, our hearers will want to know why we are going to the Bible to get our answers when there are lots of other seemingly more reliable places we could look. We should be ready to say why we are confident that the Bible provides worthwhile answers. That might mean covering the ground a bit on the inspiration and authority of the Scriptures as a whole. Or defending the reliability of a particular New Testament book by showing that it was written far earlier and with far greater accuracy than one might guess. Or unearthing archeological evidence that supports the authenticity of a particular event in biblical records.

We should be candid and honest about the struggles a modern audience faces when it encounters some of the unusual particulars in the Bible and do our best to put our listeners at ease by anticipating, affirming, and answering their questions. When we read an account from the Bible that raises some eyebrows—some counterscientific or supernatural event such as the sun stopping in its tracks for a day in Joshua 10, an ax head floating like a pool toy in 2 Kings 6, or Jesus sending a band of demons to ride herd on a bunch of pigs in Mark 5—we'd better anticipate the obstacles and respond to them. We need to be ready to account for the many things that will strike a modern reader of the Bible as outlandish. Scientific impossibilities, miracles, creation, the supernatural realm, and the demonic all scream for some sort of explanation. That doesn't necessarily mean we have to provide a convincing scientific explanation for those things. It only means that we should help provide our hearers with a biblical framework for thinking about them, one that takes both the findings of science and the teachings of Scripture seriously.

Keep close tabs on language. This point bears repeating: We will communicate best when we strip "Christianese" from our vocabulary. The lingo of the church flies about as far as a brick with today's audience. Intercede? Testimony? Ordained? Eh? Effective communication stands or falls on the ability of our words to carry our ideas across to our audience. That process is hard enough with words we all understand. Why muddy it by using words that for most people sound like they came from a technical manual written in the 1400s?

I'm not advocating throwing overboard every biblical word or phrase, or trading them all in for contemporary expressions. Certain words are tough to replace or do without, and trying to substitute other words for them—such as CEO for Lord or kindness for grace—inevitably compromises their meaning. The same would be true of words like redemption, sin, and holiness.

Here's my encouragement: Tune in to your word choice. If you're about to use a word or phrase that comes straight out of your conversational Christianese manual, stop and think about it for a moment. Can I communicate this idea faithfully without the lingo? If so, replace it with a faithful and familiar substitute. If not, use the word, and then do whatever you can to give the word a context—define it, restate it, translate it into the language of your hearers. You might think about pulling out a recent tape and listening for lingo, or asking a friend to listen for this as you talk with others. How would somebody who doesn't know the "native tongue" of the church perceive what you've said? You might be surprised by what you hear.

How We Share Faith

Several approaches to sharing faith with a secular person can be quite effective.

Ask probing questions. Perhaps the most effective approach is simply to ask questions that spark deeper thinking. Harry Blamires, in his book *The Secularist Heresy,* writes that the biggest reason people dismiss God is that they are not in touch with their finiteness. For most of us living in the Western world, life is comfortable enough, resources are abundant enough, and we are self-directed enough to feel we have no need of God. "Man behaves as though he were not a dependent creature with a limited and temporary existence in a limited and temporal universe."[5]

For most of those with whom we share life, existence is consumed with nothing deeper than the topsoil of life, things like grocery lists, sitcom plots, oil changes, and Little League schedules. Blamires' suggestion: Nudge your conversations toward consideration of the deeper, more troubling issues of life that would otherwise be given little thought. Particularly consider questions of what makes us happy, how we find meaning, and whether there is something outside of ourselves to which we can turn when life sours. "Are you satisfied with life? Are you satisfied with yourself? Isn't your heart charged with desires that never seem to be fulfilled, with hopes that life's experiences so often seem to frustrate, with aspirations life's horizons are too limited to contain? Could there be some dimension of life beyond what we see in which those longings can find full expression? Why do you exist?" These are the kinds of questions Blamires encourages us to ask.[6]

One of the most important gifts we can give the secular person is an awareness of the fact that she or he is a finite creature. Not boundless in potential and resources, not self-creating and self-sustaining, not in control, but actually limited and helpless in the face of so much that is served up by life. As they begin to grasp this, people are then open to considering—perhaps for the first time—the ideas of infinity, eternity, and divine necessity. When I discover how brief my life is, I reach for what is eternal. When I acquire a sense of having been made, I begin to wonder about my purpose. When I see life more and more as a gift, I want to know the gift giver.

It's just the kind of thing Paul was trying to do in Acts 14 with the people of Iconium: Wait a minute! Wait a minute! Don't you see it? Don't you see that you have been on the receiving end of kindnesses? Where do you think the rain comes from? What causes your crops to grow? Who provides all your food for you? And the joy you feel at being alive—where do you think that came from?

I think it is also what the author of Ecclesiastes seeks to do. "What does man gain from all his labor at which he toils under the sun? . . . Whoever loves money never has money enough. . . . Who knows what is good for a man in life, during the few and meaningless days he passes through like a shadow? . . . This is the evil in everything that happens under the sun:

the same destiny overtakes all. . . . Moreover, no man knows when his hour will come" (Eccles. 1:3; 5:10; 6:12; 9:3, 12).

In a more contemporary example, this is also exactly what Walker Percy has done in *Lost in the Cosmos,* which is nothing more than a series of probing questions, provocative multiple choice answers, and scattered wry commentary. Writing from within a Christian worldview, Percy's goal is to get people thinking about why it is that, in a world so well understood, we as humans remain such a mystery. At the end of his book he sums it up using an imaginary message sent by visitors from outer space in a series of tough questions. "Are you in trouble? How did you get in trouble? If you are in trouble, have you sought help? If you did, did help come? If it did, did you accept it? . . . Do you read me?"[7]

Good questions lead men and women to deeper thinking. But not always visibly. This summer my car broke down and I had to have it towed. The driver of the tow truck was a character, carrying on a running conversation with all the others on the road. "Look, Bud, I weigh more than ten of you combined. You better not do that." "C'mon Sally, I left you some space to get in there. That's right. C'mon." "Wake up, Sam. The light's green. What are ya, takin' a nap?"

At one point he said, "These people, they drive like nutcakes." He paused for a minute, nodding. "But ya know, ya can't blame 'em. Life is so full of stress for all of us. No time, too much to do, pressure at work, pressure at home—it makes sense that we'd get out on the road and drive like a bunch of loonies."

"So how do you deal with that kind of stress?" I asked. "Where do you look for answers to the tough stuff that life throws at you?"

He looked across at me as though he realized for the first time that I was sitting there in the cab of his truck. "Who, me?"

"Yeah."

"I like to drive cars a hundred and sixty miles an hour."

I suppose my eyes widened a bit.

"See, I build and race dragsters. That's how I deal with my stress."

I'd like to tell you that we spent the rest of the time talking about deeper issues. We didn't. We talked about engine temperatures and starting lights and how many Gs you pull when you come off the line.

But that's okay. That kind of question is like a fish hook. It grabs onto the conscience and stays there, sparking deeper thinking that can lead a person to begin to ask if there isn't something more to life than a quarter-mile drag strip.

Explore reasons for unbelief. My experience as an atheist through high school and most of college is that many people are atheists out of convenience more than conviction. Sure, they have reasons for not believing in God, but their reasons often are rationalizations built up in support of the fact that they simply don't want to believe in God.

Most of us sense that inviting God into our lives would mean some pretty major rearranging of the internal furniture. We won't get to be in charge anymore, and being in charge feels great. And we won't get to do whatever we can get away with; we'll have to trade in our comfortably broad moral latitude for something much more confining.

We simply don't like anybody else telling us what to do or what not to do, much less what to turn over control of or surrender altogether. For many—as certainly was the case for me—atheism is a convenient way of avoiding God's costly claims on one's life. According to the Bible, unbelief reveals something not about God but about those who deny him. "In his pride the wicked does not seek him; in all his thoughts there is no room for God" (Ps. 10:4).

Atheism is not only a matter of convenience; it proves to be a rather shaky belief system. For the past couple of centuries, belief in God has been ridiculed as irrational and backward, while disbelief—described as reasonable, plausible, rational, sensible—has won our culture's unthinking acceptance. But is theism really any less legitimate a worldview than naturalism? A modern person able to suspend disbelief in the supernatural would have to admit theism actually provides a compelling explanation for life as we experience it. Evidence for theism is much greater and evidence for naturalism much spottier and inconclusive than many might suppose. Belief in atheism actually requires a leap of faith every bit as sizable as that made by belief in a loving, personal God.

These things being the case, next time you talk with an atheist, you might take some time to poke around a bit. "Tell me, why do you think there isn't a God? What led you to become an atheist? Where are you getting your information about God? What makes you so sure that there is no God? Is it possible you're wrong? Is it possible there is a God, but that you are not looking in the right place to find out? If there was a God, how do you think he would make himself known? Have you ever really looked at the Bible to see what it says about God? What's kept you from doing that? Would you be willing to do that with me now?"

Expose secularism's troubling implications. Naturalism, the scientific worldview that eliminates any trace of God and the supernatural, leads down troubling corridors when we follow its conclusions to the end. The starkest are these: If life consists only of time plus matter plus chance, then I have no intrinsic value, life has no purpose, and we are alone in the universe. A universe in which there is no God means a universe devoid of meaning. I am a fluke, a quirk, an accident. "From goo to you by way of

145

the zoo," was the way Frank Peretti once put it. I am a blip on a screen that nobody is watching. I am alone and of absolutely no consequence.

In a message more sobering than funny, a billboard for the Natural History Museum in Boston expresses our alienation pointedly. "Visit the Planetarium, you tiny insignificant speck in the universe!"

Something within us screams against this. God has planted within us a sense of our unique value before him and our unique place in his universe. No, I am not alone! I am not a drifter in an empty universe!

The Bible supports our indignation. It insists that God made us and that in him we live, move, and have our being. He gives us life, breath, and everything else. And he has scattered everywhere evidence of his existence, his might, his kindness, and his artistry (Acts 17:25–28; 14:17; Rom. 1:18–20). It is not the wise one but the fool who says in his heart, "There is no god" (Ps. 14:1).

The late Carl Sagan, a secular scientist who studied the origins of the universe, insisted that the universe is all that is, or was, or ever will be. If that is true, why all the fascination with aliens? Have you noticed? Otherwise steady men and women of science grow giddy as they talk about SETI, the search for extraterrestrial intelligence. Dozens of recent movies center on this theme of the discovery of and contact with alien life-forms. Why such a keen interest in ET and his out-of-this-world friends? Because the echo of a universe without God is too much to bear.

The search for life elsewhere in the universe can be seen as the misdirected search for God. Though not a Christian, scientist Paul Davies in his book *Are We Alone?* sees the interest in contact with alien life stemming "from the need to find a wider context for our lives than this earthly existence provides. In an era when conventional religion is in sharp decline, the belief in super-advanced aliens out there somewhere in the universe can provide some measure of comfort and inspiration for people whose lives are otherwise boring and futile. This sense of religious quest may extend to scientists themselves, even though most of them are self-professed atheists."[8]

The prevailing worldview says we are alone and unimportant. We desperately need to know we are neither. That need is not just an intellectual one. It is a very real help-me-get-through-life need we all have.

Cheryl and Denny came to see me at the church, their new marriage falling apart. They pulled up to the church in Cheryl's old Pinto. Bumper stickers on the back of her car announced, "My other car is a broom" and "God is coming back . . . and is she p——ed!" Cheryl was a rough-edged bartender, a tough fidgety girl squeezed into tight jeans and a sweatshirt. A gruff, brawny biker, Denny was every bit her match. It was obvious from their nervousness that the church was not exactly a second home to them.

When I asked what led them to contact the church, they weren't sure. Denny shrugged and said, "I guess we both just felt like something was missing, and maybe it was God, and we figured, what the h——, it was worth a shot. So we flipped open the Yellow Pages, stuck our finger on the page, and here we are."

As we talked, it became obvious that Denny and Cheryl had backgrounds every bit as tough as their appearances. He'd been abused and then abandoned by his father, and had been in and out of jail and bouncing from job to job. She had been molested repeatedly by her father, raped by a stranger when she was twenty, and had been in a series of destructive relationships ever since. Now she was pregnant, but the child she carried was not her husband's; she had gotten drunk and gone off with a friend of his for a fling right after they were married. Little wonder their eight-months-old marriage was falling apart.

We talked about their marriage for a while, and I gave them some tips on forgiveness and dealing with anger, but I knew the greatest hope for their marriage lay in introducing them to the Lord. I still remember these two tough cookies coming to tears when I asked them, "What would it be like to know you were loved no matter what? No matter what you did, no matter what choices you made, no matter how unlovable you felt? What would it be like to know that someone who loved you with that kind of love was always with you? That you would never be alone, ever again? That is the kind of love that Jesus came to give us."

When I asked if I could tell them more, they were eager to hear.

Naturalism simply doesn't square with our deepest sense of what we need or with our keenest intuition about what is true. This is not a world devoid of God but *animated* by him, and life makes sense only as we come to know him.

Present evidence for a design. While it is not possible to prove to someone that God exists and should be taken seriously, there are some fruitful directions in which to move a conversation with someone open to discussion. One of the most effective apologetic approaches with the secular person is the argument from design. This says that clues everywhere in the universe point to a creative hand behind all that exists. I drew on this during a lunch with Jack, an engineer who had begun to attend church with his wife.

As we poked around the remains of our lunch, I said, "You know, Jack, my guess is that as somebody who comes with a background in science, it's tough for you to take the idea of God seriously."

"Yeah, I guess the God thing has been hard for me right from the start."

I said, "I've been reading some stuff lately that has really gotten me thinking. I don't know about you, but growing up I always got the impression that science had pretty much disproved God, that there was no place for God in the universe—it all just ran by itself.'"

Jack nodded. "Yeah, me too."

"Well, some of what I've been reading lately really gives a different picture. For instance, did you know that the people who have been studying DNA say it is organized like a language? It isn't like anything produced by chance. It's just like somebody sat down and wrote out the genetic script that is in every living thing, giving direction to its growth. The silly idea that there is a personal God who created everything doesn't seem nearly as silly to some people now.

"Scientists also talk about something called the anthropic principle.[9] They say it's almost like the universe and our solar system and the earth were specially made to support human life. The chance of the universe expanding at just the right speed to avoid recollapsing and of the earth ending up at just the right distance from the sun, at just the right angle, with just the right combination of gases in its atmosphere and water on its surface—it's infinitesimally small. You know, for years scientists tried to recreate earth's primordial soup in the hopes of creating life. But now, twenty or thirty years later, they're giving up. Even when they tried to speed up the process and jump-start the beginning of life by mixing the crucial ingredients and zapping it with electricity—nothing. So now they've stepped back and started asking a couple of questions that are pretty tough to answer. Why is the universe the way it is, as opposed to being some other way? And why is there anything at all? Researchers find more and more reasons to think the universe was made with us in mind.

"And now that evidence for the big bang keeps piling up—the idea that the universe started at a particular point in time and space fifteen billion years ago or so—scientists have a dickens of a time trying to explain the origin of life and the universe without the idea of a personal Creator.

"It's just like it says in the Bible: The heavens proclaim the glory of God. Day after day they shout about what he has done [see Ps. 19:1–2].

"It used to be easy for a scientist to think God doesn't exist. Now I think the opposite is true. There's so much order and design in the universe, so many hints of an intelligent being who made the universe just the way it is, that it gets harder and harder not to believe."

Whether it be over lunch, behind the pulpit, around discussion tables, within reading groups, through letters to the editor, or across the stage, we need to be creating forums—safe, honest, nonconfrontational settings of discussion—where a secular world can be invited to work through its toughest objections to faith and be given a clear presentation of the evidence. Creation and evolution, the origin of the universe, miracles and natural law, faith and reason, the trustworthiness of the Bible, evidence for the existence of God: all of these are topics that warrant candid conversation in a world that has ushered God off the playing field and out of the arena.

What We Communicate

Secularism could not stand more in opposition to what the Bible teaches. Here are some of the things I think bear saying to a world that has the hubris, the moxie, to deny the existence of its Maker and Sustainer.

God's existence. God is not a figment of our superstitious imaginations, nor is he the fabrication of weak minds. He is real. Philosophers call this view theistic (or metaphysical) realism: God is objectively real. Not a concept, not a fantasy, not a myth, but a real and personal spiritual being. From first to last, the Bible affirms the truth of this. It is never negotiable. As the Bible says, "In the beginning *God*," not "In the beginning *Man*" (Gen. 1:1).

God's glory. God animates and fills the whole world with his glory and grandeur. Evidence of God gleams at every turn. "The whole earth," as the seraphim proclaim, "is full of his glory" (Isa. 6:3). "For the LORD is the great God, the great King above all gods. In his hand are the depths of the earth, and the mountain peaks belong to him. The sea is his, for he made it, and his hands formed the dry land" (Ps. 95:3–5).

And God's fingerprints are everywhere. "He has not left himself without testimony," as Paul says (Acts 14:17). "God has made it plain to them. For since the creation of the world God's invisible qualities—his eternal power and divine nature—have been clearly seen, being understood from what has been made, so that men are without excuse" (Rom. 1:19–20).

God's sovereignty. God is the sovereign Lord of all. He is no pocket-sized, personal idol. He holds sway over the affairs of humanity, whether or not humanity acknowledges him. He has not been nudged aside from the universe's center, only from the hearts of women and men. "To the LORD your God belong the heavens, even the highest heavens, the earth and everything in it" (Deut. 10:14).

The bold announcement of Scripture is that God works out everything in keeping with his plan (Eph. 1:11). "The LORD brings death and makes alive; he brings down to the grave and raises up. The LORD sends poverty and wealth; he humbles and he exalts. He raises the poor from the dust and lifts the needy from the ash heap; he seats them with princes and has them inherit a throne of honor" (1 Sam. 2:6–8). "He changes times and seasons; he sets up kings and deposes them" (Dan. 2:21).

When we deny God, we place ourselves in opposition to the one who makes and sustains and orders the fortunes of all that is. "Why do the nations conspire and the peoples plot in vain? The kings of the earth take their stand and the rulers gather together against the LORD and against his Anointed One. 'Let us break their chains,' they say, 'and throw off their fetters.' The One enthroned in heaven laughs; the LORD scoffs at them. Then he rebukes them in his anger and terrifies them in his wrath" (Ps. 2:1–5). God holds sway over all.

God's claim on us. God made us and thus has a claim on each of us. We are his. "Know that the LORD is God," wrote David. "It is he who made us, and we are his" (Ps. 100:3). Jeremiah expressed a similar idea. "I know, O LORD, that a man's life is not his own; it is not for man to direct his steps" (Jer. 10:23). We are not our own. We exist for the pleasure of the one who fashioned us with his own hands (Rev. 4:11). All that we are and all that we have are his.

God's love. God created us for the purpose of showering his love on us. Love pervades every intention and every action of God toward humanity. It was love that sparked creation (Ps. 136:1–9), it was love that compelled the incarnation (John 3:16), and it is love that motivates God's every movement toward us today (Eph. 3:17–19).

A loving God runs counter to the convictions of a secular world. The God tossed overboard by the world around us is generally either a curmudgeon too distracted to notice us or a dictator too aloof to care. Yet it is the love of God that springs off nearly every page of Scripture as one of his central, defining qualities. God is love (1 John 4:16), and he looks with love on all he has made (Ps. 145:8–9). His love endures forever (Ps. 118:1).

God's holiness. God is holy, wholly unlike his creatures, free of any trace of imperfection, and morally untarnished (see James 1:17; Isa. 6:3). The arrogant rejection of his rightful place in people's lives is an affront to his holiness, an act of rebellion. "An oracle is within my heart concerning the sinfulness of the wicked: There is no fear of God before his eyes. For in his eyes he flatters himself too much to detect or hate his sin . . . he has ceased to be wise and to do good" (Ps. 36:1–3). Denying God's rightful place is a sin justly deserving of God's displeasure and punishment. God has good reason to be angry with us. "Will the one who contends with the Almighty correct him?" God asks Job, who has been questioning him. "Let him who accuses God answer him!" (Job 40:2).

The limits of science. Science and technology are not adequate answers to the deepest longings in the human heart. They may be able to prolong life and make it a bit more comfortable, but they are unable to solve any of our fundamental problems: our sin, our purpose, our eternal future, or our alienation from God. It is God who provides for our needs. "Praise the LORD, O my soul, and forget not all his benefits—who forgives all your sins and heals all your diseases, who redeems your life from the pit and crowns you with love and compassion, who satisfies your desires with good things" (Ps. 103:2–5). "He alone is my rock and my salvation" (Ps. 62:2).

Our spiritual nature. Contrary to the message we so often receive from the world, we are spiritual beings—but spiritually impoverished, parched for want of a right relationship with God. God has made provision for the nourishment of our souls by the forgiveness of our sins and reconciliation with himself through Christ. Apart from this right relationship with God, we are dead spiritually, dull and unresponsive to the things of God. "But, because of his great love for us, God, who is rich in mercy, made us alive with Christ even when we were dead in transgressions" (Eph. 2:1–5).

The authority of the Bible. The Bible can be trusted as God's reliable and adequate word to us, our final authority about spiritual issues. Though written by humans, its authorship at the same time is fully divine. In the pages of the Bible we have all we need to know about God, ourselves, and God's intentions for us—faithfully and accurately recorded. Through his use of the Bible, Jesus showed he saw it as indispensable, the very words of his Father. He based his ministry on it, answered his critics with it, and admonished his hearers to trust it. "You are in error," he said to one group, "because you do not know the Scriptures or the power of God" (Matt. 22:29).

We can look to the Bible with confidence as our final authority in all matters of faith and life. The familiar passage from Paul expresses it well. "All Scripture is God-breathed and is useful for teaching, rebuking, correcting and training in righteousness, so that the man of God may be thoroughly equipped for every good work" (2 Tim. 3:16–17).

The plausibility of miracles. The miracles described in the Bible are not scientific impossibilities.[10] Miracles are fully consistent with both the material world and the character of God because there are no natural or physical laws that somehow exist in and of themselves, inviolable properties of the universe that cannot be overruled. When scientists describe natural laws, such as gravity, they are merely talking about the consistent ways God relates to his universe, his "habit" of sustaining all that exists. Planets are not attracted to each other in and of themselves but are held by God in relationship to each other. Every atom is held together at every moment not by nuclear forces of attraction but by God's hand. A miracle is nothing more than God acting in an uncustomary way. When God raises a kindergartner from the dead or changes tap water into white zinfandel, no law has been broken. With God nothing is impossible (Luke 1:37). God is, as Asaph sings and as the Bible everywhere proclaims, "the God who performs miracles" (Ps. 77:14).

Science and the Bible. Finally, science has not disproved the Bible.[11] Nor has it eliminated the place of God in creation. Macroevolution, the theory of spontaneous creation through mutation and survival of the fittest, is not an airtight system. It is riddled with holes as an explanation of our existence and doesn't begin to give an account of creation that eliminates the need for God. To the contrary, more and more of those who study our origins—from molecular biologists to paleontologists to cosmologists—are returning to theism as the only adequate explanation for our existence. Whatever means may have been involved over whatever period of time, we exist because God brought us into existence. "Let every created thing give praise to the LORD," the psalmist writes, "for he issued his command, and they came into being" (Ps. 148:5 NLT).

Science is an amazing development unique to the Western world and a tremendous gift to each of us. But when it slides over from answering the what and how questions to attempt answering the why questions of meaning and purpose, it is wholly inadequate. Only God can account for the world that surrounds us. Any effort to explain the world without consideration of a loving, all-powerful God is arrogant and incomplete.

God's words speak as powerfully to today's brash secularist as they did to Job. "Where were you when I laid the earth's foundation? Tell me, if you understand. Who marked off its dimensions? Surely you know! Who stretched a measuring line across it? On what were its footings set, or who laid its cornerstone—while the morning stars sang together and all the angels shouted for joy?" (Job 38:4–7).

Those are questions this world needs to hear.

About Chapters 9 and 10

Concepts Worth Remembering

secularism: a worldview that acknowledges only the physical and temporal and diminishes God, faith, the supernatural, and the church

nominalism: literally "in name only," this is the practice of faith that has no transforming impact on its adherent or his or her surrounding world

authority: one's source of information about what is true

skepticism: the stance of actively doubting what we know and believe

empirical evidence: information that comes to us exclusively through our senses; "hard" measurable facts

naturalism: the closed-system view of science that holds that matter, energy, and the natural laws that govern them are all that exist

deism: the belief system common in the 1600s and 1700s that holds that God created the world and its natural laws but is otherwise uninvolved in the world

two-worlds view: the unfortunate split, common in a secularized society, between a private world in which God is active and a public world from which God is excluded

anthropic principle: the principle in cosmology that the universe was created with human observers as its aim

theistic realism: the philosophical conviction that God is objectively real

Recommended Reading

Appleyard, Bryan. *Understanding the Present: Science and the Soul of Modern Man.* New York: Doubleday, 1992. In his study of the influence of scientific thought in our culture, British journalist Appleyard makes an appeal to resist science's tendency to rob us of purpose, identity, faith, and God himself.

Carter, Stephen. *The Culture of Disbelief: How American Law and Politics Trivialize Religious Devotion.* New York: Basic, 1993. In this important book, Carter challenges the prevailing wisdom that says religion is unworthwhile as a personal pursuit and off limits in the public square.

Hummel, Charles. *The Galileo Connection: Resolving Conflicts between Science and the Bible.* Downers Grove, Ill.: InterVarsity, 1986. Hummel first highlights how four early scientists integrated their commitments to faith and science, and then—in an exceptionally clear and helpful way—wrestles with the issues of evolution, miracles, the age of the earth, and biblical authority.

Johnson, Phillip. *Darwin on Trial.* Washington, D.C.: Regnery Gateway, 1991. A Stanford law professor exposes the holes in the evidence for evolution and calls into question the naturalistic worldview that undergirds much of modern science. In his sequel, *Reason in the Balance* (Downers Grove, Ill.: InterVarsity, 1995), he further challenges the assumptions and pervasiveness of naturalism.

Newbigin, Lesslie. *Truth and Authority in Modernity.* Valley Forge, Pa.: Trinity Press International, 1996. In his customarily crisp and probing way, Newbigin challenges the prevailing confidence in science's ability to serve as our final authority.

153

Pearcey, Nancy, and Charles Thaxton. *The Soul of Science: Christian Faith and Natural Philosophy*. Wheaton: Crossway, 1994. The authors show the Christian origins of science, and then give a helpful tour—from a Christian perspective—of science's significant advances.

Updike, John. *In the Beauty of the Lilies*. New York: Fawcett Columbine, 1996. Using the fictional stories of four generations of characters, Updike tells the unsettling story of America's loss of faith in the twentieth century.

Part 6

HOW WE THINK

Beyond Right and Wrong

True pleasure is making up your own rules.

fashion ad on television

Destroy a man's belief in Immortality and not only will his ability to love wither away within him but . . . moreover, nothing would be immoral then, everything would be permitted.

Fyodor Dostoevsky, *The Brothers Karamozov*

11

Pushing Past Right and Wrong

I was flabbergasted.

I was with my family at a play place called Discovery Zone. The main feature of Discovery Zone is a huge contraption for romping and climbing that includes a maze of elevated tubes to crawl through, slides to scream down, trampolines to bounce on, and ball pits to dive into. Around the edge of this monstrous jungle gym are a number of tame and family-friendly arcade games.

In fact, the whole place has a family feel: friendly workers, home-style pizza, even knee pads for stiff-legged moms and dads who want to get in and join the fun.

That made it all the more of a shock when I glanced over and saw a dad obviously cheating on a basketball game with his son. The game's object is to make as many baskets as possible within two minutes. The more baskets made, the more tickets the game spits out. And what makes those tickets special is they can be traded for some pretty nifty toys.

So here was this dad, right out in the middle of the room, cheating. Now, he wasn't just shooting the balls for his son. ("Here, son, let your old Pop show you how it's done. I'll get you some of those tickets.") That would have been bad enough. This man was reaching over a protective barrier and dropping them in. As the balls popped up out of the machine, the son grabbed them and shoved them to his father, who then reached over the side and pushed them straight into the basket. Again and again. The two of them had it down to a science, and the tickets poured out in a steady stream.

They had quite a thing going.

The only problem was, it was quite a wrong thing they had going.

Not against the law. Not against any rules that were posted. Just plain wrong. Disregarding any sense of what is ethical, fair, honorable, virtuous, or appropriate (let alone beneficial as a model for a son), this man let what he wanted drive what he did. The end—getting as many tickets as possible in order to be a good dad for his boy—justified the means.

This man's actions exemplify the way many Americans think when it comes to issues of morality. If I had gone over and said I didn't think that was the way the game was intended to be played, I'm sure he would have been quick to reply, "Look, buster, mind your own business, would ya? Who do you think you are trying to tell me what's right and what's wrong? It's just a stupid game, anyway. It's not like I did anything illegal. I was just helping out my kid a bit. He's saving up for that Ultra Zombo Death Monster, and he just needed 140 more tickets. I thought the old dad could give him a hand."

Welcome to the gray terrain of American morality, where what we want determines what is right.

Don't get me wrong. Ours is not a country in which we have abandoned morals altogether, any more than it is a country that has abandoned God altogether. A poll by the Gallup group confirms this. In the fall of 1994, 68 percent of those polled said they believe in moral absolutes, that "some things are right or wrong regardless of the situation."[1]

The question is, which things? We have a sense of what is really bad and what is really good. With few exceptions we denounce rape or murder as wrong, and we agree that drug pushing and gang shootings cross the line. On the other end of the spectrum, we are pretty much unanimous that the late Mother Teresa's example of caring for abandoned children in the slums of India or a firefighter's death-defying rescue of a blind grandmother from a burning building are good and decent things.

It's the middle ground that's tough. And there is a lot of middle ground. It is there, in that wide expanse between the holy and the repulsive, that we spend most of our time. That is the land of everyday dilemmas and lip-chewing conundrums in which we live. There, the absolutes turn into maybe-so-maybe-nots, and our sense of right and wrong blurs. We begin to operate by a different set of moral guidelines.

In place of a scale with right on one end and wrong on the other are other lesser continuums:

Does it feel good, or does it feel crummy?

Is it beneficial to me, or does it cost me in some way?

Does it get done what I want done, or does it fail?

Does it look good, or does it look incriminating?

Do most people seem to think it's okay, or do they disapprove of it?

Categories of right and wrong have become mere safety nets, a cover-my-tail kind of concern. Is somebody going to die if I do this? Of course not. We're not talking about anything serious here. It's just a little fling (or a little stretch of the truth in my sales presentation, or a little gift on the side from a political supporter, or a little misrepresentation on my income tax, or a little help from a classmate on my exam, and on it goes).

Signs of the Times

These are the new moral considerations we live by: what feels good, what looks good, and what benefits me. You can see them at work everywhere.

In the movie *Indecent Proposal,* Robert Redford's character offers that of Demi Moore and her husband a million dollars if they will let him sleep with Demi. They accept. In a television survey on Oprah Winfrey's show, 52 percent of callers said they would have done the same thing.[2]

In a related survey, one in four Americans said that for $10 million, they would abandon their entire families. Twenty-three out of a hundred said they would become prostitutes for a week, sixteen would leave their spouses, and seven would kill a stranger.[3]

When Joan Rivers' seventeen-year-old daughter asked for contraceptives, Joan slipped her $250 for a hotel room "so it wouldn't happen in the back seat of a car."[4]

Teens in Lakewood, California, started a group during the 1990s called the Spur Posse. They had an ongoing competition to see who could have sex with the most girls, and often passed girls on to each other after they were done. Each time they had an orgasm with a different girl, they got a point. Billy, nineteen, was the high scorer with sixty-six points. "My parents were a little surprised," he said. "They thought it was more like fifty." The father of a founding member said, "Nothing my boy did was anything any red-blooded American boy wouldn't do at his age." His son had sixty-three points. The mother of another founding member likewise dismissed the whole thing. "What can you do? It's a testosterone thing."[5]

158

In the book *The Day America Told the Truth,* based on extensive surveys of two thousand Americans, authors James Patterson and Peter Kim conclude this:

> There is absolutely no moral consensus at all in the 1990s. Everybody is making up their own personal moral codes—their own Ten Commandments. . . . These are real commandments, the rules that many actually live by:
>
> 1. I don't see the point in observing the Sabbath (77 percent).
> 2. I will steal from those who won't really miss it (74 percent).
> 3. I will lie when it suits me, so long as it doesn't cause any real damage (64 percent).
> 4. I will drink and drive if I feel I can handle it. I know my limit (56 percent).
> 5. I will cheat on my spouse—after all, given the chance, he or she will do the same (53 percent).
> 6. I will procrastinate at work and do absolutely nothing about one full day in five. It's standard operating procedure (50 percent).
> 7. I will use recreational drugs (41 percent).
> 8. I will cheat on my taxes—to a point (30 percent).
> 9. I will put my lover at risk of disease. I sleep around a bit, but who doesn't (31 percent)?
> 10. Technically, I may have committed date rape, but I know that she wanted it (20 percent have been date raped).[6]

Leaping into the Gray

Hearing these things would have caused fibrillation in the heart of any common citizen just four hundred years ago. Today, it is so commonplace as to go unnoticed. How is it that concepts of right and wrong have been so vigorously elbowed aside?

There was a time when most people in the Western world lived in the same moral universe, with God at the center. Right was what he said was right. Wrong was what he showed to be wrong. The Bible served as the plumb line against which one's actions and motivations were checked. All the way up into the 1600s, most men and women agreed there were clear, God-given moral guidelines for behavior.

Moral standards were absolutes that applied to all men and women regardless of place, time, or circumstances. We found out about them through revelation. They were handed to us from outside our world in the Bible, God's revealed word.

So how have we come to where we find ourselves now? How is it that we have lost the moral anchor that once moored our society?

Enlightenment Optimism and Independence

The rope attaching our culture to its moral anchor, the Bible, began to slip with the growing optimism of the Enlightenment in the late 1600s and 1700s. This was a time of great confidence concerning the natural abilities of men and women. Scientific discoveries were announced almost daily. Technology made huge advances. Society's warring impulses seemed tamed. Medicine appeared invincible. Man was the pinnacle, the earth's pride and joy, the measure of all things. What could we not do?

Because of that, the biblical conviction that humanity was both great and fallen was abbreviated. Overboard went the ideas of fallenness, of original sin, and total, or universal, depravity. All that was left was the idea of humanity's seemingly limitless ability and potential. An unparalleled optimism gripped the imagination. This was the blossoming of humanism, and one telling expression of it was confidence in the reasoning powers of men and women.

According to this new view, humankind could trust its ability to reason clearly, to think its way to what is right and wrong. People might not agree on all the fine points; some tidbits may shift from one culture or set of circumstances to another. But they believed we could at least agree on general moral principles.

So people like John Locke and Thomas Hobbes set about developing a set of moral guidelines that would preserve each person's rights and maximize each person's benefits. They called this a social contract, a kind of handshake agreement to honor certain rights for each other. Things like protecting each other's lives and respecting each other's property and honoring each other's freedom. I'll do my thing and I'll let you do yours. I'll respect your rights, if you'll do the same with me.

Reasonable enough. But rights-based morality—as opposed to morality grounded in responsibilities and moral absolutes—soon jumps from having others as the focus to being concerned first with self.

Let me give you an illustration. One time, after a day of enjoying New England's autumn color, Sharon and I went out to dinner in a charming Vermont town. The dinner looked great, and we both wanted to share a bit of what we had. So we loaded up our forks with tasty samples and simultaneously reached across the table. But a funny thing happened. When our forks passed each other, we shifted our focus from the taste we were sharing and started looking at that morsel making its way across the table toward our own mouths. We opened our mouths and waited. Of course, as soon as we did that, our forks stopped in midair. We took our eyes off what we were giving, and started to focus on what we were getting. That is the Enlightenment legacy.

160

An optimistic view of humanity deprives us of our ability to challenge what *is* with what *ought* to be. A reason-based view of moral authority leaves behind absolutes grounded in revelation in favor of a minimalist cluster of moral universals. And a rights-based view shifts us away from thinking first of responsibilities and from what is right to what meets selfish needs. The rope is about to slip out of the anchor.

William James and Pragmatism

The shift from moral rightness to doing whatever would get the job done was furthered by the teaching of William James. He was a psychologist and philosopher whose books and lectures caught the attention of the United States around the turn of the twentieth century. His main theme, particularly toward the end of his life, was pragmatism, a radical new way of deciding what is right and true.

Pragmatism holds that an idea is only as good as the practical difference it makes in a person's life. There are no absolutes. There is no finality. Truth is what people find valuable, significant, useful, practical.

Morals, too, take on a bottom-line bent. What is right to do? What works. What is good? What is good for me. What should I do? Whatever produces the most beneficial results.

Pragmatism fits with the rubber-meets-the-road thinking typical of so many Americans. It is flexible and antidogmatic. Now, thanks to James and other pragmatists, we have come to measure the rightness of an action by its practical consequences. And there is no overarching moral framework of right and wrong to guide us in the particulars. In its place is a concern only for expedience. The pragmatism of William James began to tug the mooring line loose from our moral anchor.

Existentialism and the Authentic Act

The rope slipped free of the anchor with the rise of existentialism—the philosophy of thinkers like Jean Paul Sartre and Albert Camus—which came into public consciousness during the early to middle 1900s.

Existentialism holds that life is meaningless. The universe is absurd. There is no God, so there is no meaning or purpose inherent in life. There is nothing more solid to stand on than the fact that you exist. Because of that, it is up to you somehow to make life meaningful. Sartre's solution: authenticate your life by an act of the will. Decide to do *something,* and then do it. It doesn't matter what. The categories of right and wrong, rational or irrational, legal or illegal, are irrelevant. All that matters is asserting yourself in the face of life's absurdity, authenticating your-self through a sheer act of the will.

With existentialism we slipped free of the anchor and drifted into what some call *anomie:* lawlessness, an utter lack of moral norms that govern life.

The moral code of Sartre and Camus, perhaps more than any other, shapes the world we live in today. The '60s and '70s, with their anything-goes anarchy, were in many ways nothing more than the late flowering of existentialism at a popular level. Think of the slogans hurled from that cultural hurricane. "If it feels good, do it" and "Whatever floats your boat" probably sum up existentialism as well as anything. They also sum up the moral bent of our culture today.

In the 1940s, historian Arnold Toynbee studied twenty-one civiliza-tions. He noticed that disintegrating societies have five characteristics: They have a sense of drift, the feeling that life is meaningless and out of control. Because of that, they succumb to truancy, or escapism, retreat-ing into their distraction and entertainment. Aimless, they fall into a sort of promiscuity of thinking, an indiscriminate acceptance of anything and everything. Connected to that, they have a sense of moral abandon, ceas-ing to believe in a moral standard and yielding themselves to their impulses. Finally, they feel a huge burden of guilt, a self-loathing that comes from their moral abandon.

Toynbee describes today's moral universe.[7]

The New Morality: Take Care of Yourself

Our culture keeps using the words *right* and *wrong*. But for the most part, the words no longer mean what we think they mean. A new moral-ity guides us today. Americans determine what is right and wrong for themselves. In one survey 93 percent said they alone determine what is and isn't moral.[8]

That certainly fits with my experience. During my doctoral studies I went into the streets of Boston and Cambridge with two fellow students, a video camera, and a clipboard full of questions to survey people about their beliefs. One of the questions we asked was, How do you determine what's right and wrong; are there moral absolutes? The answer was unan-imous; here are some of the replies.

Two college students from Vermont were adamant. One said, "I don't think there's such a thing as an absolute. And I think society tries to give you their beliefs about what's right and wrong, but really, you just have to bring it down to what is morally right for you."

The other nodded in agreement. "I think it's all in your heart, what you believe is right or wrong. It can't be what the police say or what a judge says or anything. It's what you feel inside. It's whether you think what you're doing is right or what you're doing is wrong."

A black man in his thirties from Boston also agreed. "I have to judge what's right or wrong for me. No minister, no preacher, can tell me that."

A young woman waiting at the airport summed it up. "I don't think there are moral absolutes. I think a person should just be able to do what they want and justify it because they want to do it. I don't really think there's a right or wrong to anything."

The only moral absolute is personal choice. As Patterson and Kim reflected on the results of their national survey, they saw this pattern: "When we want to answer a question of right or wrong, we ask ourselves."[9]

Americans have stepped out from under the Bible and its moral authority. The natural result is that morals are relative. They are not absolute, not universally binding. You come up with your standards; I come up with mine. My standards apply only to me, and yours only to you. It is arrogant and intolerant of you to insist that I am somehow accountable to your moral norms.

Moral relativism is what breeds the kind of wacky ethical climate in which politicians can say, with all sincerity, "I personally believe that abortion is wrong, but I wouldn't think of passing a law that would prevent somebody else from exercising that right."

The new moral standard is the ethic of self-fulfillment, or what pollster Daniel Yankelovich calls the "duty-to-self ethic."[10] Our first moral obligation is to yours truly. When it comes to deciding what is right and wrong in this new ethic, here are some of the criteria we use.

It Feels Right

Feelings dominate our world. They have hijacked our language. We say "I feel" instead of "I think" or "I believe." When we have a decision to make, a belief to defend, or an action to justify, it is to our feelings we go for confirmation. If it feels good, do it. Ernest Hemingway hit it on the head: "What is moral is what you feel good after."

Few people have the self-mastery to make their feelings secondary and conduct their lives according to convictions. In a world in which self-expression and self-gratification reign, concepts like self-denial and self-control seem like antiques. Why should I mistrust my feelings when I've worked so hard to get in touch with them?

We feel obliged to do what we want to do. People have come to feel it is their "moral duty," as Yankelovich puts it, "to yield to their impulses."[11]

In the past four years I have seen four good friends let their feelings bring chaos into their marriages. They have caved in to their longings, dumped their wives, and gone off in pursuit of other women. "I just don't love her anymore," said one after the other. All four are Christians. I performed the wedding for two of them and counseled them before they got married. They all could sit across the table from me and tell me what the Bible says is true about marriage: It is a lifetime commitment. Divorce is against God's intentions for us. Adultery is wrong. But all four walked. They believed the poppycock that their feelings were right. They caved in to their desires and, against everything they knew in their heads to be right, allowed their emotions to dictate their actions.

It Brings About Good Results

If something gets good results (that is, it's beneficial, to my advantage, helpful, expedient), then it's considered okay to do. The movie *Quiz Show* is based on a scandal that resulted from just this sort of thinking in the early days of television. In the movie, when ratings for the popular game show *Twenty Questions* began to drop, a young college professor named Charles Van Doren is recruited to conquer the reigning whiz, Herb Stemple.

"What if we were to put you on the show," the producers suggest, "put you on *Twenty Questions* and ask you questions that you know, say the questions that you answered correctly on the test this morning?"

Van Doren is clearly puzzled. "I don't follow you. . . . I thought the questions were in a bank vault."

"Well, they are, in a way they are. You want to win, don't you?"

"Well, I think I'd really rather try to beat him honestly."

"What's dishonest? When Gregory Peck parachutes behind enemy lines, do you think that's really Gregory Peck? That book that Eisenhower wrote? A ghostwriter wrote it. Nobody cares. It's not like we'd be giving you the answers. Just because we know you know, you still know."

Not so long ago the phrase "the ends justify the means" was used primarily in a negative sense. We looked down on the person who was willing to let the bottom line determine his or her behavior. Today, this is considered a perfectly normal principle for making a decision.

All needs are believed to be good, as are all means to meeting those needs. Hey, whatever it takes.

In a national poll on cheating, 78 percent of students ages ten to eighteen admitted to having cheated on an exam. One of the students polled, a thirteen-year-old named Laura, spoke for a generation when she said, "I guess you do what you have to do to get what you want. . . . When you've got a legitimate reason, it's okay by me."[12]

Another survey of children showed that they decide what is right and wrong not by talking with teachers, pastors, or parents but by listening to each other and watching what goes on around them. Many more teens are guided by "what gets them ahead or what makes them feel good" than by anything else.[13]

At one time, others were central in our moral universe, which was governed by one unified moral standard (the right and the good as exemplified by God). Today our moral universe is inhabited by only one person—me—and governed by whatever it is that meets my needs.

Other People Say It's Good

In Pueblo, Colorado, the county courthouse bears the inscription "Vox populi, vox Dei." The voice of the people is the voice of God. It is the concept many of us use to decide what is right and wrong. In a land of opinion polls, we determine more and more what is right by consensus. What does everybody else think? What is everybody else doing? If other people are doing it, it must be okay. By contrast, if I am the only one doing it, I must be wrong. "Why should I drive the speed limit? Everybody else is going seventy." "Why should I report that income? Nobody else did." "Why should I be honest in my sales pitch? None of the competitors are, and it would just put me at a huge disadvantage." "What's wrong with sleeping around? Everybody's doing it; nobody's a virgin anymore."

Celebrity emulation is one particular form of this. Sitcom star Roseanne grabbing her crotch, singer Madonna parading around in her underwear, basketball superstar Charles Barkley taunting opponents with trash talk, basketball player Dennis Rodman whining and talking back to his coach, and comedians Andrew Dice Clay and Eddie Murphy rising to the top with raunchy, tasteless routines: these become the standards for behavior in our culture.

I got a taste of this several years ago as one of the leaders in our high school group helping to direct a youth mission trip. On the way there I rode with several of the high school guys. The one sitting next to me was listening to a Walkman. When I asked him what he was playing, he hemmed and hawed and tried to change the conversation. I finally got him to tell me. It was the rap group 2 Live Crew. I put it on the cassette player in the car so we could all listen to it and talk about it. The tape was angry, harsh, filled with graphic descriptions of killing cops and gang-raping women. When I asked him why he listened to that kind of music, he said all his friends listened to it, and he liked the beat.

That night, after a long day of driving, the guys went to a large dorm room on one side of the common room, the young women to a similar room on the other side. The other adult leaders and I sat in the middle room, reading. I couldn't believe it when I looked up and saw one of the young women, dressed only in a short T-shirt and underwear, walking across the room to talk to the guys. When we stopped her, she had no sense of having done anything inappropriate. "C'mon, what's the big deal? Everybody else does it!"

A few days later I came into the guys' dorm just in time to hear one of our most respected young men telling the punch line of a graphic sex joke. When I called him on it, he only felt bad that he was caught. The joke was no big deal. That night we did a sort of talent show with the whole group. Two of the young men did a series of *Saturday Night Live* takeoffs. I had to stop them halfway through because it was so crude.

It's not like I'm a lenient leader. Far from it. And it's not as though our kids were straight off the street. They came from solid homes and they were aware of my high moral standards. They just had no sense of what was appropriate. It may come as no surprise that the subject of discernment became the theme of our high school group for the next six months.

This isn't just a problem among teens. Our whole culture has bought into the everybody-is-doing-it mentality. We have lost all sense of propriety.

So here are the measuring sticks for the ethic of self-fulfillment.

- *Feelings:* It feels good. (I want to do it.)
- *Expediency:* It brings about good results. (I'll benefit if I do it.)
- *Consensus:* Others think it is good. (I'll do it because others do it.)

These are the ideas that are believed adequate to see us across that vast expanse between stark wrong and clear right. Individualistic, self-serving, flexible, undemanding . . . and incredibly wrongheaded.

12

God's Word to a World Astray

I was sitting, burger in hand, across from a single man who was wrestling with what it would mean to become a Christian. At one point he looked up, jabbed a fry at me, and said, "Can I ask your advice about something?"

"Shoot."

"Well, I'm in kind of an awkward situation. It's kind of hard to explain. There's somebody I work with who kind of likes me, and I guess I like her, too. We get along real well and we've kind of flirted around, gone out a few times.

"Anyway, she wants to have a child, and she asked me the other day if I would be a sperm donor for her, and I'm not sure what I should do."

I nodded. "Man, that's quite a decision!"

"Well, that's not the whole story. She's not just talking about the test tube and *in vitro* stuff. She wants me to sleep with her and get her pregnant."

"Oh, man. That raises a—"

"Hang on. There's more. She's married. And her husband is a real jerk. She doesn't love him anymore, but she doesn't want to deal with the hassle of a divorce. I was over at their house the other night, and she pulled me into the kitchen and told me she would really like it if I would be the father of her next child.

"What do you think I should do? What does Christianity have to say about something like this?"

Great question. How do we bring the moral truth of the Bible to bear in a world where the Scriptures are written off, right and wrong are vague and distant concepts, moral norms are all cattywampus, and real-life ethical guidelines look more like ways to get our needs met than guides by which to choose what is right?

Holding Up a Mirror

Perhaps the most important thing to communicate in such a world is the reality of sin and moral failure.

The Ivory soap 99.44 percent pure view of humanity doesn't cut it. This Enlightenment notion of the goodness of humankind must be dismantled. We must expose the hollowness of the idea that—as one of the first positive thinkers, Emile Loué, put it in the 1930s—"Every day in every way I'm getting better and better."

That's bunk. As Solomon wrote, "There is not a righteous man on earth who does what is right and never sins" (Eccles. 7:20). It takes some mighty extensive editing of ourselves to assert that we are good and getting ever better. Twisted motives, selfish relationships, compromised choices, and dishonest dealings are at every turn. We may be able to keep up the appearance of being good, or have one part of our lives fairly intact, but to look at the whole of our lives and to conclude that we are good is more of a reflection of what we wish than what we are.

The same is true when we look more broadly at our culture as a whole. The only way we can assert progress and optimism is to ignore a handful of details to the contrary, such as political corruption, racial tensions, gang violence, insider trading on the stock exchange, crass rap music, and a couple of world wars.

It seems like one careful reading of the newspaper should be enough to challenge too rosy an idea of human nature. Sitting through an hour of Sally or Geraldo should do the same. But it doesn't. Most men and women today still hold to a pretty high view of themselves, in spite of the overwhelming evidence to the contrary.

I believe several things make it hard for us to own up to our shortcomings. First, our emphasis on externals makes it easy for us to think we are good because we look good. We devote a lot of time and energy to our facades, taking regular inventory of the exterior: clothes matched and in fashion (check), tummies girdled and trim (check), facial flaws buried under makeup (check), teeth flossed and free of any unsightly leftovers from breakfast (check).

We know the outside inch by inch. But we are out of touch with what goes on inside. We manage to miss the darkness there because, in our concern with the surface trim, we so rarely peek through the windows.

The second thing that stands in the way of our fessing up to our flawed nature is that we feel we have to choose between saying we are either all good or all bad. All good doesn't quite fit the facts, but it is a lot more pleasant than saying we are all bad (read: miserable worms deserving of God's fury and eternal damnation). Nobody seems to have done a good job of accounting for what most of us, if we are honest, believe is the truth: We are both quite good and quite bad.

Biblical communicators have the challenge of helping seekers see that Christianity provides a convincing explanation for why we are the way we are. Created in glory but broken in a mighty fall, majestic and ugly, grand and puny. If men and women can be made to see why they are the way they are, it is not such a big distance from there to an explanation of what can be done to solve the problem and restore them to their former glory.

A third reason we tend to have a positive view of ourselves is that most of us decide we are good by comparing ourselves to others. And compared to most of the menaces of society we read about in the paper or see on the news, we come out looking not half bad. In fact, we come out smelling pretty good. "Hey, at least I'm not a billion-dollar bank embezzler or a serial killer!"

Among the most awkward—and important—things we can do for a seeker is to help him come face to face with his moral debility. That happens through good probing questions and, sometimes, uncomfortable conversations. Chuck Colson tells the wonderful story of a lunch with a collection of bigwigs from Hong Kong's banking and finance community. Ten of them were seated around a table at an exclusive rooftop executive club. Among them was a poised and polished English woman, the wife of the chairman of Lloyd's of London. At one point she leaned across the table to Colson and said, "Mr. Colson, you seem so intelligent, so well read. You're not one of those who goes around doing hellfire and brimstone preaching, are you?"

When he asked what she meant, she said, "Well, calling people sinners and that sort of thing." Colson looked across the table at her and asked, "Have you ever thought about yourself?" The other diners around the table grew still. Silverware was lowered and tensions began to rise. "You know," Colson went on, "man is not morally neutral. You are either disposed to sin or you are disposed to good. Now, look through the history of the twentieth century and tell me persons are disposed to good."

She thought about that for a moment and then said, "Well, I think man *is* morally neutral." Colson answered, "Two Jewish psychologists have just done a brilliant study in America on the criminal personality, and they've discovered that man has a disposition to evil. If you put him in a room, lock up everything, give him two choices, and let him know that he has nobody watching him, he'll always do the wrong thing."

She laughed, "I don't believe that for a moment. I am a good person." Colson shook his head. "I don't want to do anything that's going to ruin this lunch, but I must tell you that if you stop and think about it you are more like Adolf Hitler than you are like Jesus Christ." She dropped her fork, and the clang of silver against fine china rang through the lunch room. She didn't take another bite.[1]

In a world infatuated with appearances, we present a gift when we ask the questions that help people begin to understand what's clicking on the inside.

Ultimately, helping people face up to their moral depravity means helping them realize that the standard they are being held to is not the national moral average but God's moral perfection. And compared to that plumb line, we're quite off center. It is not about appearances. Nor is it about how we fare compared to others. It is how we line up with the character of God and his perfect moral standard made known in the Bible. "Be perfect, as your heavenly Father is perfect," Jesus says in Matthew 5:48. Those are high standards. Our sense of moral failure comes only when we see God for who he is: holy, mighty, and morally perfect.

We need to help people see God for who he is and—in that light—see themselves for who they are. That opens the way for people to see Jesus for who he is and to understand why he came.

Not long ago we developed a worship service to do just this, to walk people from the holiness of God to the sinfulness of humanity to the provision of God in Christ. We began by reading portions of Psalm 96 describing the splendor and majesty of the Lord. Then, after reading the psalm and singing together about God's perfection, we shifted the focus to our contrasting lack of holiness. I gave a short pointed message about the reality of sin and about the consequences of sin in our relationship with God. This was followed by an extended time of silence—at least five minutes—during which we invited people to catalog their failure to live up to God's perfect moral standard. In the third part of the service, I gave another short message, this time on the grace and forgiveness we find in Christ. We concluded with an invitation for seeking people to come to Christ and believers to come to communion.

In the first brief message, I began by talking about how consumed we are with appearances. Then I said, "But our concern with appearances puts us at odds with God in a big way. In Samuel it says that men and women look at outward appearances, but the Lord looks at the heart (1 Sam. 16:7). For us, appearance is everything. For God, appearance is nothing and character is everything. And when God looks past our appearances to our hearts, he doesn't like what he sees.

"So God created a mirror that would let us look past the surface to the heart. In dim enough light, from far enough away, every one of us can feel confident that we are basically good, decent folks, capable of right choices and able to love each other in caring, selfless ways. In the soft incandescent light of our surrounding world, we all come out looking pretty good.

"But in the piercing halogen light of his holiness, God sees something different . . . and he uses his Word as a mirror to help us see what he sees when he looks at us.

"In the movie *Outbreak,* a killer virus is spreading across the country. It begins harmlessly enough, with a few open sores on the person's face, but within twenty-four hours, the person is dead. There is no known cure. At one point in the movie, one of the key people fighting against the virus slips when she is taking blood from a patient and jabs her finger with a contaminated needle. She sloughs it off and presses on with her work, seemingly unconcerned. A little later, though, she goes into the bathroom and stands in front of the mirror. She pulls off her protective mask and inspects her face. And there are the first of the sores beginning to break out.

"God's Word is like that mirror. When we look into it, we see glimpses of ourselves. And if we will look closely, we can see evidence of a lethal disease at work in us. But for this disease there is a cure."

I then turned to Isaiah 59:3–8 and said, "This passage is like a full-length mirror for our hearts and souls. It describes people just like you and me. It reflects what is true about us. Let's see what it says."

We can help those who are morally befuddled and out of touch with their sinfulness by speaking "exposingly." With tough questions, probing illustrations, honest personal examples, and time for silent reflection, our messages can probe the ways of the heart, giving our hearers the opportunity to rummage around a bit in their souls.

But when we finally begin to probe around on the inside, most of us aren't sure what we're doing. We have no way of talking about or making sense of what we trip over in the dark recesses of our souls. What are my temptations? My passions? My motivations? Biblical communicators can help by providing listeners with a language of the interior, a language of self-examination and confession.

In the early and middle ages of the church, thoughtful Christians came up with a list of what they saw as the most common and costly sins. They called them the seven deadly sins: pride, anger, greed, lust, envy, gluttony, and slothfulness (spiritual indifference). There isn't one action on the list; these are motivations and dispositions. They are the soil in which sin takes root.

I've found consciousness of the seven deadly sins to be helpful in my prayer and reflection, something of a sonar scope that lets me see what lies on the murky bottom of my heart. I will sometimes think over recent days and ask the Lord to show me where any of these killer sins may lie just under the surface. Then they become helpful categories for framing my confession.

With a bit of nervousness over how it might be received, I recently preached a sermon series on the seven deadly sins. The result? We sold more tapes of those sermons than of any previous series. Our hearers long to make sense of the passions and motives at work within them.

Unless we come to grips with our own fallenness, our moral failure, the cross will forever be a mystery to us, and the gospel will remain nothing but a self-help program. It's time we reclaimed the word *sin* from the dessert menu and reinvested it with some substance.

Getting Our Bearings

We live in a world that has lost its moral bearings. Apart from raising awareness of sin, what else should we have in mind as we try to orient this world to a moral North Pole?

How We Preach and Teach

Accept without conditions. Perhaps our most important sensitivity is to remember that we do not share the same moral code with unbelievers. And it is unfair for us to insist that people without the Lord act like Christians before we befriend them.

Unlike a lot of Christians, most unchurched people live morally consistent lives. Their actions line up with their moral standards. Sleeping around, lashing out in anger, cheating on taxes, having an abortion, and "borrowing" supplies from the office—that kind of behavior makes perfect sense to a person who doesn't live under the biblical moral code.

That doesn't make such choices right. Non-Christians are still ultimately accountable to God's standard, whether or not they admit it. But is it our place to judge their behavior and to pull away because we disapprove of the choices they're making? Aren't these the people who need our love and acceptance most?

In one of our PrimeTime programs, we presented a play called "Whatever Happened to Compassion?" In the play, Jenny, a Christian college student, brings home a friend who is HIV positive, and her family wrestles with what to do. Finally her mother draws the line.

"I will not have a homosexual stay in this house," she announces.

Jenny counters "Is that what it means to respond in a Christian way? With condemnation and judgment? That's a scary thought!"

"It *means* we don't associate with immoral people," her mother says.

"Don't tell Jesus that, because he sure didn't act like a Christian. He spent a lot of time with filthy old prostitutes and tax collectors and people like that. I wonder if *his* parents knew who *he* was spending time with."

When Jenny's father interrupts and tells her to change her tone, she responds with exasperation, "Daddy, I don't mean to be sarcastic. I just think we've missed the boat on this. All of us. Me included. You know, Jesus wouldn't have approved of women selling their bodies for money. But he still spent time with the prostitutes. He accepted them and loved them. Same with the tax collectors. He would've been ticked off at the way they hit people up for money. But he still welcomed them and spent time with them. Since when does being a Christian mean pushing away people we don't approve of?"[2]

Acceptance doesn't mean condoning sin. We have a responsibility to show those who follow the ethic of self-fulfillment that their moral codes are inadequate and that the moral norms of the Bible are to their advantage to follow. But I think we cross a line when we insist that unbelievers live as Christians. Our responsibility is to accept people right where they are, speak God's moral standard with grace and understanding, and let God be the one who convicts them of sin.

Make sensitive use of the Scriptures. A second implication of our conflicting moral codes is that we need sensitivity and wisdom when it comes time to introduce the Bible into a conversation or message about moral conduct. We shouldn't hesitate to give people an opportunity to hear what the Bible says about their moral state. It is one of the most important things we can do because it desperately needs to be heard. But we must do it thoughtfully. That means keeping in mind that things are in the Bible because they are true, not the other way around.

God's moral parameters make good sense. God gave commandments for the same reason the city has provided curbs on our streets. They direct where we should go, and they keep us and others safe in the process. If we choose, we can bounce over them and drive down the sidewalk, but it is rarely safe and usually costly when we do so. It is important that we help people see the benefits of obedience to God's moral law.

Here is one way you might point to the Bible's standard without alienating those who haven't taken its truthfulness into their lives. I spoke a few times with a non-Christian woman who had some big questions about the man with whom she lived. Should she marry him or break up with him? She was very confused. I encouraged her to think about asking the man to move out while she tried to sort out her feelings for him. But I didn't say, "Look, toots, the Bible calls what you're doing sin. Kick the bum out and repent." Had she been a Christian, something along those lines (though, obviously, more gracious) might have been appropriate. But for Karen, who had many painful experiences with the church as she grew up, it only would have reinforced her distance from Christianity.

Instead, I said something like this: "You know, Karen, when you're in a relationship where there's sexual intimacy, the water gets really muddy. Sex is a powerful thing, and it makes it tough to see what is really going on. Do I love this man? Or do I love how I feel when I'm with this man? Are we really close? Do we have real intimacy? Or is the closeness I feel just a matter of having someone close in the middle of the night? Feelings can really get mixed up, and you can end up marrying your feelings instead of a person.

"The other thing that can happen when you live together is that it becomes like a test. Can you meet my needs? Are you good enough? If so, we'll get married; if not, you're outta here. That's a pretty tough way to start a relationship, because that meet-my-standards attitude carries over into the marriage. The whole thing is based on performance instead of acceptance and forgiveness. What happens when two years (or two weeks) into the marriage I blow it?

"I don't know if you know this, but when you compare married couples who lived together with married people who didn't, you see some surprising things. Studies show that the ones who lived together first are less happy with their marriages, enjoy sex less, and are more likely to be critical of their spouses. And they are more likely to have their marriage end up in divorce. I think that's why the Bible encourages people not to live together and to save sex for marriage. God really knows what's best for us. He knows we need to be in a relationship that's built on more than some passion in the middle of the night, one where there's an unconditional commitment to stay together no matter what."

Don't hesitate to bring God's Word to bear in conversations about morality, but when you do, always explain the why along with the what.

Model a faith congruent with life. There is a third implication of the fact that Christians are committed to a different moral code: They had best be consistent with that higher standard. What do we have to say to the world if we follow its self-serving moral code?

One day I asked Mindy, a non-Christian with whom I'd had a lot of contact through my work at the church, why she didn't take Christianity more seriously. "Why should I? Most of the Christians I know are jerks!" There is something wrong when the behavior of Christians is one of the best reasons not to believe in Christianity.

The world around us rightly expects us to live in a way consistent with our convictions. Why should it take our faith seriously if we don't? One of the most disheartening things I have ever heard is that, when it comes to the choices we make and the way we live our lives, Christians cannot be statistically distinguished from non-Christians. As one of many examples, Josh McDowell studied thousands of teens actively involved in evangelical churches. He found that during the three months before the survey, two out of three had lied to their parents, one in three had cheated on an exam, one out of four had smoked a cigarette, one in five had tried to hurt someone, and every ninth student had gotten drunk. More than half will be sexually active by the time they reach age eighteen. Adult Christians bear out the same pattern of blending into the prevailing moral climate.[3]

Something is wrong here. The gospel doesn't make us perfect. But it should make us noticeably different from those around us who don't share our faith in Christ. I'm sure you've seen the bumper sticker that says, "Christians aren't perfect, just forgiven." That is absolutely right. Unfortunately, many of us live as though it says, "Christians aren't any different, just forgiven." When we act just like everybody else, we have nothing convincing to say. Or more accurately, we have no one who will listen.

"Whoever claims to live in him must walk as Jesus did," wrote the apostle John (1 John 2:6). We are called to go against the flow, to swim against the current of our culture. There is no excuse for a church that blends into the world.

How We Share Faith

Get people to ponder the source of our conscience. When I came to actively consider Christianity for the first time, someone handed me *Mere Christianity* by C. S. Lewis. In spite of the fact that everything he said went against everything I wanted to hear, I couldn't put the book down. And part of the reason—beyond exceptional writing—was the argument at the beginning of the book. It is a compelling use of the issue of morals to point people to Christ.

Our culture is fond of boasting that we share no moral consensus. Lewis disagrees. Notice, he says, the way people quarrel. "'How'd you like it if anyone did the same to you?'—'That's my seat, I was there first.'—'Leave him alone, he isn't doing you any harm.'—'Why should you shove in first?'—'Give me a bit of your orange, I gave you a bit of mine.'—'Come on, you promised.'

"Now what interests me about all these remarks," says Lewis, "is that the man who makes them is not merely saying that the other man's behaviour does not happen to please him. He is appealing to some kind of standard of behaviour which he expects the other man to know about. And the other man very seldom replies: 'To [h——] with your standard.'"

Lewis uses that observation from everyday life to argue that there is a moral law, a rule of right and wrong, that we all seem to carry with us. We don't manage to live up to it very well, but it is there, and we use it as the basis for our getting along with each other. Our moral sense is not an instinct—it often runs against what we might think of as instinctual behavior—and it is not merely a consensus of how to get along. It runs much deeper. This conscience, this rule of decent behavior, seems to have come from outside of us. We did not invent it, but we know we ought to obey it.

Lewis then shifts his focus. He points out that there are two ways of making sense of what this universe really is and how it came to be. The first is a materialist view that space and matter just happen to exist. The other is the religious view that holds there is a mind behind the creation of the universe and it has personal purposes and preferences. Conventional science cannot tell us which is the right view. Science explains how things behave, but it does not answer why things exist and why they are as they are, instead of something else.

Where do we look, then, for answers? To ourselves. "If there was a controlling power outside the universe," Lewis concludes, "it could not show itself to us as one of the facts inside the universe—no more than an architect of a house could actually be a wall or staircase or fireplace in that house. The only way in which we could expect it to show itself would be inside ourselves as an influence or command trying to get us to behave in a certain way. And that is just what we do find inside ourselves. Surely this ought to arouse our suspicions?"

Our conscience—the innate sense of right and wrong that we all share—is, as Lewis argues, compelling evidence of a personal God who has left his mark on those he has made.[4]

Explore the outcome of moral ambiguity. Another approach to evangelism with people who argue there is no shared moral standard is to help them see what an unsatisfactory life results from simply seeking to meet our own needs. A life worth living cannot be built on thinking first and only about oneself. It may be fun for a while. But in the end there is an emptiness in thinking only of ourselves, and that emptiness will make itself known.

Skirting around moral categories and making decisions on the basis of what is expedient does not make moral issues go away. Jeff Goldblum, who plays a proponent of chaos theory in the movie *Jurassic Park,* expresses grave concern about some scientific experiments. "We've been driven by asking what we *could* do and never stopped to ask what we *should* do." The results, as the movie shows, are disastrous. When we live in a way that ignores God's moral order, there is eventually a moral emergency, an experience of ethical bankruptcy, that can grind us to a halt and throw wide open the doors to faith.

I remember when Jon came storming into our church. I had met him the Sunday before and had a chance to talk with him briefly after the service about Christianity. But now he was furious, throwing things around and threatening to kill his roommate, who had run off with his girlfriend. Jon was ready to get even in a big way. "Why shouldn't I? I'm sick of people running over me, doing whatever they want to do. You talk about God. God has forgotten me. He's not stopping this from happening. He doesn't care. Well I do, and I'm going to do something about it."

I was at a complete loss for what to say. (They don't cover homicide intervention in seminary.) Finally I said, "Jon, you've been talking a lot about right and wrong. I agree, what your roommate did was a wrong thing to do. It was really low. But Jon, when you think about killing your roommate, does that feel right? I know it feels good, I know it feels fair. But does it feel right? How are you going to live with yourself when you realize that you did the same thing your roommate did? He followed his feelings. He didn't care about anybody else. He just did what he wanted.

"Now, what if you go and do the same thing? You feel like you want to get even, so you go blow him away. Isn't there something inside you that tells you that—even though that's what he did to you, even though that's what he deserves—it isn't right? It isn't your place to do it?

"The Bible says that God operates on that same sense of right and wrong that we have. In fact, he put it there in us. And he promises that he will punish every single act of wrongdoing, every act of injustice, that is ever done. That means God will make sure your roommate will get what he deserves. It's hard, Jon, but I think you've got to let God take care of it."

By the grace of God, Jon was able to hear that. It registered.

Once Jon calmed down, he told me that when he was six, his mother and father divorced. When it came time for the judge to award custody of the children, Jon's father and mother divided up the other children, and left Jon sitting on the bench. "What about him?" the judge asked. "I don't want him," Jon's father said. His mother shook her head. "Neither do I." Jon had lived with that rejection ever since. And now he was left in the dust again, this time by the first woman he ever loved. It wasn't his roommate he wanted to kill but his pain, the pain of rejection.

In conversations that followed, I was able to tell Jon about a God who says, "Never will I leave you; never will I forsake you" (Heb. 13:5). Today Jon is a Christian.

The ethic of self-fulfillment is no ethic at all but a ticking time bomb. Sooner or later it will blow. And when it does, we have words of hope.

What We Communicate

The relationship of faith to morality. One of the American myths is that Christianity is really just about living a decent, upright life of honesty and integrity. But as you well know, the Bible says that isn't so. The world around us needs to hear that moral living is to Christianity as foam is to a root beer float. When you get the right ingredients together, it will always be there. It bubbles to the surface and is always the first thing you taste. But the foam isn't the float. It is a by-product. The same is true of a moral life.

Christianity is not first about decent living but about rebellious men and women being restored to their loving Father through the death of his Son in their place. We have nothing to do with this restored relationship between God and us. It isn't God's reward to us for getting our act together; it is God's gift to us because we clearly could not. We are right with God because of our faith in *his* good work, not ours. Once we commit our lives to Christ, by his Spirit he begins the lifelong transforming work of making us more and more like himself. The moral life is a response to and the fruit of our relationship with Christ, not the basis for it.

Definition of sin. Whenever we relate with people who are stuck in a moral quagmire, we need to use the word *sin* carefully and define what we mean. I'm not saying we need to tiptoe through our culture in dread fear of offending someone's self-esteem. Sin needs to be discussed. We need to shoot straight and say the hard things. But we need to use the word carefully because it is so easily misunderstood. We've lost consensus about what those three letters mean.

For some, the word brings to mind petty rules, an arbitrary list of dos and don'ts. A ditty like this might pop into mind: "Don't drink, don't smoke, don't chew, and don't go with girls who do." Or our hearers might think of the Catholic church and its old ban on eating meat on Fridays or its laws against the use of contraception—two rules that make no sense whatever to the modern mind. For these folks, sin means breaking trivial, nonsensical regulations, stepping over a line that shouldn't be there in the first place. According to Patterson and Kim, five out of six Americans have no qualms about violating an established rule of their religion if they think it is wrong.[5]

For others, on the other hand, *sin* brings to mind the really big stuff, the Ten Commandments. You know: don't murder, don't uh, don't uh, well, don't murder. For this group, sin has a capital *S*. It means binding somebody's feet in concrete and dumping him into a river. Are you kidding? Not something I would ever do.

The only thing most people are agreed on is that sin is about what we do (or shouldn't do, but do anyway).

The Bible says sin is more than that, deeper than that. At its root, sin is an attitude, not an action. As I often say to my congregation, the essence of sin is our decision to push God out of the center of our lives and to take the place that is rightfully his. It is our proud and defiant act of saying to God, "Look, thanks for everything, but I think I know better than you do how to run my life, so ta-ta. Close the door on your way out." That central sin of independence from God then spills over into a thousand and one wrong choices, thoughts, and actions every day.

Confession and repentance. For many, confession is some sort of mysterious rite that involves dark corners, stuffy booths, and bored priests. But in the Scriptures confession is simply owning up to our fallenness. It is the age-old practice of saying to God and to others, "Of course. It figures. I can do no better. Listen to what I did this time." Confession is counterintuitive; when we blow it, we want to run and hide and point the finger at someone else. Confessing our sins to God is doing just the opposite. It is going to God, telling him everything we've done, and taking responsibility for it.

For someone who doesn't have a clear understanding of the gospel, that makes not one bit of sense. But when we remember that the gospel is about God's gracious intervention as we make a mess of our lives, we see why confession is so important. It is a way of drawing close to the one who saved us by shoving aside our shame and laying hold of his grace. "If we confess our sins, he is faithful and just and will forgive us our sins and purify us from all unrighteousness" (1 John 1:9).

The Bible urges us to confess not only to God but also to each other. The reason? To keep us from pretending to be better than we are, to free us from the burden of carrying our pain alone, to bring our sin out into the light, and to invite others to hold us accountable for different choices in the future.

Repentance is another valuable biblical discipline, one that parallels confession. It simply means doing an about-face, turning around 180 degrees. Acts 3:19 explains the importance of repentance: "Repent, then, and turn to God, so that your sins may be wiped out, that times of refreshing may come from the LORD." Repentance means resolutely turning from living for ourselves and stepping toward God's way of life. Confession says, "This was wrong." Repentance says, "I want to change; I resolve to be different."

The source of God's moral standards. We need to communicate that God is at the center of the moral universe, and it is from God that we take our standards for what is right and wrong. Every moral guideline and ethical standard threads through him. Because God is morally perfect, our moral standards originate in what is true about him. There is nothing fickle or arbitrary about the ethical guidelines put before us. God has not pulled them out of thin air. Goodness, purity, appropriateness, and rightness are different ways of expressing the same thing: doing things as God does them. For Christians, the words *moral* and *godly* mean the same thing. That is why Jesus wraps up his discussion about morality in the Sermon on the Mount with this: "Be perfect, therefore, as your heavenly Father is perfect" (Matt. 5:48).

The Ten Commandments, then, are not an outdated moral code. They are something of a moral portrait, showing God for who he is. That being the case, and God being the same yesterday, today, and forever, the Ten Commandments still bind us today. As ABC's *Nightline* host, Ted Koppel, pointed out in his commencement address at Duke University some years back, "What Moses brought down from Mount Sinai were not the Ten Suggestions. . . . They are Commandments. *Are,* not were."[6]

Morality expressed in service. To be moral means to reclaim the emphasis Christianity puts on others. A moral framework built on answering what is good for me is utterly inadequate for a planet on which more than one person lives. God's moral standards always encompass others. Ethics, from the perspective of the Bible, are primarily relational, and begin with the attitude described in this passage in Philippians: "Do nothing out of selfish ambition or vain conceit, but in humility consider others better than yourselves. Each of you should look not only to your own interests, but also to the interests of others" (Phil. 2:3–4).

The "one another" passages of Paul's letters flesh out the specifics of our moral and ethical duty. Care for one another, serve one another, build each other up. Love one another, give preference to one another, tell the truth to each other. Accept one another, forgive one another, bear with one another. Submit to one another out of reverence for Christ.

Virtue is not a solo venture. It can never be achieved alone.

The place of feelings. In a world consumed and driven by feeling, it needs to be said again and again that we cannot trust our feelings to tell us what is true or right. In the Proverbs we are cautioned not to rely on our own insights and feelings. Instead, we are to look outside of ourselves to God and let him direct us in what to do (Prov. 3:5–6). Our feelings are a gift from God, and they are valuable. But in spite of the message from our culture, following our feelings does not set us free. Feelings can mislead us and, if we're not careful, enslave us. This is the mistake Peter addresses when he warns about false teachers who advocate following one's passions. They encourage people to chase after their feelings, promising that those who do so will experience freedom. But in the end, if we let ourselves be driven by what we feel, we will *lose* freedom—"for a man is a slave to whatever has mastered him" (2 Peter 2:17–19).

Only God's Word can tell us for sure what is wrong and what is right to do. "How can a young man keep his way pure? By living according to your word" (Ps. 119:9).

Great freedom comes from living within the constraints God has put out for us. When I was filling out an application for a mortgage, I got to talking with Rick, my loan officer, about the issue of integrity. He told me his partner crossed the line constantly. He failed to insure his loans and he regularly ignored current credit rates. He was incredibly successful because he always had the lowest rates in town. But he was a great risk to the people who got loans through him. More than one had been forced to default on a loan because of his unethical practices.

Rick looked at me across the table and said, "He'll die wealthy. I'll die poor. But I'll be smiling."

About Chapters 11 and 12

Concepts Worth Remembering

moral absolutes: moral norms that are given to us from outside of us and that apply to all men and women regardless of place, time, or circumstances

social contract: an agreement to honor one another's rights

pragmatism: the philosophy that practical results alone determine the truth or worth of an idea; when applied to morals, the idea that what works is what is good and right to do

existentialism: the worldview of the early- to mid-1900s that life is absurd and meaningless, that existence precedes essence (who we are is not grounded in any overarching notion of humanness or meaning; we simply exist), and that our lives are authenticated through random acts of the will

anomie: lawlessness, lack of moral norms governing life

moral relativism: the belief that morals are not absolute or universally binding but dependent completely on the individual and his or her circumstances; what is right for me may or may not be right for you

ethic of self-fulfillment: the new moral standard in which personal choice is the only absolute and in which feelings, expediency, and consensus are the criteria for the right and the good

Recommended Reading

Collier, James Lincoln. *The Rise of Selfishness in America*. New York: Oxford University, 1991. Carefully researched and easily read, this book is a study of the movement in our culture from a moral code of self-restraint, which was prominent in the Victorian era, to the self-gratification of the present.

Peters, Ted. *Sin: Radical Evil in Soul and Society*. Grand Rapids: Eerdmans, 1994. Peters' book is something of a topographical map of wrongdoing, charting the seven-step erosion of character from anxiousness into blatant sin.

Plantinga, Cornelius. *Not the Way It's Supposed to Be: A Breviary of Sin*. Grand Rapids: Eerdmans, 1995. With engaging style, Plantinga beautifully unfolds a picture of what God originally intended for his creation and the way sin has conspired to undermine that original *shalom*.

Stivers, Richard. *The Culture of Cynicism: American Morality in Decline*. Cambridge, Mass.: Blackwell, 1994. Stivers charts the ways we have shifted from concern for morality and integrity to concerns for happiness, power, technique, and self-absorption.

Wells, David F. *Losing Our Virtue: Why the Church Must Recover Its Moral Vision*. Grand Rapids: Eerdmans, 1998. Dr. Wells maps the loss of our culture's moral imagination and argues forcefully for the need of the church to recover its moral character within our fraying social fabric.

Yankelovich, Daniel. *New Rules: Searching for Self-Fulfillment in a World Turned Upside Down*. New York: Random House, 1981. Probing reflections on our shifting moral grounds, based on extensive polls over more than two decades. (Out of print but well worth searching out.)

I also recommend three classic books of fiction that deeply probe this area of morality and society:

Dostoevsky, Fyodor. *The Brothers Karamozov*. New York: Bantam, 1981.

———. *The Idiot*. New York: Bantam, 1981.

Golding, William. *Lord of the Flies*. New York: Riverhead Books, 1997.

Part 7

HOW **WE THINK**

Beyond Meaning and Purpose

I don't know what I believe in. And if I believe—I believe there's some Higher Power, I think. But I don't know. Like right now I'm at a point where I don't know what I believe, but I'm open to everything. So I like to believe in everything, because I don't know what it is I truly believe in.

> Twenty-something backpacker
> in a man-on-the-street interview in Boston

When the old God leaves the world, what happens to all the expended faith? . . . When the old God goes, they pray to flies and bottletops.

> Don DeLillo, *Mao II*

13

Leaving **Meaning Behind**

In the fall of 1995, a rare event happened on television. A serious topic was taken up by a sitcom. With unusual insight for prime time television, the show, "Cybill Discovers the Meaning of Life," explored the different ways we try to fill our lives and give them meaning.

The show begins with Cybill hitting something of a crisis in her acting career. Chagrined, she gets reflective with her friend Maryann. Life isn't turning out the way she hoped it would. Her career is a failure, she isn't the mother she wanted to be, her marriage is a mess, and she's getting older every day.

"Maryann, I used to have such dreams. Now I'm a big old, sloppy, floppy failure. I used to know who I was, where my life was going. Now I feel lost. Maybe I need to see a psychiatrist."

"Dr. Gold has always worked wonders for me." Maryann grins.

"You have a therapist?"

"The best. Let me introduce you." Out of her purse Maryann pulls a Visa Gold credit card. "Cybill, meet Dr. Gold."

After an afternoon of shopping, eating out, pedicures, facials, and massages, Maryann sighs. "Ah, that was great. I, for one, feel closer to God."

"That's because you have the same credit limit!" Cybill quips.

Then Maryann gives Cybill a gift, a pricey purse she has always wanted. "Just think of it as a prescription for happiness from the good Dr. Gold."

Cybill is overjoyed. But when her daughter pokes fun at her "toy purse," Cybill shouts, "It's not a toy! It's very chic and fashionable . . . " then glumly mumbles, "and empty and useless, like my life."

As she stands there, despondent, her family members fly through the house, heading off to this party and that fishing trip. Cybill turns to Maryann.

"Do you see what's going on here? All the people in my life have lives of their own that don't include me. I'm an asterisk, a footnote, a blonde afterthought."

Maryann looks up from the table where she is sitting, and considers her friend for a moment. Then she hands her a glass.

"Ah, poor baby. Drink this. It's called alcohol. It'll make you not care."

Cybill is confused, frustrated.

"No! No more drinking, no more eating, no more shopping. All that does is fill up your closet and your stomach. Not your soul. Maryann, I feel empty. Family doesn't fill the void. Work doesn't fill the void. . . . I know what I have to do. I've got to get out of here. I've got to go somewhere where there's no distractions, where there are some answers, where I can be totally alone."

"Oh, goody!" chirps Maryann. "Where are we going?"

"On a spiritual retreat—to the desert!"

Once they get to the desert, Cybill rolls out a mat and plunks down, eager to get started, but her friend is reluctant.

"Come on! Open yourself up! The desert is a power place. You'll thank me, you'll see. We're gonna meditate, we're gonna fast . . . "

Maryann looks at her. "What do you mean 'fast'? What do you mean 'we'?"

When Cybill closes her eyes to begin meditating, Maryann quietly reaches into her purse and pulls out a candy bar. Cybill, hearing the crinkling paper, opens her eyes and looks over. "You big cheater!" she says.

"Surely you don't expect me to fast on an empty stomach!"

Cybill grabs the candy bar and launches it out into the night. Maryann is appalled. "I cannot believe you did that!"

"You can't have a spiritual experience with a mouth full of chocolate!"

Maryann disagrees. "You can if it has a creamy nougat center."

They continue to jab at each other, and eventually their bickering turns into an all-out fight. Cybill snaps, "You know, I'd be making a lot more progress if you weren't here."

"Fine, give me the keys to the car and I won't be. I'm not the one looking for answers to her empty life."

"Well, maybe you should be!"

"What's that supposed to mean?"

"Well, what do you do all day? Shop, get your hair done, b—— about your ex."

"That's not empty. That's busy. Busy, busy, busy."

Finally, after a long night of trying to meditate, punctuated by fighting and making up with her friend, Cybill gives up.

"You were right. What did I expect? Some blinding insight? Some ancient spirit is going to rise up out of the ground and tell me the meaning of life?"

Maryann gives her a hug and says, "You were right about one thing. My life is sad and empty, too. All I do is shop for fabulous clothes, eat in the best restaurants, get pampered in the finest salons." Throwing her arms open and looking up, she yells, "Why me, God?"

They roll up their ground pads and head for home, having decided that there aren't any answers after all. Maybe all that makes life bearable is having a friend at one's side.

Our lives, like our Daytimers, are busy, busy, busy, full of things to do and places to go and people to see. Many of us, convinced that the opposite of an empty life is a full schedule, remain content to press on and ignore the deeper questions. Perhaps it is out of fear that we stuff our lives to the walls—fear that, were we to stop and ask the big questions, we would discover there are no satisfying answers after all.

In the movie *Say Anything,* one kid explains to another why it's easier simply not to think about it. "You get to be thinkin' about how short life is, and how maybe everything has no meaning, because you wake up, and then you're fryin' burgers, and you're like sixty or seventy, and then you check out. . . . I just don't need to be thinking about those kinds of things."

As a sophomore in college I was involved in intramural sports, started a high adventure club called CHUTE ONCE (College Humans Usually Try Everything Once), worked as a workshop presenter at a peer counseling office, participated in a couple of honor societies, and served as a resident assistant in one of the freshman dorms. My life was, well, busy. One night I was visiting the young women on my exchange corridor when one of them—a Christian, as I was later to find out—looked at me and said, "David, what are you running from?" I had no idea what she was talking about.

A Joke without a Punchline

Why are we here? When we asked that question of a stewardess at a Boston airport, she stared off into space, silent for a long moment. "What is my purpose in life?" She paused again, a long pause. "What makes life worth living?" She laughed awkwardly. Finally, with troubled eyes, she answered. "I haven't figured that one out yet. I suppose it is trying to get up each day and make it through the day, and going to bed every night thankful that I made it. I don't know what makes life worth living!"

When we take the time to look, which we don't often do, we begin to see that, while our lives are full of activities, they are often empty of purpose.

T-shirts and TV commercials capture the urgency of a life whose script has been lost.

Just do it.

Life's short. Play hard.

Life's not too short, it's just that death's so long.

The one who has the most toys—dies anyway.

It's not the pace of life that bothers me—it's the sudden stop at the end.

Lack of meaning in our lives is especially obvious in modern art. I had the opportunity to visit the National Gallery of Art in Washington, D.C., but had only two hours. I decided to tour the gallery in a different way. Instead of going to the Impressionists, say, or the works of the early Renaissance, I went to the end of the gallery, where the medieval art was displayed. Then, without stopping, I walked through the entire gallery in chronological order, ending with the present. I would encourage you to do the same sometime in a museum near you. The experience is sobering and disconcerting.

All through the Middle Ages, art is simple, even stark. Scenes are somber, quiet, beautiful, filled with God. Angels, Jesus, Mary, and the saints appear again and again. As you enter the Renaissance, you begin to notice the change. It is like going from a book to an epic 1950s movie. Now the art is grander, more elaborate, refined, polished, true to life. Nature and humanity come to the fore, with the Bible stories and the ancient legends of the gods now serving as mere backdrops. By the time you reach the grand works of the Romantic period, vast canvases spill over with biceps and battlegrounds and beckoning frontiers. Man looms large.

When you pass from the Romantics through the Impressionists into modern art, the next change is obvious. We jump from Cecil B. DeMille to MTV. Modern art abandons the real world. In rapid succession, the works lose the grand themes, lose focus, lose resemblance to real life, lose a single point of perspective, and ultimately lose coherence. Chaotic, broken, and dark, they evoke and provoke, teasing the eye, taunting the mind, tearing at the heart.

William Barrett has written the best short critique of modern art I've read. It is as much an expression of what has become of our world as an observation of what has happened in the realm of art. Modern art, like the modern world, flattens space, collapsing near and far onto each other. This means collapsing time as well, the past blurring into the present. Beyond that, it flattens significance. Beginning, middle, and end are lost; background and subject become equally important. Plot and climax disappear, and along with them any sense that the art is saying something understandable. Art loses intelligibility as boundaries are blurred and connections are abandoned. Finally, modern art flattens a sense of value. The unimportant and important seep together, the ordinary and the extraordinary blend in. There is no hierarchy, no way to sift out what matters from what doesn't.[1]

All of the same dynamics are at work with MTV, where logic and reason are put aside and anything can happen. MTV is a jumble of images that has no story to follow, no connection to reality. It is an explosive montage of disconnected sensations and emotions. Nothing is still. Cameras bounce, zoom in and out, spin around, bouncing graphics appear and disappear, angles shift, subjects transform, cuts are abrupt, focus comes in and out. No continuity, no point, no time to reflect. Just the eternal present in which we get swept along. Richard Corliss, a film critic, describes what it is like to enter into this world: "Each MTV video says, 'I got three, maybe four minutes, and in that time my sights and sounds are gonna blitz your brain.' The next video does the same thing, and the next and the next. MTV doesn't exhale."

Our world is a hodgepodge of fleeting images, with no more substance than a puff of smoke. What's the point?

This Is Not Your Father's Worldview

Several centuries ago, life's purpose was not a mystery. The first question of the Westminster Catechism sums up what generations of men and women knew to be true. "The chief end of man is to glorify God and enjoy Him forever." We exist to love and honor God, to live our lives for him.

But through the years, as humankind drifted away from a worldview with God at its center, the period changed to a question mark. We were made to live our lives for God? Ah, I don't think so.

Over its long history, Western civilization has been shaped by three major ways of making sense of reality. The first, typically referred to as the premodern worldview, was the God-centered, biblically based perspective that primarily shaped our culture beginning in the fourth century. In this view God is the defining reality out of which our understanding of self, others, and the universe grows.

Then began the first shift of worldviews, a lurching transition starting with the Renaissance and culminating during the Enlightenment. Humanity and the physical world began to loom ever larger, moving more and more into the center of the picture, while God—initially relegated to the fringes—eventually was lopped out of the scene altogether. When the dust settled, we found ourselves looking through new glasses, standing within what came to be known as the modern worldview. A naturalistic worldview that had no place for the supernatural, the modern view was dominated by self, which occupied center stage, and reason, which emerged as the new authority.

Then began the second shift, beginning with the expressiveness of romanticism and culminating in the anything-goes permissiveness of the sixties. This time the modern world was being bumped aside for a new one, the postmodern world. Postmodernism ushered in a world that hums with the supernatural but is absent of God, is filled with opportunity but lacks any inherent meaning, replaces responsibility to others with an ethic of self-fulfillment, and rejects reason in favor of intuition and feelings as its final authority.

Like a hippo diving into a bathtub, the arrival of this new worldview had a way of rearranging everything. Nothing remains untouched.

The Roots of Rootlessness

How is it that we have made this move from lives filled with meaning to lives devoid of it?

Nietzsche, the Death of God, and the Loss of Certainty

In a series of dark works written in the several decades leading up to 1900, Friedrich Nietzsche began to dismantle Christianity and its God-centered worldview. Christianity, as he saw it, was not a good thing. Much of the world's troubles could be traced to the Christian faith. With its ethic of self-sacrifice and concern for others, it had managed to compromise the enormous potential of humanity, bringing humanity down rather than raising it up. It didn't set us free; it bound us, stifled us, pulled us down.

It was time, said Nietzsche, to rid ourselves of the idea of God and of a worldview built around him. It was time to stop being our master's shadow and start being the master of our shadow instead. It was time to acknowledge that God was just a convenient myth, a myth that needed to die.

What that leaves is a world with no purpose, no center, no source, no hope. This is nihilism, the view that nothing of meaning exists. "Do we not now wander through an endless Nothingness?" screams a character in one of Nietzsche's books.[2]

According to this dark thinker, if God is dead, meaning is not a given. It is not something intrinsic that is handed to us. It is forged by our own hands. We have to bring forth a new superhumanity by a sheer act of the will.

Nietzsche's philosophy also discusses life's lack of certainty. During his day there was a heated debate about what we can know without question. Is there objective truth which is certain, impersonal, true for everybody? Some said that there is and that reason is the way to arrive at objective truth. Others contended that we can only know something with certainty by using our senses, through empirical evidence. Nietzsche said both are wrong. He argued that there is no such thing as objective truth. We can never get beyond our own perspective. There are no facts, only interpretations. This is perspectivism, the idea that we can have many perspectives of the world, but none is objective and none can be shown to be more valid than any other.

A bizarre and despondent man who bordered on insanity, Nietzsche was written off in his day. But as the world has discovered since, he came up with virtually all the ideas that now shape our postmodern age. A worldview devoid of God, meaning that is created rather than received, and the concept that what is true depends on where you are standing: these are views that are common today.

The Fuzziness of Math and Physics

Since the earliest days of modern science, going all the way back to Galileo and his telescope or Newton and his apple, the scientific venture has been built on the idea of a sane, predictable world operating under predictable natural laws. The world is solid, lines are straight, and time never wavers.

But this steady outlook was shaken in 1905 when Albert Einstein announced his theory of relativity. Space and time, he said, are not absolute but relative, stretching and squeezing in unaccountable ways. In certain circumstances, because matter and energy are related, light bends, lengths shorten, space curves, and time slows down. There is no fixed point to stand on, nothing solid we can grasp. Everything moves, nothing is sure. In an unsettling way Einstein seemed to confirm the nihilism Nietzsche proclaimed. We are adrift, alone, with no solid rock on which to firmly plant our feet.

Not much later, in 1920, studies in atomic physics caused the world even more consternation. In his study of light Werner Heisenberg found it impossible to determine the position and speed of subatomic particles.

Measured in one way, light appeared to be made up of electronic particles. But looked at in another way, it was clearly a series of electromag-
netic waves. It seemed the act of observing light caused light to change.
In the subatomic world of quantum physics, you cannot get an objective
measure of anything; what is true depends completely on your perspective. This is Heisenberg's uncertainty principle, and it sounds disconcert-
ingly like Nietzsche's perspectivism: There is no objective truth. Perspective is everything. There is nothing we can know with certainty.

Math, like physics, used to be a predictable realm in which two added
to two always gave you four. But recently, mathematicians began to see
that math, like science, is not such certain territory. In some areas of the-
oretical mathematics, results are not certain at all but instead are unpredictable, haphazard, random. The mathematicians who work in this area
call this chaos theory, and a new breed of mathematicians called chaoti-
cians emerged. But as with Einstein's relativity and Heisenberg's uncertainty, chaos theory crept past its own discipline and captured the imagination of the broader public. Life was out of control. Everything was a
result of chance.

Relativity. Uncertainty. Chaos. What has become of our predictable
world? I don't think we're in Kansas anymore, Toto.

Though he wrote a hundred years ago, Nietzsche's words capture the
spirit of the times in an uncanny, unsettling way. "Is there still any up or
down? Are we not straying as through an infinite nothing? Do we not feel
the breath of empty space? Has it not become colder? Is not night continually closing in on us?"[3]

For so long, the universe seemed to be a steady, certain structure on
which we could firmly plant our feet. Now, all of a sudden, it seems like
a rickety, creaking suspension bridge stretched high over a chasm that
looks a long way down.

The Arrival of Postmodernism

In the course of our interviews with people on the streets of Boston
and Cambridge, we talked with one young woman who told us she was
a postmodernist. When we asked her what she thought God is like, she
replied, "I'm a philosophy major, and I'm heavy into the twentieth century with Nietzsche and Gadamer and whatnot. And honestly, I believe
God is dead. And I think that religion and whatever is important, but I
don't think that there is a heaven and that you go up to whatever and that
there'll be a God that's overlooking everything. I think that there is a Being,
but the basis of all things is a No-Thing, a Nothing. . . . I think people are
afraid of there not being anything beyond. They really shouldn't. They're

basing their happiness on something beyond this life. But they should be happy in this life, because this life is all there is."

Welcome to postmodernism, the philosophy of our day. You might call it the philosophy of dancing on the suspension bridge.

At bedrock, postmodernism is the affirmation that there are no absolutes. Postmodernism is not so much a new worldview as it is the death of any coherent worldview.

Postmodernism is a rejection of Enlightenment thinking, the rationalism and optimism of the modern world. Purpose, design, objective truth, absolutes, and any idea of overarching "metanarratives" or "totalizing discourses" are thrown out the window. Instead, postmodernism embraces the nihilism and perspectivism of Nietzsche and the existentialism of Sartre. Life is pointless. There is no inherent meaning or purpose in life, and there is no truth.

But postmodernism doesn't stop there. It unites existentialism, nihilism, and perspectivism with three modern cousins: pluralism, multiculturalism, and deconstructionism.

Deconstructionism is a perspectivist way of looking at literature, an approach that took shape in the middle of the twentieth century. For the deconstructionist, reality is not only meaningless, it is unknowable. If reality is not knowable, then language doesn't tell us anything about what is out there. It can't. Instead, language is simply a matter of power; it is a means of controlling the chaos of reality by labeling and categorizing it, declaring what is important and what is not. This way of thinking leads to what is called the reader-response theory of meaning. That is a fancy way of saying that when you read something, you can never know for sure what the writer meant. Meaning is determined by the reader. I decide what Jesus meant when he said, "If anyone would come after me, he must deny himself and take up his cross daily and follow me" (Luke 9:23). Nothing is clear. Nothing is certain. Everything is interpretation.

Pluralism and multiculturalism further the aggressive debunking of any one way of making sense of the world. Pluralism holds that all belief systems are equally true. Multiculturalism insists that every culture is equally worthwhile. Because everything is a matter of perspective, we are backward if we insist on teaching Christianity as the only true religion, or the history and literature of the Western world as that most worthy of study. There is no exclusive truth. There is no superior culture. We need to embrace them all. This leads, of course, to elevating tolerance and acceptance as our most important societal virtues. Since everything is a matter of perspective, who are you to tell me that you're right and I'm wrong? We are all equally right, and it is arrogant and judgmental of you to insist otherwise. A Christian staff member at Stanford encapsulates the challenge: "It's fine to pursue truth as long as you don't find it."[4]

In the end, with its mixture of nihilism and deconstructionism, post-modernism becomes a word game in the dark, a game of Scrabble on the deck of the Titanic.

Stuff happens. Whatever.

This is where we now stand:

There is no God. God is dead.

There is no meaning or purpose. Life is absurd.

There is no predictability. The world is chaotic.

And there is no truth. Perspective is everything.

Fragments of a Torn World

All of this has been fairly abstract and conceptual. Let's see some of the important practical ways that the postmodern mind is evident in every-day life. Above all, postmodernism shows itself in the questions that have begun to bubble to the surface around us. Timeless certainties have been replaced by troubled doubts and painful questions for which postmod-ernism is unable to provide any coherent answers.

Why Am I Here?

If there is any meaning to be found in life, it cannot come from out-side ourselves. There is nothing "out there" to look to. We're on our own. Meaning is not supplied for us.

A teenager in the movie *River's Edge* expresses it starkly: "I've got this philosophy. You do s———. Then it's done. Then you die."

The alternative rock group Bad Religion captures the prevailing sense of aimlessness in one of its songs: "If there's a purpose for us all / It remains a secret to me."[5]

Life begins to feel like a joke whose punch line has been forgotten. It rambles on and on, and then comes to an awkward, halting end. Like a suspenseful novel with its last ten pages torn off, our lives lack resolution.

Who Am I?

We have less and less of a sense of identity today. So much emphasis is put on the externals of appearances and first impressions. Ads tell us that we are what we wear (or drive, or eat, or have on our face). Cosmetic surgery is available to suck, tuck, trim, and boost us into "a better you." An exercise equipment ad says, "A flower is perfect in every way. You, on the other hand, could use some work." With fashions changing monthly, Madonna and Dennis Rodman remaking themselves weekly, and TV ads changing daily, we are more and more at a loss as to who we really are.

Robert Jay Lifton says that we live what he calls protean lives. Like Proteus, the Greek sea god who could change his shape at will from wild boar to dragon to fire to flood, we refashion ourselves continually. We have a continuous flow of being, out of one personality into another without an obvious connection between them.[6]

Can Anything Be Certain?

Skepticism and doubt have become a way of life. How *do* you know? Isn't it all opinion anyway? I mean, who are you to say that you are right and I am wrong? Or that anybody is wrong?

We accept it as a given that two people can believe radically different things and both be right. We're no longer bound by what is rational, logical, or sensible. All we know is that lots of people have lots of ideas, and somehow everybody is right.

I had lunch one day with a neighbor before he became a Christian. As we often did, we got to talking about religious things. This time I asked him, "Gary, where would you say you get your answers about what is true about spiritual things? Would you say it is from inside you, something you feel, something that makes sense to you? Or would you say it comes from outside you, from the Bible or something like that?"

"Oh, I'd say it's based on what I feel is right. You know, just that sense you have on the inside."

"What do you do," I asked him, "with the fact that what you feel is right is different from what somebody else feels is right? How do you deal with that contradiction?"

Gary shrugged his shoulders. "That's not a problem for me. I mean, if someone is sincere in what he believes, who am I to tell him what he believes is wrong? I can't. I can only speak for myself."

"But, Gary, if one person believes that God is a person and another that God is not, or if one person thinks God is perfectly good and another that God is the author of good and evil, isn't it possible that, even though they are both sincere about what they believe, one of them is sincerely wrong?"

"Not necessarily."

"But something can't be true and not be true at the same time!"

"Maybe in heaven it can."

Gary is not nuts. He is a delightful guy whose company I greatly enjoy. He was simply expressing the confusion of his skeptical, irrational, pluralistic world. Truth doesn't matter, and neither does contradiction. All that matters is what you personally believe.

In 1991, two out of three Americans surveyed said they agreed with the statement, "There is no absolute truth; different people can define truth in conflicting ways and still be correct."[7]

"Whatever," the word tossed around at every turn, captures the spirit of the age better than any other. It sums up our beliefs, our moral standards, and our evaluation of what is true.

Which End Is Up?

There was a day when we had the sense that things held together. You could trust what you saw. Things were solid, predictable. There was comfort in knowing that a table was made of wood, not atomic particles whirling around each other.

Now, the world seems like the mystical land of Oz. There is nothing normal, nothing predictable, nothing knowable, nothing sure. Time and order and sense have collapsed in on one another, and things don't much hang together anymore. We live in the unpredictable world of computer morphing and cross-dressing and black holes, and we long to get back to the black and white world of Kansas.

Our culture's loss of certainty is powerfully captured in the conversation in DeLillo's *White Noise* between Jack Gladney and his son Heinrich as they drive to school in the rain. Heinrich has told his dad that, in spite of what looks like rain on the windshield, the radio said it wasn't going to rain until that night. His dad is frustrated.

"Just because it's on the radio doesn't mean we have to suspend belief in the evidence of our senses."

"Our senses? Our senses are wrong a lot more often than they're right. This has been proved in the laboratory. Don't you know about all those theorems that say nothing is what it seems? There's no past, present or future outside our own mind. The so-called laws of motion are a big hoax. . . ."

"Is it raining," I said, "or isn't it?"

"I wouldn't want to have to say."

"What if someone held a gun to your head . . . a man in a trenchcoat and smoky glasses. He holds a gun to your head and says, 'Is it raining or isn't it? All you have to do is tell the truth and I'll put away my gun and take the next flight out of here.'"

"What truth does he want? Does he want the truth of someone traveling at almost the speed of light in another galaxy? Does he want the

195

truth of someone orbiting around a neutron star? Maybe if these people could see us through a telescope we might look like we were two feet, two inches tall and it might be raining yesterday instead of today."

"He's holding a gun to *your* head. He wants your truth."

"What good is my truth? My truth means nothing. What if this guy comes from a planet in a whole different solar system? What we call rain he calls soap. What we call apples he calls rain. So what am I supposed to tell him?"

"His name is Frank J. Smalley and he comes from St. Louis."

"He wants to know if it's raining *now,* at this very minute?"

"Here and now. That's right. . . . Is there rain here, in this precise locality, at whatever time within the next two minutes that you choose to respond to the question?"

"If you want to talk about this precise location while you're in a vehicle that's obviously moving, then I think that's the trouble with this discussion."

"Just give me an answer, okay, Heinrich?"

"The best I could do is make a guess."

"Either it's raining or it isn't," I said.

"Exactly. That's my whole point. You'd be guessing. Six of one, half dozen of the other."

"But you *see* it's raining!"

"You see the sun moving across the sky. But is the sun moving across the sky, or is the earth turning? . . . How do I know that what you call rain is really rain? What *is* rain anyways?"

"It's the stuff that falls from the sky and gets you what is called wet."

"I'm not wet. Are you wet?"[8]

Nothing glues us to reality anymore. The linchpin has been pulled and misplaced, and everything falls apart. We are lost, removed, adrift. Normal life no longer seems possible, and we hover on the edge of sanity. In a provocative study, schizophrenia expert Louis Sass notes the similarities between our culture and madness. We don't know how to relate to our world freely, spontaneously. We are hesitant, detached, hyper-self-conscious. We find ourselves divided from our feelings, from other human beings, from the external world. We bounce from one perspective to another, from cerebral, cold detachment to frenzied and irrational involvement.[9]

The confusion is captured on a T-shirt I saw that said, "A man's got to believe in something. I believe I'll have another beer."

The bewilderment shows up, too, in the song "If I Ever Lose My Faith in You" by the popular musician Sting.

> You could say I've lost my faith in science and progress.
> You could say I lost my belief in the Holy Church.

196

You could say I've lost my sense of direction.
Yes, you could say all of this and worse.[10]

Aimlessness and disillusionment are particularly evident among those in the generation known as the baby busters, generation 13, or generation x. The effects range from mild cynicism to outright darkness, the sense of despondency that comes from walking on the edge of insanity, sentenced to a meaningless existence. You see it in the black clothing, black hair, black lipstick. You hear it in the music that blares around the clock from the stereo. It is behind the body piercing, tattooing, and branding that have become so popular. Matt is a teenager from Colorado Springs whose tongue is pierced and who sports seven other piercings in more inaccessible places. When asked if he thought he might regret the piercings fifteen years down the road, he laughed. "I don't think we'll be around in fifteen years."[11]

Woody Allen captured the pulse of our day when he wrote, "Civilization stands at the crossroads. Down one road is despondency and despair, and down the other is total annihilation. Let us pray that we choose the right road."

The musical group Faith No More sums up the hopelessness.

Guess what? It never ends . . .
The pain, the torment and torture, profanity,
Nausea, suffering, perversion, calamity.
You can't get away.[12]

In the face of life's ultimate questions, a world without God ultimately comes up empty handed.

Where Can I Turn for Answers?

After long years of spiritual neglect, we are witnessing today an enormous rebound into the spiritual, a huge corrective nudge in the human trajectory.

This is the day of the virtual sacred. The spiritual realm has oozed into the ordinary stuff of life, and we can find sacred connections with the cosmos at every turn. So long thought to be empty of any spiritual dimension, the universe now is believed to be filled with the extraordinary, the paranormal, the supernatural, the metaphysical. Interest in the paranormal, the occult, astrology, Eastern mysticism, and the New Age movement are all expressions of this dimension.

The universe is a haunted house, a magical, mystical, spirit-filled domain in which anything can happen. There is fairy dust on everything.

Ghosts and goblins, angels and aliens, superstitions and spirit guides, crystals and channels, horoscopes and harmonic convergence, ESP and Elvis are all part of this wonderful existence. In the panoply of spirits, only God is absent.

The enormous popularity of angels today is a direct result of this sanitized spirituality. Where aliens are the perfect substitute for God in a secular, modern world, angels are the ideal replacement for him in a spiritual, postmodern one. "For those who choke too easily on God and his rules," writes *Newsweek* correspondent Nancy Gibbs, "angels are the handy compromise, all fluff and meringue, kind, nonjudgmental."[13] Caring and comforting, they help everyone and impose on no one.

We are in the middle of a clamoring for spiritual meaning. This generation is rushing the gates of heaven, searching for a connection to something bigger than the ground we stroll upon. But while it is for God that souls thirst, many have decided that God is not really an option anymore. God is the stuff of religion, and this is the day of spirituality. According to Sam Keen, who wrote *Hymns to an Unknown God,* the two ideas could not be more different. Religion is based on revelation from a knowable God, a word that charts a clear map to a known destination and gives authoritative answers to questions. Its main virtue is obedience, and when it is boiled down, it is all about authority.

Spirituality, in Keen's mind, is just the opposite. "The quest begins when an individual falls into a spiritual 'black hole' in which everything that was solid vaporizes. Certainties vanish, authorities are questioned, all the usual comforts and assurances of religion fail, and the path disappears."[14]

The adventure begins with doubt, not with revelation, and its chief virtue is openness. What matters here is not some external authority but an internal drive, a mystical quest for a taste of the transcendent.

Spirituality flourishes and religion flounders in our day. We want to populate the heavens again . . . but following God is just too much to ask. Too dogmatic. Too exclusive. Too demanding. Too distant and unapproachable. We need something chummier, more comfortable and user friendly. The old God has a PR problem. He needs to loosen his tie, lighten up, get a tan. Let's dispense with the fire and brimstone, lose the rigid rules. It's time for some God Lite: less demanding, feels great.

David Addison on the 1980s television show *Moonlighting* captured the tone of the West's spiritual pursuit. "I'm going to take a moment to contemplate most of the Western religions. I'm looking for something soft on morality, generous with holidays, and with a very short initiation period."

What happens when we are spiritually ravenous, but when God is not an option to meet the hunger of our souls? A syncretic made-to-order religion is the result. This mix and match approach to faith spins out of the bumper sticker concern: "God is too big to fit inside one religion." Rather than submitting ourselves to the truth and discipline of one faith, we make an omelette out of a variety of traditions, mixing, say, two parts Islamic ritual, one part Zen meditation, a dash of psychic self-defense, and a shake of Native American spirituality.

More and more people approach spiritual matters in this way. I like how Kenneth Woodward put it in a series in *Newsweek,* "The Search of the Sacred: America's Quest for Spiritual Meaning." He said that, in a climate of religious pluralism, "many searching Americans flit from one tradition to the next, tasting now the nectar of this traditional wisdom, now of that. But, like butterflies, they remain mostly up in the air."[15]

Whatever.

This is the postmodern world. In it, we are alone, confused, disillusioned, and adrift. We are dying of thirst, and yet we push away the one sure source of life.

What do we say to a society that says God is dead and Elvis is alive?

14

God's Word
to a World Adrift

In the spring of 1983 I went to Fort Lauderdale to share Christ with college kids on the beach. The first night we were there we had a short training session, and then we were given a simple assignment: Head uptown to where the bars are and strike up a conversation with three people.

Obedient but terrified, I headed out of the hotel and ran right into a young man in his mid-twenties, standing on the street corner with a beer in his hand. He was dressed in black leather and had a spiked orange mohawk and a safety pin through his nose. Now, this was in the days when hair came in four standard colors: blonde, brown, black, and gray. The punk movement had barely hit the U.S., let alone Cincinnati, and I had no idea what to make of this guy.

And I'm sure he had no idea what to make of me, standing there in my khaki shorts, preppy button-down shirt, and Reeboks. But somehow we struck up a warm conversation. I ended up spending the whole evening with him, talking with him about his life and about the gospel. It was one of the most interesting conversations I've ever had.

Craig grew up in Philadelphia, in a home similar to mine: middle income, church going, suburban. But his was a broken home, and he hated it. Home life was the pits, and middle-class suburbia felt inauthentic and shallow to him. He felt imprisoned, confined to a painful and superficial existence. So one day he escaped. He grabbed his jacket, walked out to the highway, and hitchhiked to Florida. A year and a half had gone by since then, and he still hadn't been in touch with his parents to let them know where he was or that he was okay. Now he lived with some other punkers in a cheap apartment, making just enough money at odd jobs during the day to pay for a couple of brews at the punk bar where they would go every night.

At this bar they would crank up their tunes and dance. But what they called dancing was a little different from what I was used to. Two people line up in opposite corners of the "pit," run at each other as fast as they can, and smash their heads together. "The pain feels cool," Craig laughed. "Kinda reminds you you're still alive, ya know?"

Later in the conversation I asked him, "How have your thoughts about God changed since you ran away from home and moved down here?"

"I grew up going to church, but I gave up on that crap a long time ago. Everybody I knew back home was all into God, and they were the biggest hypocrites I ever saw. They didn't care about anything but their own comfort, ya know? It's like the country club and the bank and the church all mixed into one. Forget that.

"But ever since I got into the punk scene, I have been like so into the story of Cain and Abel. That is the coolest thing. Cain goes and smashes in his brother's head, and then God curses him and puts this mark on his face. And then he's different than everybody else and everybody stays away from him. God sets him apart, ya know? He makes him different. He's kind of above everybody else, ya know? I can relate to that so much. That would be the coolest thing, to be cursed by God like that. Isn't that cool?"

I don't remember what I said. I don't expect I said much. I was saddened and dumbfounded—and I had no idea how to speak with someone whose worldview was so at odds with my own. How could I share the gospel with someone who rejects God, throws out the Bible, mocks conventional ideas of right and wrong, thinks it's cool to smash headfirst into somebody else, and identifies with one of the loneliest and most forlorn men ever to walk the planet? Where could I even begin?

Meaning-Makers

All these years later I still think the challenge of engaging the postmodern mind is one of the hardest. There are perhaps more obstacles to gaining a hearing for the Bible than there have ever been. Oddly enough, because of the way meaning has been stripped from life in our world, I think there also may be more open doors to hearing and responding to the Bible than there have been for a long time.

Where do we begin? More than anything else, I believe the most important thing we can communicate to the postmodern world is a coherent and compelling Christian worldview. We have the challenge and privilege of inviting people to occupy with us a biblical way of answering the questions of who made us, why we exist, how we are to live, and what happens when we die.

Even though God is a distant mystery at best and a sick joke at worst to many in our world, deep within each of us lie both the belief that life ought to be meaningful and the desire to experience a life that reflects that. In the movie *Papillon,* the main character, who has been imprisoned for life, dreams he is dragged before the courts to be tried. He pleads with the judge that he is not guilty of the charge against him. But the judge cuts him off, telling him that's not the crime for which he is now being tried. He is being charged instead with the most heinous crime of the human race. Papillon nervously glances at the judge and asks what that crime is. The judge answers, "The crime of a wasted life." Papillon breaks down weeping. "Guilty," he cries. "Guilty."

The greatest gift we can give to this world adrift is a sense of meaning. Listen to the wonderful way Donald Posterski puts this: "We need to become Christian *meaning-makers.* Meaning-makers are people who make sense of life, people who make sense of God, people whose lives ring with clarity in the midst of contemporary ambiguity, people who have integrity, people who reside in today's world revealing with their living and their lips that Jesus' death is the source of vital life."[1]

This world ripples with meaning simply because God *is.* His very existence means that meaning and purpose permeate all that he has made. Life is the furthest thing from meaningless. It is just that, for so many, meaning remains a mystery. God drops people in our laps so we can point them to the meaning he has already provided. Nothing is more important in our preaching, speaking, and sharing of faith.

I think being a meaning-maker begins with simply asking good questions and then listening, asking more questions and listening some more—all the way down to the darkness. As we do this we slowly unearth the other person's worldview. What frame of reference shapes why this person lives as he or she does? Is this person a theist, believing in a personal God? A naturalist (or materialist), believing that the physical world is all there is? Perhaps a monist, someone who believes God and himself and the world all to be one? Or is this person a true postmodernist, believing nothing to be true and all things to be merely a matter of perspective?

Once we've been able to dig to those bedrock convictions, we can begin to show the flaws in them. In a process Francis Schaeffer describes as "taking the roof off,"[2] and David Wells captures with the image of loosening the dirt and preparing the soil,[3] we need to help people see their beliefs for what they are—and to recognize, perhaps for the first time, their inadequacies.

For instance, we might ask a secular humanist how she makes sense of all the evil in the world (and in her), given her belief that people are good and the world is getting better and better. Or we could help a naturalist who operates out of a scientific worldview see that science fails to give a convincing account of how time plus matter plus chance could produce a being as complex as a human. Or if we're speaking with a New Ager with a monistic bent, we can ask if it isn't a bit tough to believe we are God when we are powerless to prevent ourselves from getting a common cold, let alone shape the events around us or manage to live forever.

The soil prepared, we can now begin to plant seed. Once we've asked lots of questions and identified some of the inadequacies of the other person's worldview, we can then draw that person into the pages of the Bible and show how well it accounts for the way we are and the way the universe is. Only Christianity gives an adequate and coherent explanation for life.

In the jumble of images and emotions and experiences that make up the present world, we have the privilege of holding out meaning.

Let me give you an example of how the Bible might be used to bring meaning into a potentially meaningless experience. Kim, a thirty-nine-year-old man who was part of our congregation, collapsed playing racquetball. He died instantly, killed by massive heart failure. When I prepared the funeral message, I was aware that several members of Kim's broader family, most of whom were Buddhist, and many folks from Kim's workplace, almost all indifferent to religious issues, would be there. Here is how I sought to bring meaning to that moment.

"Kim is dead," I began, "and we are here this afternoon to put his life and death into perspective."

I talked briefly about his full and happy life, and our special memories of the man he was.

Then I said, "Kim's was a life well lived. His death, though, is harder to put into perspective. Suddenly everything is brought to an end. Thirty-nine years old, married just ten years, two small children: It feels like a life cut short.

"In fact, a brief life and unexpected death shows death for what it is: an intruder, an interrupter, a disrupter. Death surrounds us, we hear about it every day, but still it seems to break in from the outside, a trespasser. Everything in us pursues life, and everything in us recoils at death.

"Little wonder why; it is so confoundedly final. Death is dark and stubborn and can't be sideslipped. We can relate to Woody Allen when he says, 'It's not that I'm afraid to die; it's just that I don't want to be there when it happens.' Death seems in every way to have the last word. With stubborn persistence it fractures every family, breaks every friendship, quiets every hand, cuts short every life.

"In our world there are two main ways to look at time and history. The Eastern way is to see history as a circle. Time is an endless circle of comings and goings, of appearing and disappearing. That seems encouraging at first as we face death. It seems to comfort us with the idea that Kim will return. But the Eastern view of history as a wheel is really no comfort at death. His life is still cut short, interrupted, and nothing of this life carries over into the next: no memory, no personality, only the purest of life-forms is passed on. Even if he were incarnated next door, we would never know it—and he wouldn't either. Far from being a source of comfort to us at death, the Eastern idea of the wheel begins to feel more like a trap, a roller coaster gone bad. We can't get off, and we spin around and around. There is no hope here.

"The Western way to see history is even less comforting. Life is a series of splashes thrown at random against a wall, like a Jackson Pollock painting. There is no overall design, no meaning, no movement toward some end. Just a series of overlapping splashes of paint, a random collection of individuals, each one of whom is either frantically wrestling to determine some meaning for this short existence or frantically wrestling to ignore death and its finality, drowning out the discomfort of death with work, or things, or something from the medicine cabinet. In the contemporary Western view of history, life has no purpose, and death is just a cold, stark period at the end of a brief sentence. There is no hope here, either.

"Little wonder that the only response we know in the face of death is despair. But into the confusion and fear of death that is all around us God brings a third view of life and death. And it flies in the face of the endless repetition of an Eastern view and the painful randomness of the Western view. You get a glimpse of it in this passage from the Bible, that says, 'Our friends, we want you to know the truth about those who have died, so that you will not be sad, as are those who have no hope' [1 Thess. 4:13 TEV]. The Christian views death in an utterly unique way—not with despair but with hope. There is still deep, deep sadness at the loss of Kim. Our lives are emptier because he is gone. But for the Christian there is hope. Why?

"'We believe that Jesus died and rose again' [4:14], the passage goes on. It says that on a Sunday morning nearly two thousand years ago in the little country of Palestine, a dead man stepped out of a tomb alive. Three days before, his body had been taken down from a cross and placed in a grave . . . and now he lives! Jesus, the Son of God, conquered death.

"But listen to what that means for us. The passage goes on: 'We believe that Jesus died and rose again . . . and so we believe that God will take back with Jesus those who have died believing in him' [4:14]. With Jesus are raised those who believe in him, those who have put their faith, their trust, their hope in him. Jesus, through his death on the cross and his being raised again, shattered the finality of death. He broke death's hold on himself, and when we become his followers, when we believe in him, he breaks loose death's hold on us as well. The Christian view is that time and history are a line—and our individual histories too—a line that breaks through death as though it wasn't there, a line of life that continues un-interrupted in spite of death."

I then went on to tell the story of how Kim became a Christian, and closed the message with this: "I grin thinking about Kim's first moments in heaven. He died playing racquetball. Bob hit a shot off the front wall, and Kim raced back to get it. And suddenly he found himself backpedal-ing through very different courts. I can picture him looking around, a growing grin on his face. Kim isn't dead. He's alive.

"From our perspective, death is like watching an airplane leave the gate at the airport. We wave good-bye, it rolls down the runway and climbs into the sky, and gradually disappears. It's a painful good-bye. But God reminds us that, for the believer, just at the point where we say, 'Well, it's gone,' someone else in a faraway city spots it on the distant horizon and says, 'Here it comes! Here it comes!'

"The day Kim died, Kim's daughter Melissa and I were talking. She turned to me and said, 'Well, I know what the saddest day of my life is.' I put my arms around her and I said, 'It is, Melissa. This is the saddest day you've ever had.' I held her in silence for a while, and then I said, 'But do you know what, Melissa? This is the happiest day of your father's life.'

"Kim isn't dead. He's alive."

God invites us to be meaning-makers in a meaningless world: to make sense of what makes no sense, to piece together what seems long ago to have fallen apart, to show the way where there is no way to be found.

When I lived in Colorado, one of my favorite ways to spend a day was to go hiking in the mountains. "Doing a fourteener," hiking to the top of one of Colorado's fourteen thousand-foot peaks, was a particular joy. But high-altitude hiking has its challenges. At the base of the mountain, where there is soil, the trails are usually well marked and easily walked. But once you get above timberline, which you hit at about eleven thou-sand feet, there are virtually no trails. You're on your own, picking your way through gravel slips or over boulder fields as you slog your way toward the top. It can get frustrating, especially if you find yourself inside a cloud or a surprise snowfall with no way to look ahead and see where you are going. When you add to that the low temperatures and reduced oxygen encountered at higher altitudes, it can become quite uncomfortable, confusing, and even dangerous.

Trying to find one's way in the postmodern world is like hiking a mountain above timberline. It is cold, disorienting, and unforgiving, and the path is nowhere to be seen. You're on your own—aimless, stumbling, desperately in need of someone to point the way.

Years ago, hikers developed a system of marking the way through high-altitude terrain where a trail is impossible to make out. Small piles of stones called cairns are placed every ten yards or so along the trail. That way, even in the worst of conditions, it is possible to pick out the next cairn in the distance and make your way to it. They are lifesavers.

God invites us to be cairns. The way I put it in a prayer not long after I became a Christian was this: "Oh, my Lord, that I might be / But an arrow that points to Thee."

Truth-Tellers

In our efforts to be meaning-makers, the obstacle that looms larger than any other is the postmodern concept of truth. In a world of perspectivism, when you have your truth and I have mine, what's to be said? And why try?

There are no easy answers for a society that sniffs dismissingly, together with Pilate, "What is truth?" (John 18:38). But there are answers nonetheless. And providing them begins with taking people back to where their bedrock beliefs take shape.

I've found that when someone insists it is not possible to know anything for sure about religious things, it can be helpful to probe that a bit. "Where are you getting that idea? I may have missed something, but it sounds as if you just said that the only thing we can know with certainty about religious things is that we cannot know anything for certain about religious things." Why is truth not even an option?

I've also found it helpful to point out the big, glaring mistake that lies behind pluralism. That is the leap that so many make from the fact of diversity (there are many faith options, all sincerely held by thousands of people) to the belief in pluralism (everybody's faith is equally valid and true).

If you were to ask a class of first graders what four plus four equals and get seven different answers, would that mean that all of them were true in their own way because each answer was sincere? Or that none of them was true, because each person's answer was shaped by his own perspective and probably doesn't have much to do with what is real? Do you see the leap? It doesn't make sense to jump from the fact that there is more than one answer to the belief that each, or none, is right.

To take this idea a little further, I'm sure you're aware that the debate about whether there is life on Mars has been revived. Now, if I asked you whether there is life on Mars, I'm sure you would have an opinion. Say, for the sake of the argument, that you don't believe there is life on Mars. Now say I ask somebody else, and she believes there is life on Mars.

I'm sure you are both sincere in your beliefs. But if you say no and she says yes, one of you is sincerely wrong. Sincerity does not determine truth. Reality does. Either there is life on Mars or there is not. Truth is whatever corresponds with reality.

The same is true in the realm of spiritual things. Either there is a personal God or there is not. Either Jesus is God with Us or he is not. Either I will live past death or I will not. Either the tomb was empty or it was not. When it comes to reality, the answer can never be "all of the above."

So how do we know which beliefs are true and which ones are false?

Most of us answer that question by consulting one source of authority: ourselves. We rely for answers on our feelings, our reason, our experience. But as natural as that is, it has some real problems. I can tell you that I feel deeply that there is no life on Mars. Or that I have thought long and hard about it, and I believe it is unreasonable to think life exists on Mars. Or that my experience—seeing as how I have never met a Martian—suggests there is not life on Mars.

But if I am relying solely on myself as the authority, I'm not any closer to knowing whether life exists on Mars or not. And if you and I disagree, all we are disagreeing about is uninformed opinion. You don't know, and neither do I.

See the parallel with matters of the faith? There may or may not be a God, but my opinion doesn't tell me much. While reason, feelings, and experience may suggest to me what is true, they can never—with matters of the faith—*tell* me. Looking only to myself to decide if there are little green men running around on that far red planet doesn't get me very far toward the truth. It's also a lousy way to decide if there is a God and what he is like and what he might require of us.

The only option is to look to some source of information outside ourselves. If I want to know if there are Martians, I need to don my spacesuit and go there. Short of that, all I have is an opinion that may have nothing to do with reality.

The problem, of course, is that personal observation is not an option. United Airlines doesn't run flights there yet. The same is true of matters of the faith. We can't hop in a shuttle, program in H-E-A-V-E-N, and go get the proof we want.

If I want to know if there is a God, I need to find some sort of outside evidence that would support the idea. I find it interesting that, when you move past opinion and feelings and reasoned thinking, and you begin to poke around for outside evidence, you don't have to look very far. Does the world reflect an artist's design and skill? Cosmologists and physical scientists confirm what Paul writes in Romans: "Since the creation of the world God's invisible qualities—his eternal power and divine nature—have been clearly seen, being understood from what has been made" (Rom. 1:20).

Are there places in history where it seems possible that God has impacted the course of human or natural affairs? As one example among many, the resurrection of Jesus, well attested historically, has never been given an adequate natural explanation—or anything even close. According to Paul, more than five hundred people were eyewitnesses of the resurrected Christ, most of whom were still alive when he wrote his first letter to the Corinthians (1 Cor. 15:4–5).

Do we have any evidence to suggest that God has made an effort to communicate with us? That is exactly what the Bible claims to be, the Word of God—the work of a divine hand and not merely the reflections of human authors. "All Scripture is God-breathed," writes Paul to Timothy (2 Tim. 3:16). The remarkable consistency of its message in spite of having been penned over more than a thousand years, its amazing historical accuracy, confirmed daily by archeological findings, and the undeniable way that the wisdom of the Scriptures squares with our life experience all give us reason to take Paul's claim seriously.

And is there anything to suggest that God may have come and revealed himself to us directly? The life, death, and resurrection of Jesus are unparalleled in human history. The evidence abounds. "In the beginning was the Word . . . and the Word was God . . . and the Word became flesh and made his dwelling among us" (John 1:1, 14).

As Christians we lack definitive proof that God exists and that he has spoken to us in the Bible. But we have some mighty convincing reasons to take both possibilities seriously. James Sire, in his excellent book *Why Should Anyone Believe Anything at All?* digs into all this far more deeply than I can here. But let me share with you his conclusions. He suggests that, barring certainty, the best way to decide if something is true is to ask these questions:

- Is it reasonable? Does it have a good shot at being true?
- Is it logical? Does it keep from contradicting itself?
- Is there empirical evidence for it? Does it fit with other things I know?

- Have I experienced it? Do my experiences fit with what this suggests I should expect?
- And finally, does it give the best explanation for the way things are and for the tough issues of life? In other words, does it fit with all the data and does it give a better account of the world, ourselves, and others, than any other explanation?

Sire argues—and I believe deeply he is right—that orthodox, biblical Christianity fits the bill better than any other option. Jesus announces, "I am the way, and the *truth,* and the life" (John 14:6).[4]

Supplying the Missing Thread

The need for meaning-makers and truth-tellers is certainly great, but we face other tough challenges. Our postmodern world is skittish about people who seem to be pushing their faith, skeptical about the Bible, and downright cynical toward claims of exclusive answers. Here are some ways for us to communicate God's truth to our changing world.

How We Preach and Teach

Be honest about struggles. Engaging the postmodern world begins with taking its questions and reservations seriously and answering them with candor and honesty. The mood among those around us hovers between realism and pessimism, mixed with large doses of cynicism. This is a world filled with pain and struggle, and its upcoming generations are shell-shocked from the explosion of society. The disruptions of frequent moves, lower standards of living, tougher job markets, the pain of divorce, suicide, and sexual abuse are all within the common experience of so many today. Our streets, homes, and churches are filled with the walking wounded.

That being the case, a talk titled "Three Easy Steps to the Victorious Life in Jesus" probably wouldn't gain much of a hearing these days. Pat answers that don't give elbow room for the complexities and difficulties of real life will fly about as far as an ostrich egg. We need to own up to our struggles, admit our doubts, and avoid easy answers in our communication. Avoiding pedestal perching and discarding "you" language in favor of "we" language will also help open cynical ears. Sharing the pulpit or lectern with men and women who are not "professional Christians," giving them opportunities to talk about their struggles to integrate faith and life, also will lend credence to our words.

Start from scratch. It is important to remember that there is a good chance the people we are speaking with have no frame of reference for what we are talking about. The Bible is as foreign and strange a place as Tanzania. Don't assume your hearers know New Testament from Old, or where one might find Ezemiah (or whatever it's called). Give them page numbers and some points of reference for getting around. "First Samuel is about a fourth of the way in from the front cover, right after Ruth. If you're flipping around in Kings or Chronicles, you're close but you've gone too far." We may find we need to give that same kind of guided tour whether we're picking our way through doctrine, church history, events in the life of Jesus, or our Sunday morning liturgy.

Establish common ground through popular culture. Every so often, take some time to tune in to our culture. Listen to the top three radio stations in your community, watch the TV shows with the highest ratings, catch Siskel and Ebert's favorite movies, or read a best-seller. You might also think about having someone in your congregation tape the top one hundred music videos on MTV at the end of the year, and take some time to watch them.

Why? Two simple reasons. First, the media form our society's common ground. There is probably no better way to keep your finger on the pulse of our ever-changing culture than to flip on the radio or TV.

Second, if you listen in on the cultural pipelines long enough, you may find that a TV show or current song provides just the right quote or anecdote to bring a message to life. Those familiar points of reference cannot help but build a point of connection between us and our listeners. I think that is exactly what Paul is doing in Acts 17:28 as he addresses the people of Athens. First he takes a line from a Top 40 hit called "Cretica" by the rock group Epimenides: "In him we live and move and have our being." Then he follows that up with a quote from the journalist Aratus, taken from a recent cover story in the weekly news magazine *Phenomena:* "We are his offspring." (Paul actually cited familiar works of philosophy and poetry, but you get the point.) When we can express our ideas in the language of popular culture, ears get unstopped in a hurry.

How We Share Faith

Keep Jesus at the center. The most important question a person can answer is, Who is this Jesus, and what does that mean for me? If nothing else stays with you from this book, I hope that this will. As you talk with people about the faith, as you proclaim God's Word from the pulpit, keep circling back to this central question. Who is Jesus, and what does that mean for me?

Every person has unanswered questions about God and spiritual things, and those need careful listening and faithful answering. If God is so good, why do so many bad things happen? Why should I take Christianity seriously when the church is so full of hypocrites? How can you be so brash as to claim that Jesus is the only way? Why should I believe in the Bible when science has disproved it?

"Great question," I will often say. "Great question. I'm happy to talk with you about that. But before I do, I just need to say that I think there is another question that is even more important than that. When you boil it all down, Christianity is really just about one thing: Who is this Jesus, and what does that mean for me? After I answer your question, could we talk about that?"

The more we can keep our conversation focused on this amazing man from Galilee, the more effective our evangelism will be. There are many other important issues for us to work through in conversations with others—the role of the church, the nature of God, how faith and science intersect, the problem of evil, the environment—but we will be most effective when we begin with Jesus and work outward from that central starting point.

Rethink our approach to evangelism. I think it's time to reconsider the traditional approach to evangelism. The old gospel two-step—single somebody out and hit him with the gospel—doesn't fly. People today are skeptical of easy answers, protective of their privacy, and intolerant of aggressive "religious types," regardless of what brand of religion they may be pushing.

In a pluralistic, perspectivist world in which all authority is suspect and nothing is certain, I believe gaining a hearing involves five things.

1. *Building strong friendships.* Begin by making genuine friendships with non-Christians. In today's guarded climate, no relationship means no hearing. Only within the context of an authentic friendship will we win the right to be heard. Our friendships cannot be acquaintances for Christ but instead must be genuine relationships marked by the same vulnerability and availability and honesty that mark our other friendships.

   There is nothing wrong with building a friendship with a non-Christian specifically with the idea that at some point you might have the opportunity to share the gospel. But if the friendship flounders when religious discussions get put off, and if it screeches to a halt right after the "friend" has failed to respond to a gospel presentation, then perhaps something is wrong.

   Shortly after Kurt came to Christ, he said to me, "You know, I've thought a lot about what it was that turned me around. You know what made the difference? The fact that you were so loyal as a friend. I never once felt like our friendship hung on whether or not I agreed with you." We cannot let gospel-sharing opportunities drive the friendship, or our acquaintances will go from feeling like friends to feeling like projects in a big hurry. Skittish as people are, they can sniff a person with a religious agenda from a thousand yards away. We need to broaden the way we think about what it means to share Christ to include our lives and not just our words.

2. *Living an attractive life.* Live a compelling life in front of your friends. The lives of most people around us look like MTV: a bunch of garbled images with no thread that holds them together. When you come along with a meaningful existence that seems to have a center, that forces people to stop and take notice. What makes your life hang together in a world that is falling apart? In an era of chaos and uncertainty, a connected life stands out like a lighted candle in a power outage.

   Just the other day a friend said to my wife and me, "If it is Jesus who makes you the way you are, that's what I want." We are called to the kind of life through which God shines onto the world around us.

3. *Asking good questions.* Ask thoughtful questions and listen carefully to the answers. If you have ten minutes to share the gospel with someone, spend the first nine asking questions and listening. Only then can we speak words on target. When we speak more than we listen, it is like flying a kite in the dark. Our words go out, but we have no idea if they ever get off the ground. "We often think of evangelists as good speakers," Leighton Ford once said. "But first they need to be good listeners."

   Gently and patiently take time to probe around. What does this person believe about God? Is God present, absent, dead? Where does the emptiness of the person's life apart from Christ show itself? In broken relationships, teetering esteem, a sense of purposelessness? What kinds of spiritual issues has your friend wrestled with? Come to know the person's heart and history. The better you do, the more ready you will be to speak when the time is right.

4. *Telling about your experience.* Talk openly and honestly about your experience of Christ. Feet get fidgety when a tract gets pulled out or a Bible is flipped open. Religious dogma gets shot down in a moment. But nobody can deny your experience, not even the most ardent New Ager or most stubborn Scientologist. In a world where truth is nothing and experience is everything, our "testimony"—

describing in fresh ways the difference Jesus has made in our lives—is one of the most important tools we have for reaching people. I call this first-person evangelism, a nonthreatening and indirect way to present friends with the truth of the gospel.

The effectiveness of sharing is doubled when we are able to include a short summary of the gospel as it was first explained to us. For example: "So John asked me if anybody had ever explained to me why Jesus died on the cross. No, nobody ever had. So what he explained to me was that, because we've chosen to turn our backs on God . . ." and so on. Skeptical people who will derail a conversation the instant they hear any second-person efforts to share the gospel with them ("*You* need to accept Christ today because . . . ") will listen intently to a personal anecdote ("I came to realize that I needed to accept Christ because . . . "). When others walk in the footprints of our experience, they not only put their feet where ours were, their hearts walk the same path, their ears hear the same words of truth. And it is possible that their souls will make the same step of faith.

Sharing our Christian experience has even greater power when we are able to show that the struggles and questions our friend is wrestling with are similar to ones we asked at the same point in the process. If we can let our friend listen in on our struggles with Christianity and the way we worked through them, it can help the person do the same without feeling put on the defensive.

5. *Encouraging your friend to read the Bible.* When the time is right, invite your friends to get their noses into the Bible, and let it convince them of its own authority. In the past, we might have spent quite a bit of time explaining to people why the Bible was worth taking seriously before we ever opened its pages together. Experience tells me that is increasingly hard to do. People find so many reasons to be distrustful of the Bible's authority that we may never convince them of anything and never get the cover opened. But what would happen if you were simply to ask, "Would you be willing to look with me at what the Bible says about Jesus? We've talked about him a lot but we haven't taken any time to look at the firsthand accounts of what he said and did. You game?" Or you could say, "I understand you are skeptical about Christianity, but before you reject it, it might make sense to find out what you're saying you don't believe. How about if we read part of the gospel accounts together?" Part of why I became a Christian was because someone extended that kind of invitation to me.

I'm not saying we can't be direct about the gospel and its claims on our lives. We can. We tell the truth rather than qualifying it. Nor am I saying we need to cater to the needs and feelings of our hearers and "sell" the Good News. We don't. We are truth-tellers, not hawkers of spiritual wares. All I'm talking about is being sensitive to our hearers. One of the bottom-line communication principles is to begin where your hearers are, not where you wish they were (or where you are).

Hearers today don't begin anywhere near where we do. For them there is no truth, no God, no certainty, no authority, no objective reality, no purpose. The only sure thing for the postmodern person is his or her experience.

So we begin there, with the hearer's experience and ours. It would be nice to begin evangelistic conversations with the existence of God as a given, or the Word of God as the accepted final authority, but we can't. The world has moved on, and more and more traditional presentations of the gospel get returned to the sender unopened. We can't afford to send our mail to where the world used to be. We have to address it to where the world is today.

For a further development of these principles, check out the appendix, where I explore them more specifically.

Address the problem of exclusivity. You won't have to venture far into conversation before you encounter one of your biggest communication challenges. Because of this world's struggle with the idea of truth, Christianity's claim that salvation is found in Christ alone (John 14:6; Acts 4:12) is met with a combination of laughter and indignation.

What do we say to the person who believes every religion is a different road to the same mountaintop or a different facet of the same diamond or a different access code to the same computer file?

First, when people say those things, they usually assume (without having looked into it much) that all religions teach basically the same thing. That's true, they do—if you throw out their beliefs and keep only the ethical teaching, the shoulds and shouldn'ts. When you reduce the world's religions to moral codes, they come out surprisingly alike. (Perhaps it's not quite so much of a surprise when we remember that God has planted within all of us the same moral sensor, our conscience.)

But as soon as you move past ethics and begin to talk about differences in worldview—what is true about time, reality, God, humanity, death, matter, the supernatural, the goal of life—the various religions could not be more different in their teachings. Most people are surprised to see just how much they differ. And once those variations are spelled out, it becomes harder to hold that all of those conflicting views are true. It just doesn't make sense. Some of them have to be wrong.

Which begs the next question: If only one religion is right, how could so many people be so wrong? Where did all the false religions come from? An approach I take to answering that is to point out that every culture has some sort of belief in God. The Creator has put in us all a spiritual hunger, along with a sense that he is somehow the satisfaction for that appetite. But nobody has seen God. He is distant, not a part of our lives. It makes sense to me that, in trying to solve that problem, people would come up with some way they think might bring them closer to God. Couldn't that be the source of the different world religions?

I think that is exactly what you begin to see when you study them. The striking thing is that, in broad strokes, every major world religion but one arrives at the same solution—the idea of man, through his efforts, becoming like God. We work, or fast, or meditate, or serve our way into God's good graces.

Christianity comes at it from the opposite direction. It is not we who do the work but God. Broadly speaking, only Christianity holds the belief that God has become a man, taking upon himself the responsibility of bringing us into his grace. That distinction, running as it does against the grain of all the other religions, makes Christianity warrant careful consideration. The fact that it is so counter to what we might expect of a supreme being gives it a certain plausibility and invites a closer look.

What We Communicate

Our identity is found in God. It is not necessary for us to grope for a sense of identity, endlessly remaking ourselves like chameleons in a box of crayons. Identity is woven into our fabric as created beings. The question is not one of making our identity but discovering it. In the same way an artist values a work of art, God delights in and values us. Identity cannot be found outside of the one who made us. We are derivative, his unique handiwork, "knit together" by him, "fearfully and wonderfully made" (Ps. 139:13–14).

But who we are is ultimately defined by our having been made right with God through Jesus Christ. Who I am has everything to do with who he is. And those who put their confidence in Christ now live in him as new creations (2 Cor. 5:17). But from a broader biblical perspective, we are not so much made new as "re-newed," restored to wholeness, becoming the men and women God intended us to be from the start. That is what speaking the truth of God's Word is all about: "We proclaim him, admonishing and teaching everyone with all wisdom, so that we may present everyone perfect [mature, complete, whole, restored, fulfilled] in Christ" (Col. 1:28).

215

God has made a place for us. We were not created to spiral alone through a void. God's purpose is to ground us, giving us a place in relation to himself and others. We are adopted into his family (Eph. 1:5), children of God (1 John 3:1), and brother and sister to one another (1 Peter 2:17). In this relationship we find a secure place to be ourselves, to serve each other, to be tended to and cared for, to be gently prodded toward maturity. True, sin mucks up the body of Christ, but God's Spirit still allows us to find safety in one another, fallen though we are.

God gives us meaning. Finally, it is unnecessary for us to fumble for meaning, purpose, or hope. Meaning is inherent in the world because God made the world on purpose. The universe is teeming with evidence of the intentions of God, from the formation of the first molecule to the latest creation of a baby. And we are invited to join in, to discover and become part of the purpose of all creation. "For he chose us in him before the creation of the world to be holy and blameless in his sight. In love he predestined us to be adopted as his sons through Jesus Christ, in accordance with his pleasure and will" (Eph. 1:4–5).

The existence of God gives meaning to the universe, and that meaning translates into purpose for each of us. "He died for all, that those who live should no longer live for themselves but for him who died for them and was raised again" (2 Cor. 5:15; see also 1 Cor. 10:31; Col. 3:17). In Christ we discover God's mission for our lives.

And confidence in God's purposes for us gives us reason to be encouraged as we face a world that is dark and a future that is uncertain. A sense of purpose waters the seed of hope and brings it to life. "I know the plans I have for you," says God to those who live within his purposes, "plans to prosper you and not to harm you, plans to give you hope . . . and a future" (Jer. 29:11).

About Chapters 13 and 14

Concepts Worth Remembering

nihilism: the view that, with God removed from the picture, there is nothing that gives meaning to life

objective truth: something that we can all agree is certain, impersonal, true-for-everybody truth

perspectivism: the belief that there are many subjective perspectives on the world, none objectively true and none any more valid than any of the others *postmodernism:* the contemporary philosophical view that affirms that there are no absolutes, there is no objective truth, there is no inherent meaning, and all of life is a matter of perspective

deconstructionism: the contemporary view in literary criticism that all language is subjective, incapable of conveying objective ideas and subject to the interpretation of the reader

reader-response theory of meaning: an approach to interpretation that says the meaning of any given work is determined by the reader, not the author

pluralism: a social climate affirming a diversity of beliefs and the right of any individual to believe as he or she wishes; this can mutate into a philosophy that holds that all beliefs are equally valid, that truth cannot be found in one belief system to the exclusion of others, and that tolerance and uncritical acceptance are the central social virtues

multiculturalism: the view that all cultural heritages are uniformly valid and valuable, that all are equally deserving of our study and appreciation, and that none should be elevated above any of the others as more virtuous or worthy of study

law of noncontradiction: the principle of informal logic that holds that something cannot simultaneously be x and not be x

Recommended Reading

Beaudoin, Tom. *Virtual Faith: The Irreverent Spiritual Quest of Generation X.* San Francisco: Jossey-Bass, 1998. Beaudoin engagingly explains the suspicion of religion, hunger for spiritual experience, and acceptance of ambiguity that define his generation's theology—as well as the crucial role of popular culture in shaping it.

DeLillo, Don. *White Noise.* New York: Penguin, 1984. This is a remarkable novel, filled with tongue-in-cheek observations about the shallow consumerism of our society and probing insights into the darkness of the postmodern mind.

Gergen, Kenneth. *The Saturated Self: Dilemmas of Identity in Contemporary Life.* New York: Basic, 1991. An enthusiastic advocate of postmodern developments writing from outside a Christian perspective, Gergen provides a powerful introduction to the postmodern frame of mind that has captured our age.

Howe, Neil, and Bill Strauss. *Thirteenth Gen: Abort, Retry, Ignore, Fail?* New York: Vintage, 1993. This book is jammed with quotes and features that shed clear light on a prominent generation now on the scene.

217

Netland, Harold. *Dissonant Voices: Religious Pluralism and the Question of Truth*. Grand Rapids: Eerdmans, 1991. In this thorough study, Netland explores pluralism in general, the competing claims of the various world religions in particular, and reasons for believing Christianity's exclusive claims to truth.

Percy, Walker. *The Moviegoer*. New York: Fawcett Columbine, 1989. A compelling fictional expression of modern man's loss of place and identity and of the resulting malaise that grips him.

Roof, Wade Clark. *A Generation of Seekers: The Spiritual Journeys of the Baby Boom Generation*. San Francisco: Harper San Francisco, 1993. In this important book, based on extensive surveys of Americans across the country, Roof summarizes the various ways Americans make sense of spiritual issues. A valuable resource.

Sire, James. *Why Should Anyone Believe Anything at All?* Downers Grove, Ill.: InterVarsity, 1994. Sire describes the reasons people give for mistrusting truth claims and explains compellingly why he thinks it is reasonable to be confident about Christianity's claims to truth.

Strohmer, Charles. *The Gospel and the New Spirituality: Communicating the Truth in a World of Spiritual Seekers*. Nashville: Thomas Nelson, 1996. Strohmer provides a faithful introduction to the New Age mind, as well as a whole host of valuable suggestions for communicating effectively with people of a spiritual bent.

Veith, Gene Edward. *Postmodern Times: A Christian Guide to Contemporary Thought and Culture*. Wheaton: Crossway, 1994. A clear, insightful introduction to postmodernism from a Christian perspective.

EPILOGUE

Bridging Heaven and Earth

The Word of God and the gospel it contains are as true and crucial today as when they were spoken a couple of thousand years ago.

The world's self-reliance and complacency can make us forget how much the gospel is needed. And the skepticism and relativism with which this world greets us can prompt us to be timid and apologetic.

It's easy to second-guess ourselves. Is this really all that important, my wrestling so hard to gain a hearing for God's Word?

Yes! Yes, yes, yes! Don't be misled by the casual gruffness of our world. Underneath it are parched souls gasping for life. The words of the Bible have never been more relevant, more timely, or more needed. The Bible simply begs to be proclaimed.

Let me give you three quick glimpses past the rough exterior of our world and into its heart.

Douglas Coupland (born in 1961) is considered by many to be the mouthpiece of the baby busters' generation. He voices its dark humor, its not very subtle cynicism, and its bottom-line brusqueness. But he also expresses something of its heart. Look at this remarkably candid passage with which he ends his book *Life after God:* "Now—here is my secret: I tell it to you with an openness of heart that I doubt I shall ever achieve again, so I pray that you are in a quiet room as you hear these words. My secret is that I need God—that I am sick and can no longer make it alone. I need God to help me give, because I no longer seem to be capable of giving; to help me be kind, as I no longer seem capable of kindness; to help me love, as I am beyond being able to love."[1]

Dennis DeYoung, lead singer for the rock band Styx, wrote a hit song called "Show Me the Way." Here are some of the words to that haunting song:

> Every night I say a prayer
> In the hopes that there's a heaven
> But every day I'm more confused . . .
>
> And I feel this empty place inside
> So afraid that I've lost my faith
> Show me the way[2]

Now consider some of the words to a sudden hit song by Joan Osborne. "One of Us" gave Osborne two Grammy nominations and was performed live in front of more than a billion TV viewers on the 1996 Grammy Awards show.

> If God had a name, what would it be
> And would you call it to his face
> If you were faced with him in all his glory
> What would you ask him if you had just one question?
>
> If God had a face, what would it look like
> And would you want to see
> If seeing meant that you would
> have to believe in things like heaven
> And in Jesus and the saints and all of the prophets?
>
> What if God was one of us?[3]

These are only three of hundreds of similar expressions of thirst and longing that well up in the throats of our culture.

God's Word is for today's world. It holds answers that this world longs for. It contains within it the power to send men and women into the future changed. It is a bolt of lightning sizzling with the promise of hope and meaning and new life. And when we, standing high on the narrow ledge, faithfully bring Word and world together, God's Word courses through people with power and hits home.

And that is precisely what this world longs for from us. This remarkable quote from Albert Camus, one of history's most outspoken atheists, speaks volumes: "What the world expects of Christians is that Christians should speak out loud and clear . . . in such a way that never a doubt, never the slightest doubt, could rise in the heart of the simplest man."[4]

But sometimes—perhaps too often—when we speak God's Word, it is no electric moment. We don't generate anything close to 1.21 gigawatts of power. It is more like a small buzz than a bolt of lightning.

One of my favorite wintertime amusements as a kid was shuffling my feet around the carpeted parts of our house and then touching the light switch (or my sister). I was fascinated by the little purplish spark that would shoot between the screw on the light switch and my fingertip.

Lightning and static shocks are, in one small respect, the same thing. They are electrical discharges leaping between negative and positive fields. But the similarity ends there. Static electricity produces a tiny pop, the mildest of nuisances. I'm told that even the heartiest of static shocks amounts to only about a half a joule of power. That is just enough energy to run a typical electric clock for about a quarter of a second.

Lightning, on the other hand, is a one-inch-thick bolt that can carry as much as 110 billion joules of power and reach temperatures as high as 50,000 degrees. That's five times hotter than the surface of the sun. One bolt of lightning has enough energy to make a car crisscross the United States three times or to run an electric clock for 1,712 years.[5]

Static amuses or annoys. Lightning disrupts, electrifies, and transforms.

We are the Doc Browns of the kingdom. When we use the Bible to preach, teach, or share faith, we connect heaven and earth. God speaks, and we bridge the gap between time and eternity. The question is, What will result when we open our mouths? Will it be lightning? Or will it be static? When we open the Word to this world, will the world be annoyed and amused, or will it be disrupted, electrified, and transformed?

I believe two things make all the difference.

First, how well do you know your world? How clear is your understanding of the people you are trying to reach? If you know your audience like you know your Bible, God's Word will hit home to the heart and lightning will strike. Know your surrounding world like a meteorologist knows the shape of the clouds, like a gardener knows the texture of the soil, like a mechanic knows the purr of an engine, like a mother knows the voice of her child. Be an ardent student of your world.

Second, how clearly do you represent God? How big is the God you make known? Because, in the end, it is not so much God's Word and this world that we want to connect, but God himself and this world. And if the God we teach and preach and share is small, so will be the impact of our words. If we make God out to be little more than the God portrayed in *Oh, God* by George Burns—approachable, absent-minded, and a little out of touch—our electrical charge will be only a handful of annoying crackles.

In previous eras, when a person came before God there was a clear sense of disproportion. God was huge, vast, filling the universe with his majesty and might. He spoke, and worlds came into existence. He judged, and nations ground to a halt. He moved, and the entire course of human history moved with him. A human, by contrast, was minuscule, finite, dependent, fragile. Aware of the purity of God's heart and the darkness of his own, he approached God with a heart both timid and penitent. Conscious of the paltry proportions of his own resources and the limitless scale of God's, he approached God with deep trust and dependence. And mindful of the enormity of Christ's gift on the cross—as well as of his own unworthiness—the human approached God with a gratitude that extended beyond words to result in a life committed to the Lord.

That was yesterday. Today, when the world bumps into God, it yawns and wanders past. He is not the ground of all being. He is little more than a dirt clod kicked up from the dusty past.

I think it could be argued that, more than any other single factor, the history of the Western world in the past five hundred years has been shaped by this one dynamic: the diminishing of God and the concurrent inflating of man. That is the overarching theme that runs through these pages. God has been whittled down to a safe, convenient, bite-sized deity. Meanwhile, humanity has blown itself up to huge proportions, so that we are now, like Macy's parade balloons, enormous . . . and hollow.

That is where we are today. When self-absorbed, individualistic consumers and spectators move beyond God, beyond right and wrong, and beyond meaning and purpose, then what becomes of the spiritual life? It undergoes a bizarre twist and eventually gets reduced to this: I will do whatever works for me until I find something better. And God, uh . . . God, umm . . . well, I'm not quite sure how God fits into the picture.

The only antidote for this kind of ingrown pragmatism is to reintroduce God in all his glory and majesty and limitlessness to the men and women he has made. It is time this world was put back in its rightful place . . . and God was restored to his.

And the best place for us to be is on that narrow ledge, the Word in one hand and the world in the other, bridging heaven and earth.

APPENDIX

The Human Dilemma

believe the way we share the content of the gospel needs to change. When the tracts *The Four Spiritual Laws, Steps to Peace with God,* and *The Bridge* were written several decades ago, their authors correctly read where our culture was. At that time, most people believed in a personal God and were confident that the Bible was God's Word. What was missing was only that people lacked a clear presentation of the gospel content. So the authors developed ways to present the basics of the gospel in a straightforward way. These three excellent presentations of Christianity are the result. They are biblically based and have been used to bring thousands of people to the Lord. God has greatly used them, and they remain valuable resources today.

But, for several reasons, I believe it is time to develop a new way to present the content of the gospel, an approach that could be used alongside these others. The tracts all begin with a personal God; today's world doubts that such a being exists. They appeal to spiritual "laws," but the world has rejected the idea that there is such a thing as an absolute. And they use the Bible as an authoritative source in a world that dismisses it as irrelevant.

These great evangelistic tools were written to speak to the heart and mind of people who occupied a different world from the one we know. In an environment that has bumped off God, abandoned the idea of binding laws, and dismissed the Bible as dated fiction, it is tough to get very far with these approaches.

So what is the alternative? I believe the only thing that is authoritative for people today is their experience. So if we take seriously the idea of beginning where our hearers are, that means beginning with their experience and taking them from there to the content of the gospel.

Let me suggest a way we might do that.

The Seven Dimensions of the Human Dilemma

Every person who is outside of a relationship with Christ is experiencing the negative consequences of that missing connection. The relationship with God is seriously damaged, the ability to relate with others is derailed, and life is thrown out of kilter. I call this the "human dilemma." It is what is inevitably true about human beings apart from Christ.

As I've thought about this, it seems to me that the human dilemma manifests itself in seven areas or dimensions (fig. 4).

Alienation from others: Friendships are fleeting, filled with tension, and a constant source of struggle.

Bad experiences: Painful losses and unfair life experiences trip us up routinely.

Conflict between intentions and actions: I don't do what I want to do, and I'm forever doing what I shouldn't do.

Direction lacking in life: If there is a point to our existence, I missed the announcement.

Esteem in crisis: Am I worthwhile, valuable, unique?

Future uncertain: What happens when I die?

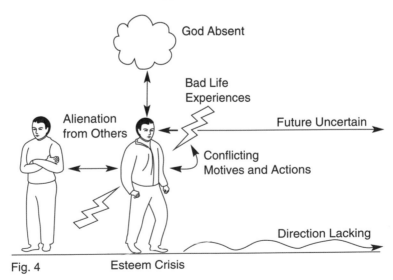

Fig. 4

224

God absent: God seems distant, his voice is silent, he is missing from my daily experience.

The Starting Point and Four Responses

This approach seeks to begin evangelism not by pointing to God but by identifying which of the seven aspects of the human dilemma is most real to the person with whom we're speaking. Which of these places of struggle has begun to surface in the life of this person? To answer that takes time, insightful questions, and a willingness to listen.

Every person apart from Christ experiences these aspects of the human dilemma, but not everybody is aware of them. Good questions can help us discover where the human condition shows itself in a person's life and help those we're speaking with become aware of those struggles. Both open the door for us to share our experience of Christ and the difference he has made in our lives.

If the human dilemma is a reality, why is it that the world is not flocking to us for answers? For one thing, people are experts at not facing up to what is going on in their lives. ("Problem? What problem?") Beyond that, they're so self-reliant they would only ask for help as a last resort. ("I'm fine. I can handle it on my own. I've got everything under control.") Those things were certainly true for me before I became a Christian.

For those reasons, when a problem bubbles up in a person's life, I think there are four possible responses to it.

Denial: There is no problem, in spite of the evidence to the contrary.

Resignation: There is a problem, but nothing can be done about it.

Effort: There is a problem, but if I work hard, I can eliminate it through my own effort.

Seeking help: There is a problem, and I am unable to fix it, so I will seek help.

The fourth is the one that most often is opted for last, and usually only after every other option has been exhausted. Figure 5 shows how the other three responses might express themselves.

Once we have zeroed in on which dimension of the human dilemma the person is most conscious of, we can begin to probe how he or she is choosing to respond to this pain or frustration. "I'm picking up that this is a tough part of life for you. How do you deal with that? Has that made a difference?" The more we can gently help the other person see that none of the first three options is a satisfying solution, the more that person will be ready to seek help. And we can help show what it is like to do that by sharing our experience of coming to Christ.

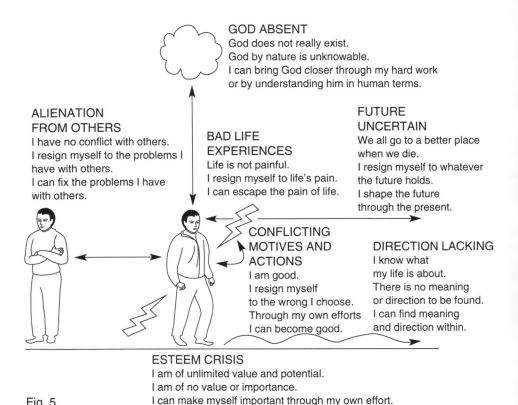

GOD ABSENT
God does not really exist.
God by nature is unknowable.
I can bring God closer through my hard work
or by understanding him in human terms.

ALIENATION FROM OTHERS
I have no conflict with others.
I resign myself to the problems I have with others.
I can fix the problems I have with others.

BAD LIFE EXPERIENCES
Life is not painful.
I resign myself to life's pain.
I can escape the pain of life.

FUTURE UNCERTAIN
We all go to a better place when we die.
I resign myself to whatever the future holds.
I shape the future through the present.

CONFLICTING MOTIVES AND ACTIONS
I am good.
I resign myself to the wrong I choose.
Through my own efforts I can become good.

DIRECTION LACKING
I know what my life is about.
There is no meaning or direction to be found.
I can find meaning and direction within.

ESTEEM CRISIS
I am of unlimited value and potential.
I am of no value or importance.
I can make myself important through my own effort.

Fig. 5

Our Experience and Jesus' Answer

The next step is to share with that person our experience of the same dimension of the human dilemma. How did I experience it? What did I choose to do about it? How effective was that? How did I come to see Christ as an answer in that particular struggle? And now that I have become a Christian, what difference has Christ made in that area of my life? While my main struggle in life may not have been the same as this person's, it was a struggle nonetheless, and that experience can be shared.

It would be counterproductive to give too simplistic an account of how Christ has made a difference in one of these dimensions. It is true that sometimes Jesus radically transforms a part of our lives. More often,

226

that area continues to be a place of conflict for years, even the rest of our lives. But in the midst of that, Jesus gives courage to face it, power to begin changing, and hope that one day—whether in this life or in eternity—the struggle will be put to rest. Too simplistic an account can misrepresent the gospel (we *don't* come to Christ as a quick fix to get our needs met) and create misleading impressions of what to expect once we become a Christian (life will *not* suddenly become perfect or easy or comfortable).

Surviving the Struggle

Up to this point, we have remained in the realm of experience. Now we begin to move to the solution, pointing to the Bible as providing relevant answers to real experiences. What we discover when we open the pages of the Bible is the promise that when we come to Christ, each one of these dimensions of the human dilemma is brought back into line.

When we talk about the seven dimensions, we are not talking about surface needs, like a desire for prestige or more discretionary income or personal comfort. Each dimension is a bedrock spiritual consequence of alienation from God. They are direct consequences of the fall. All are issues that the Bible openly addresses, and for which the Bible presents the antidote.

To alienation from others Jesus brings forgiveness and reconciliation.

To the pain of bad experiences Jesus brings comfort and the promise of ultimate justice.

To conflicting intentions and actions Jesus brings wholeness and forgiveness of sins.

To direction that is lacking Jesus brings meaning and purpose for living.

To a crisis of esteem Jesus brings assurance of our belovedness.

To an uncertain future Jesus brings hope for eternal life.

To separation from God Jesus brings redemption—God and man made right through Christ.

Once we've identified the primary place where a friend is experiencing the pain of life without Christ, and help the person see how unsatisfying it is to rely on self for answers, we can show how the Bible suggests an answer: Jesus Christ (fig. 6).

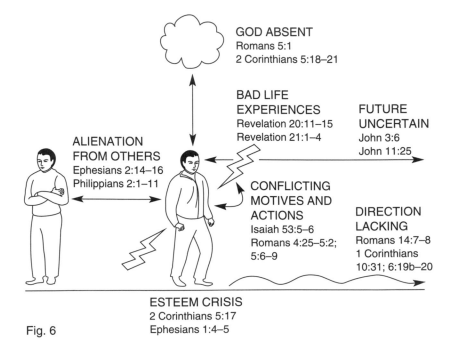

GOD ABSENT
Romans 5:1
2 Corinthians 5:18–21

BAD LIFE
EXPERIENCES
Revelation 20:11–15
Revelation 21:1–4

FUTURE
UNCERTAIN
John 3:6
John 11:25

ALIENATION
FROM OTHERS
Ephesians 2:14–16
Philippians 2:1–11

CONFLICTING
MOTIVES AND
ACTIONS
Isaiah 53:5–6
Romans 4:25–5:2;
5:6–9

DIRECTION
LACKING
Romans 14:7–8
1 Corinthians
10:31; 6:19b–20

ESTEEM CRISIS
2 Corinthians 5:17
Ephesians 1:4–5

Fig. 6

The Solution to the Dilemma

The final step in the process is to supply the missing pieces for the person, to round out the gospel. The person we're speaking with has seen how Jesus claims to be the answer for this aspect of the human dilemma. Now we need to step back and show more fully who Jesus is and why he came. This would be the perfect place to use the presentation of the gospel that is provided in *The Bridge, Steps to Peace with God,* or *The Four Spiritual Laws.*

Or at this point in the conversation you may want to develop your discussion in the following way. This is how I usually explain the basics of Christianity.

1. First, God made us to live for him. He created us, and he has a claim on us. We are his.
2. But we decided we would rather live for ourselves than for him. We pushed God out of his rightful place at the center of our lives and took his place. (This we call sin.)
3. The result of our decision to push God out of the center is twofold. First, we have made a mess of our lives. With God pushed out, life

doesn't go well. It makes no sense and is a constant struggle. We were made to live for God, and we don't have to look far to see the consequences of our not doing that. The human dilemma is what we all experience apart from Christ. Second, we have offended God. We have broken our relationship with the one who made us and now find ourselves rightly deserving of God's anger and punishment. We have made a mess of our lives.

4. Jesus came to us as God's solution both for the mess we've made of our lives and for our broken relationship with God. He came to restore us to God's original intention for us by pointing us back toward living our lives for him. And he came to restore our relationship with God by bearing on the cross the punishment we rightly deserve.

5. We need to respond in two ways. First, we need to put our trust in Jesus as the only way to be made right with the Father whom we have so deeply wronged. Second, we need to decide not to live for ourselves anymore but to turn away from that focus and live for him from this point on in submission, trust, and obedience.

All of this leads the person, Lord willing, into a new experience—being made new and whole and right in Christ.

N⦾TES

Chapter 1: Walking the Narrow Ledge of Relevance

1. Thanks to my friend Bill Tibert for this wonderful analogy.
2. Haddon Robinson, class lecture, 25 May 1993.
3. P. T. Forsyth, *Positive Preaching and the Modern Mind* (Grand Rapids: Baker, 1980), 207.
4. Robinson, class lecture, 17 May 1993.

Chapter 2: Bringing the Truth to Bear on Our World

1. Stephen Crane, "The Open Boat," *The American Tradition in Literature,* 6th ed., ed. George Perkins, et al. (New York: Random House, 1985), 1046.
2. Roy Clements, "The Nature of Expository Preaching," *Contact* 19, no. 2 (summer 1990), 4.
3. P. T. Forsyth, *Positive Preaching and the Modern Mind* (Grand Rapids: Baker, 1980), 8, 131.

Chapter 3: Manufacturing the Consumer

1. Myron Magnet, "The Money Society," *Fortune* 6 (July 1987), 26.
2. Juliet B. Schor, *The Overworked American* (New York: Basic, 1992), 107.
3. "Five Top Tourist Spots," *react* (25 September–1 October 1995), 5.
4. See Kenneth Lux's helpful explanation of these ideas in *Adam Smith's Mistake* (Boston: Shambhala, 1990), 13–27.
5. Jonathan Lerner, "The South: Thirty-Five Fascinating Facts," *Hemispheres* (April 1995), 27.
6. James Lincoln Collier does a nice job covering these developments in *The Rise of Selfishness in America* (New York: Oxford University, 1991), 19–48. See also "Industrialization, Business and Consumerism," in *Modern American Culture,* ed. Mick Gidley (London: Longman, 1993), 166–88.
7. Sue Ellyn Scaletta, "Better Junk Junk Mail before It Buries You," *Gazette Telegraph* (16 November 1993), D3.
8. George Ritzer, *The McDonaldization of America* (Thousand Oaks, Calif.: Pine Forge, 1993), 29.
9. Tom Heymann, *On an Average Day* (New York: Fawcett Columbine, 1989), 102.
10. Steven Lagerfeld describes this and other mall methods in "What Main Street Can Learn from the Mall," *The Atlantic Monthly* (November 1995), 110–20.
11. Laurence Shames, *The Hunger for More* (New York: Vintage, 1991), 33.
12. Heymann, *Average Day,* 101.

13. Tom Parker, *In One Day* (Boston: Houghton Mifflin, 1984), 47.

14. Heymann, *Average Day,* 154. More recent estimates say the figure is closer to three to four thousand.

15. Eric Clark, *The Want Makers* (New York: Penguin, 1988), 62.

16. Collier, *Rise of Selfishness,* 243.

17. "Didya Know?" *Gazette Telegraph* (24 January 1993), A2.

18. Take a peek at Leslie Savan's great essay about the lengths advertisers go to do this: "Listless Is More," *The Sponsored Life* (Philadelphia: Temple University, 1994), 43–46.

19. Clark, *Want Makers,* 27.

20. Ibid., 23–24.

21. Christopher Lasch, *Culture of Narcissism* (New York: Warner, 1979), 138.

22. Paul Wachtel, *The Poverty of Affluence* (Philadelphia: New Society, 1989), 39.

Chapter 4: God's Word to a Discontented World

1. Thomas Morris does an excellent job of introducing this aspect of Pascal's thinking (as well as many other of his ideas) in his superb little book *Making Sense of It All: Pascal and the Meaning of Life* (Grand Rapids: Eerdmans, 1992), 109–27.

Chapter 5: Bringing the Spectator into Focus

1. Bill McKibben, *The Age of Missing Information* (New York: Plume, 1993), 18.

2. Don DeLillo, *White Noise* (New York: Penguin, 1985), 22.

3. Ninety-nine percent of homes have a TV set, nearly two-thirds have two or more, 58 percent have cable, and 70 percent a VCR, as of 1992. Don R. Pember, *Mass Media in America,* 6th ed. (New York: Macmillan, 1992), 300.

4. Conversations with Beryl Gulya of the Colorado Springs Homebuilders Association and with Bill Forsyth and Mike Roberts, realtors in the Colorado Springs area.

5. Estimates range between twenty-five and thirty hours a week, but most land at about twenty-eight. Patrick Barwise and Andrew Ehrenberg, *Television and Its Audience* (Newbury Park, Calif.: Sage, 1988), 12.

6. Ibid.

7. Tom Heymann, *On an Average Day* (New York: Fawcett Columbine, 1989), 183.

8. Ibid., 202.

9. "Five Top Tourist Spots," *react* (25 September–1 October 1995), 5.

10. See the probing analyses of Neil Postman and Daniel Boorstin in Neil Postman, *Amusing Ourselves to Death* (New York: Penguin, 1985), 64–80, and in Daniel Boorstin, *The Image* (New York: Vintage, 1961), 12–14.

11. Postman, *Amusing Ourselves to Death,* 69.

12. Ibid., 76.

13. Walker Percy says the word didn't enter our language until the eighteenth century in his *Lost in the Cosmos: The Last Self-Help Book* (New York: Noonday Press, 1983), 70.

14. See the excellent discussion of the way we view and use leisure time in Witold Rybczynski, *Waiting for the Weekend* (New York: Penguin, 1991). Especially pertinent are pages 132–44.

15. James Lincoln Collier has done a masterful job of chronicling these developments in his book *The Rise of Selfishness in America* (New York: Oxford University, 1991), 93–104, 168–80, 239–45.

16. See McKibben, *The Age of Missing Information,* 54–55.

17. James B. Twitchell, *Carnival Culture: The Trashing of Taste in America* (New York: Columbia University, 1992), 197.

18. Robert Kubey and Mihaly Csikszentmihalyi, *Television and the Quality of Life* (Hillsdale, N.J.: Laurence Erlbaum Associates, 1990), 74.

19. Ibid., 171.

20. Thanks to Larry Douglas, station manager of Fox 21 in Colorado Springs, for these insights.

21. Ken Myers, *Television and Christian Discipleship,* audiotape (Powhatan, Va.: Mars Hill Lectures).

22. Haddon Robinson, doctor of ministry class lecture, Gordon-Conwell Theological Seminary, 17 May 1994.

23. From "Time to Kick the Habit for Trial Junkies," *Gazette Telegraph* (4 October 1995), A4.

24. Kubey and Csikszentmihalyi, *Television and the Quality of Life,* 79, 104, 134.

Chapter 6: God's Word to a Distracted World

1. By Brown Bannister and Amy Grant, "Fairytale," *Father's Eyes,* Amy Grant (Home Sweet Home Productions).

2. For more information about this play and other creative approaches to sharing the gospel, contact Stan Nussbaum at 5355 Astronomy Court, Colorado Springs, CO 80917, or at his e-mail address: stan@gmi.org.

Chapter 7: Isolating the Individual

1. John Locke, *The Second Treatise of Civil Government* (New York: Hafner, 1964), 122–24.

2. Ralph Waldo Emerson, "Historic Notes" and "Self-Reliance," in *The Complete Writings of Ralph Waldo Emerson* (New York: William Wise, 1929).

3. David Henry Thoreau, "Walden," in *The American Tradition in Literature,* 6th ed., ed. George Perkins, et al. (New York: Random House, 1985).

4. Walt Whitman, "Songs of the Open Road," "Song of Myself," and "Assurances," in *Leaves of Grass* (Boston: Small, Maynard, and Co., 1897).

5. This poem was included in class handouts in a leadership class taught by Mary Ruth Lembright, Miami University, 1979–80. Source unknown.

6. Carl Rogers, *On Becoming a Person* (Boston: Houghton Mifflin, 1961), 130.

7. This is a phrase from Robert Wuthnow's portion of the article "The Scandal of the Evangelical Mind," *First Things* (March 1995), 41.

8. According to James Patterson and Peter Kim, 72 percent don't have a friendship with their next-door neighbors, 45 percent have never spent an evening with them, 27 percent have never been inside their homes, and 15 percent don't even know their names. *The Day America Told the Truth* (New York: Prentice-Hall, 1991), 172.

9. For example, Andres Tapia (see "Reaching the First Post-Christian Generation," *Christianity Today* 38, no. 10 [12 September 1994], 18–23) and Dieter Zander ("The Gospel for Generation X," *Leadership* 16, no. 2 [spring 1995], 36–42).

10. If you want to learn more about some of the identity twisting that takes place on-line, see Sherry Turkle's *Life on the Screen: Identity in the Age of the Internet* (New York: Simon and Schuster, 1995). Articles about virtual relationships, on-line sex, and identity blurring can be found in the winter 1996 issue of *Virtual City* (pp. 34–42, 56–58) and the February 1996 issue of *The Net* (vol. 1, no. 9, pp. 44–57).

11. According to a 1988 Roper poll. This and other valuable insights into our world can be found in Ralph Keyes' delightful book *Timelock* (New York: HarperCollins, 1991), 149.

12. Paul Leinberger and Bruce Tucker, *The New Individualists* (New York: HarperCollins, 1991), 232–39.

13. Daniel Yankelovich describes the way people have come to feel a moral obligation to yield to their impulses in his *New Rules* (New York: Random House, 1991), 86.

14. This idea is forcefully communicated in Tony Walter's *Need: The New Religion* (Downers Grove, Ill.: InterVarsity, 1985), 1–10.

Chapter 8: God's Word to a Disconnected World

1. From "Whitman's Manuscripts" and "As I Ebb'd with the Ocean of Life," cited in Wilfred M. McClay, *The Masterless: Self and Society in Modern America* (Chapel Hill: University of North Carolina, 1994), 67.

Chapter 9: Shoving God Aside

1. George Gallup Jr. and Jim Castelli, *The People's Religion: American Faith in the Nineties* (New York: Macmillan, 1989), 45.

2. George Barna, *What Americans Believe: An Annual Survey of Values and Religious Views in the United States* (Ventura, Calif.: Regal, 1991), 207.

3. Gallup and Castelli, *The People's Religion,* 21.

4. Stephen L. Carter, *Culture of Disbelief: How American Law and Politics Trivialize Religious Devotion* (New York: Basic, HarperCollins, 1993), 15.

5. Clifton Fadiman, ed., *The Little, Brown Book of Anecdotes* (Boston: Little, Brown and Company, 1985), 343.

6. Carter, *Culture of Disbelief,* 24.

7. Robert Frost, "Fireflies in the Garden," in *The Poetry of Robert Frost,* ed. Edward Connery Lathem (New York: Henry Holt and Company, 1969).

8. Carter, *Culture of Disbelief,* 22.

Chapter 10: God's Word to a World Alone

1. Donald Sunukjian, doctor of ministry class lecture, Gordon-Conwell Theological Seminary, 17 May 1994.

2. Haddon Robinson, doctor of ministry class lecture, Gordon-Conwell Theological Seminary, 24 May 1993.

3. Ibid.

4. These examples were shared by Robinson over several sessions, class lectures, 24 and 27 May 1993 and 24 May 1994.

5. Harry Blamires, *The Secularist Heresy: The Erosion of the Gospel in the Twentieth Century* (London: SPCK, 1956), 13–14.

6. This paragraph is a paraphrase of Blamires, *The Secularist Heresy,* 31–32.

7. Walker Percy, *Lost in the Cosmos: The Last Self-Help Book* (New York: Noonday, 1983), 262.

8. Paul Davies, *Are We Alone? The Philosophical Implications of the Discovery of Extraterrestrial Life* (New York: Basic, 1995), 136. See also Anthony Mansueto "Visions of Cosmopolis: Does UFO Fascination Reflect Our Need for God?" *Omni* 17, no. 1 (October 1994), 64–69, 110.

9. The anthropic principle and other evidence for a changing view of the universe is presented in Robert M. Augros and George N. Stanciu, *The New Story of Science: Mind and the Universe* (New York: Bantam, 1984), 53–82, and throughout Hugh Ross, *The Fingerprint of God* (Orange, Calif.: Promise Publishing Company, 1989).

10. More on the plausibility of miracles can be found in Charles Hummel's wonderful book *Galileo Connection: Resolving Conflicts between Science and the Bible* (Downers Grove, Ill.: Inter-Varsity, 1986).

11. For exceptional background on the issue of evolution in particular, see Phillip Johnson, *Darwin on Trial* (Washington, D.C.: Regnery Gateway, 1991).

Chapter 11: Pushing Past Right and Wrong

1. "Moral Absolutes Returning," *Gazette Telegraph* (29 December 1994), A1.

2. "Indecent Proposals," *Parade Magazine* (14 July 1993), 17.

3. James Patterson and Peter Kim, *The Day America Told the Truth* (New York: Prentice-Hall, 1991), 36.

4. "Who Said That?" *Gazette Telegraph* (18 June 1993), A2.

5. "Sex with a Scorecard," *Time* (5 April 1993), 41.

6. Patterson and Kim, *The Day America Told the Truth,* 25–26.

7. Historian Arnold Toynbee's insights are helpfully summarized in Gene Edwards Veith Jr., *Postmodern Times: A Christian Guide to Contemporary Thought and Culture* (Wheaton: Crossway, 1994), 44–46.

8. Patterson and Kim, *The Day America Told the Truth,* 27.

9. Ibid., 6.

10. Daniel Yankelovich, *New Rules: Searching for Self-Fulfillment in a World Turned Upside Down* (New York: Random House, 1981), 245.

11. Ibid., 86.

12. "Who Cheats?" *react* (23–29 October 1995), 10–11.

13. "Children: 'But Everybody Else Is Doing It,'" *Gazette Telegraph* (30 September 1990), and "Self-Gratification, Not Morals, Guides More Kids' Behavior," *Gazette Telegraph* (4 November 1990).

Chapter 12: God's Word to a World Astray

1. Chuck Colson, *America without God?* (Wheaton: Tyndale, 1993), audiocassette, tape 1, side 2.

2. Dean Ridings and David Henderson, *Whatever Happened to Compassion?* scene 6.

3. Josh McDowell, "Right from Wrong: The Campaign for Truth," *Parentlife* (June 1995), 30–32.

4. C. S. Lewis, *Mere Christianity* (New York: Macmillan, 1981), 3–28. Quotes are from pages 3 and 21.

5. James Patterson and Peter Kim, *The Day America Told the Truth* (New York: Prentice-Hall, 1991), 27.

6. Noted by Cal Thomas in "Woodstock Generation Comes to Regret Its Relativism," *Gazette Telegraph* (4 February 1994).

Chapter 13: Leaving Meaning Behind

1. William Barrett, "The Testimony of Modern Art," in *The Irrational Man: A Study in Existential Philosophy* (New York: Anchor, 1958), 185. If you're interested in digging into this further, look at three other books. H. R. Rookmaaker has written a superb history and critique of modern art from a Christian perspective: *Modern Art and the Death of a Culture* (Wheaton: Crossway, 1970). Along similar lines, Frances Schaeffer wrote *How Should We Then Live?* (Old Tappan, N.J.: Revell, 1976), a history of art and culture from ancient Greek and Roman culture to the present, also from a Christian perspective. Finally, Louis Sass has written a provocative book called *Madness and Modernism: Insanity in the Light of Modern Art, Literature, and Thought* (Cambridge: Harvard University, 1992). On pages 28–36 he presents, like Barrett, an insightful set of characteristics of modern art.

2. From section 125 of Friedrich Nietzsche's *The Joyful Wisdom*, cited in William Barrett, *The Irrational Man: A Study in Existential Philosophy* (New York: Anchor, 1958), 185.

3. Friedrich Nietzsche, *The Gay Science,* trans. W. Kaufman (New York: Random House, 1974), 181.

4. Mary K. Wilson, quoted in Tim Stafford, "Campus Christians and the New Thought Police," *Christianity Today* (10 February 1992), 19.

5. Dave Graffin, "Struck a Nerve," *Recipe for Hate,* Bad Religion (Atlantic).

6. Cited in Kenneth Gergen, *The Saturated Self: Dilemmas of Identity in Contemporary Life* (New York: Basic, 1991), 248–49.

7. Sixty-six percent agreed somewhat or strongly with the statement. Among those affiliated with an evangelical church, 53 percent agreed, 23 percent strongly, and 30 percent somewhat. George Barna, *What Americans Believe* (Ventura, Calif.: Regal, 1991), 83–85.

8. Don DeLillo, *White Noise* (New York: Penguin, 1984), 22–24.

9. Louis Sass, *Madness and Modernism: Insanity in the Light of Modern Art, Literature, and Thought* (Cambridge: Harvard University, 1992), 37.

10. Sting, "If I Ever Lose My Faith in You" *Fields of Gold* (A&M).

11. Greg Worthen, "Pierced Tattooed Branded Scarred," *The Colorado Springs Independent* 3, no. 43 (25–31 October 1995), 11–13.

12. Faith No More, "Surprise! You're Dead!" *The Real Thing* (Slash Records).

13. Nancy Gibbs, "Angels among Us," *Newsweek* (27 December 1993), 56.

14. Sam Keen, *Hymns to an Unknown God: Awakening the Spirit in Everyday Life* (New York: Bantam, 1994), 76–78.

15. Kenneth L. Woodward, "On the Road Again," *Newsweek* (28 November 1994), 62.

Chapter 14: God's Word to a World Adrift

1. Donald C. Posterski, *Reinventing Evangelism: New Strategies for Presenting Christ in Today's World* (Downers Grove, Ill.: InterVarsity, 1989), 15.

2. Francis Schaeffer, *The God Who Is There* in *Francis A. Schaeffer Trilogy* (Westchester, Ill.: Crossway, 1990), 140.

3. This was shared during conversations with Dr. Wells at Gordon-Conwell Theological Seminary, May 1995.

4. James W. Sire, *Why Should Anyone Believe Anything at All?* (Downers Grove, Ill.: InterVarsity, 1994), 78–90.

Epilogue: Bridging Heaven and Earth

1. Douglas Coupland, *Life after God* (New York: Pocket, 1994), 359.

2. Dennis DeYoung, "Show Me the Way," *Edge of the Century* (A&M Records).

3. Eric Bazilian, "One of Us," *Relish,* Joan Osborne (PolyGram).

4. Cited in Albert M. Wells Jr., *Inspiring Quotations Contemporary and Classical* (Nashville: Thomas Nelson, 1988), 35.

5. Thanks to my brother, Bill Henderson, for providing me with these shocking (or are they striking?) bits of information.

SUGGESTED READING

Gaining a Hearing

Preaching and Communication Today

Abbey, Merrill R. *Preaching to the Contemporary Mind: Interpreting the Gospel Today.* New York: Abingdon, 1963.

Brown, Steve, Haddon Robinson, and William Willimon. *A Voice in the Wilderness: Clear Preaching in a Complicated World.* Sisters, Ore.: Multnomah, 1993.

Buechner, Frederick. *Telling the Truth: The Gospel as Tragedy, Comedy, and Fairy Tale.* New York: Harper and Row, 1977.

Davis, H. Grady. *Design for Preaching.* Philadelphia: Fortress, 1958.

Decker, Bert. *You've Got to Be Believed to Be Heard.* New York: St. Martin's Press, 1992.

Duffett, Robert G. *A Relevant Word: Communicating the Gospel to Seekers.* Valley Forge, Pa.: Judson Press, 1996.

Forsyth, P. T. *Positive Preaching and the Modern Mind.* Grand Rapids: Baker, 1980.

Galli, Mark, and Craig Brian Larson. *Preaching That Connects.* Grand Rapids: Zondervan, 1994.

Greidanus, Sidney. *The Modern Preacher and the Ancient Text: Interpreting and Preaching Biblical Literature.* Grand Rapids: Eerdmans, 1988.

Hybels, Bill, Stuart Briscoe, and Haddon Robinson. *Mastering Contemporary Preaching.* Portland, Ore.: Multnomah, 1989.

Kraft, Charles. *Communication Theory for Christian Witness.* Rev. ed. Maryknoll, N.Y.: Orbis, 1991.

Lewis, Ralph L., and Gregg Lewis. *Inductive Preaching: Helping People Listen.* Westchester, Ill.: Crossway, 1983.

Lowry, Eugene L. *Doing Time in the Pulpit: The Relationship between Narrative and Preaching.* Nashville: Abingdon, 1985.

———. *The Homiletical Plot: The Sermon as Narrative Art Form.* Atlanta: John Knox, 1980.

Marquart, Edward F. *Quest for Better Preaching: Resources for Renewal in the Pulpit.* Minneapolis: Augsburg, 1985.

Miller, Calvin. *The Empowered Communicator: Seven Keys to Unlocking an Audience.* Nashville: Broadman and Holman, 1994.

Rogness, Michael. *Preaching to a TV Generation.* Lima, Ohio: CSS, 1994.

Smith, Donald K. *Creating Understanding: A Handbook for Christian Communication across Cultural Landscapes.* Grand Rapids: Zondervan, 1992.

Stott, John. *Between Two Worlds: The Art of Preaching in the Twentieth Century.* Grand Rapids: Eerdmans, 1982.

Willimon, William H. *The Intrusive Word: Preaching to the Unbaptized.* Grand Rapids: Eerdmans, 1994.

———. *Peculiar Speech: Preaching to the Baptized.* Grand Rapids: Eerdmans, 1992.

Thinking Christianly and Understanding Worldviews

Blamires, Harry. *The Christian Mind: How Should a Christian Think?* Ann Arbor: Servant, 1963.

———. *Recovering the Christian Mind: Meeting the Challenges of Secularism.* Downers Grove, Ill.: InterVarsity, 1988.

Burnett, David. *Clash of Worlds: A Christian's Handbook on Cultures.* World Religions and Evangelism. Nashville: Oliver Nelson, 1990.

Dyrness, William A. *How Does America Hear the Gospel?* Grand Rapids: Eerdmans, 1989.

McCullough, Donald W. *The Trivialization of God: The Dangerous Illusion of a Manageable Deity.* Colorado Springs: NavPress, 1995.

Moore, Peter C. *Disarming the Secular Gods: How to Talk So Skeptics Will Listen.* Downers Grove, Ill.: InterVarsity, 1989.

Mouw, Richard J. *Distorted Truth: What Every Christian Should Know about the Battle for the Mind.* San Francisco: Harper and Row, 1989.

Sampson, Philip, Vinay Samuel, and Chris Sugden, eds. *Faith and Modernity.* Oxford: Regnum Books, 1994.

Shelley, Bruce L. *The Gospel and the American Dream.* Portland, Ore.: Multnomah, 1989.

Sire, James W. *Chris Chrisman Goes to College . . . and Faces the Challenges of Relativism, Individualism, and Pluralism.* Downers Grove, Ill.: InterVarsity, 1993.

———. *The Universe Next Door: A Basic Worldview Catalog.* Downers Grove, Ill.: InterVarsity, 1988.

Smith, Joanmarie. *A Context for Christianity in the 21st Century.* Allen, Tx.: Thomas More, 1995.

Stott, John. *The Contemporary Christian: Applying God's Word to Today's World.* Downers Grove, Ill.: InterVarsity, 1992.

Contemporary Culture (General)

Barna, George. *The Frog in the Kettle.* Ventura, Calif.: Regal, 1990.

Chandler, Russell. *Racing toward 2001: The Forces Shaping America's Religious Future.* Grand Rapids: Zondervan, 1992.

Collier, James Lincoln. *The Rise of Selfishness in America.* New York: Oxford University, 1991.

Colson, Charles. *America without God.* Wheaton: Tyndale, 1993. Audiocassettes.

Guinness, Os. *The American Hour: A Time of Reckoning and the Once and Future Role of Faith.* New York: Free Press, 1993.

———. *The Dust of Death: The Sixties Counterculture and How It Changed America Forever.* Wheaton: Crossway, 1994.

Hammond, Josh, and James Morrison. *The Stuff Americans Are Made Of.* New York: Macmillan, 1996.

Hunter, James Davison. *Culture Wars: The Struggle to Define America.* New York: Basic, 1991.

Johnson, Paul. *Modern Times: The World from the Twenties to the Eighties.* Rev. ed. New York: HarperCollins, 1991.

Keyes, Ralph. *Timelock: How Life Got So Hectic and What You Can Do about It.* New York: HarperCollins, 1991.

Roof, Wade Clark. *A Generation of Seekers: The Spiritual Journeys of the Baby Boom Generation.* New York: Harper San Francisco, 1993.

Rookmaaker, H. R. *Modern Art and the Death of a Culture.* Wheaton: Crossway, 1970.

Rybczynski, Witold. *Waiting for the Weekend.* New York: Penguin, 1991.

Veith, Gene Edward Jr., *State of the Arts: From Bezalel to Mapplethorpe.* Wheaton: Crossway, 1991.

American Culture from a Foreign Perspective

de Tocqueville, Alexis. *Democracy in America*. Translated by George Lawrence. Edited by J. P. Mayer. New York: Doubleday, Anchor, 1969.

DeVita, Philip R., and James D. Armstrong, eds. *Distant Mirrors: America as a Foreign Culture*. Belmont, Calif.: Wadsworth, 1993.

Gidley, Mick, ed. *Modern American Culture: An Introduction*. New York: Longman, 1993.

Ideas Shaping Our World

Brown, Harold O. J. *The Sensate Culture: Western Civilization between Chaos and Transformation*. Dallas: Word, 1996.

Gaarder, Jostein. *Sophie's World: A Novel about the History of Philosophy*. New York: Farrar, Straus, and Giroux, 1994.

Houston, James. *The Mind on Fire: An Anthology of the Writings of Blaise Pascal*. Portland, Ore.: Multnomah, 1989.

Morris, Thomas V. *Making Sense of It All: Pascal and the Meaning of Life*. Grand Rapids: Eerdmans, 1992.

Schaeffer, Francis A. *How Should We Then Live? The Rise and Decline of Western Thought and Culture*. Old Tappan, N.J.: Revell, 1976.

Apologetics and Evangelism

Aldrich, Joseph C. *Lifestyle Evangelism: Crossing Traditional Boundaries to Reach the Unbelieving World*. Portland, Ore.: Multnomah, 1981.

Barna, George. *Evangelism That Works: How to Reach Changing Generations with the Unchanging Gospel*. Ventura, Calif.: Regal, 1995.

Briner, Bob. *Roaring Lambs: A Gentle Plan to Radically Change Your World*. Grand Rapids: Zondervan, 1993.

Ford, Leighton. *Good News Is for Sharing*. Elgin, Ill.: David C. Cook, 1977.

Green, Michael. *Evangelism through the Local Church*. Nashville: Oliver Nelson, 1990.

Green, Michael, and Alister McGrath. *How Shall We Reach Them? Defending and Communicating the Christian Faith to Nonbelievers*. Nashville: Oliver Nelson, 1995.

Jacks, Bob, and Betty Jacks. *Your Home a Lighthouse: Hosting an Evangelistic Bible Study*. Colorado Springs: NavPress, 1986.

Metzger, Will. *Tell the Truth: The Whole Gospel to the Whole Person by Whole People*. Downers Grove, Ill.: InterVarsity, 1981.

Moreland, J. P. *Scaling the Secular City: A Defense of Christianity*. Grand Rapids: Baker, 1987.

Morgenthaler, Sally. *Worship Evangelism: Inviting Unbelievers into the Presence of God*. Grand Rapids: Zondervan, 1995.

Newbigin, Lesslie. *Foolishness to the Greeks: The Gospel and Western Culture*. Grand Rapids: Eerdmans, 1986.

Petersen, Jim. *Evangelism as a Lifestyle: Reaching into Your World with the Gospel*. Colorado Springs: NavPress, 1980.

———. *Evangelism for Our Generation: Practical Ways to Make Evangelism Your Lifestyle*. Colorado Springs: NavPress, 1985.

Phillips, Tom, and Bob Norsworthy, with W. Terry Whalin. *The World at Your Door*. Minneapolis: Bethany House, 1997.

Pippert, Becky. *Out of the Salt Shaker and into the World: Evangelism as a Way of Life*. Downers Grove, Ill.: InterVarsity, 1979.

Posterski, Donald C. *Reinventing Evangelism: New Strategies for Presenting Christ in Today's World*. Downers Grove, Ill.: InterVarsity, 1989.

Ratz, Calvin, Frank Tillapaugh, and Myron Augsburger. *Mastering Outreach and Evangelism*. Portland, Ore.: Multnomah, 1990.

Roxburgh, Alan J. *Reaching a New Generation: Strategies for Tomorrow's Church*. Downers Grove, Ill.: InterVarsity, 1993.

Sjogren, Steve. *Conspiracy of Kindness*. Ann Arbor: Servant, 1993.

Wells, David F. *Turning to God: Biblical Conversion in the Modern World*. Grand Rapids: Baker, 1989.

The Church's Place in a Changing Culture

Clapp, Rodney. *A Peculiar People: The Church as Culture in a Post-Christian Society*. Downers Grove, Ill.: InterVarsity, 1996.

Colson, Chuck. *The Body: Being Light in Darkness*. Dallas: Word, 1992.

Crabb, William, and Jeff Jernigan. *The Church in Ruins: Foundations for the Future*. Colorado Springs: NavPress, 1991.

Guinness, Os, and John Seel, eds. *No God but God: Breaking with the Idols of Our Age*. Chicago: Moody, 1992.

Hauerwas, Stanley, and William H. Willimon. *Resident Aliens: Life in the Christian Colony*. Nashville: Abingdon, 1989.

———. *Where Resident Aliens Live: Exercises for Christian Practice*. Nashville: Abingdon, 1996.

Hendricks, William D. *Exit Interviews: Revealing Stories of Why People Are Leaving the Church*. Chicago: Moody, 1993.

Hunsberger, George R., and Craig Van Gelder. *The Church between Gospel and Culture: The Emerging Mission in North America*. Grand Rapids: Eerdmans, 1996.

Hunter, George G. III. *Church for the Unchurched*. Nashville: Abingdon, 1996.

Hybels, Lynne, and Bill Hybels. *Rediscovering Church: The Story and Vision of Willow Creek Community Church*. Grand Rapids: Zondervan, 1995.

Mead, Loren D. *The Once and Future Church: Reinventing the Congregation for a New Mission Frontier*. Washington, D.C.: Alban Institute, 1991.

Miller, C. John. *Outgrowing the Ingrown Church*. Grand Rapids: Zondervan, 1986.

Miller, Donald E. *Reinventing American Protestantism: Christianity in the New Millennium*. Berkeley: University of California, 1997.

Petersen, Jim. *Church without Walls: Moving beyond Traditional Boundaries*. Colorado Springs: NavPress, 1992.

Regele, Mike. *Death of the Church*. Grand Rapids: Zondervan, 1995.

Seel, John. *The Evangelical Forfeit: Can We Recover?* Grand Rapids: Baker, 1993.

Van Engen, Charles. *God's Missionary People: Rethinking the Purpose of the Local Church*. Grand Rapids: Baker, 1991.

White, James Emery. *Reinventing the Church: A Challenge to Creative Redesign in an Age of Transition*. Grand Rapids: Baker, 1997.

Resources to Share with Seekers

Chesterton, G. K. *Orthodoxy*. New York: Doubleday, 1959.

Craig, William L. *Knowing the Truth about the Resurrection: Our Response to the Empty Tomb*. Ann Arbor: Servant, 1981.

Green, Michael. *My God*. Nashville: Oliver Nelson, 1993.

———. *Who Is This Jesus?* Nashville: Oliver Nelson, 1990.

Guest, John. *Risking Faith: Personal Answers for Weary Skeptics*. Grand Rapids: Baker, 1993.

Henderson, David W. *Discovering Ancient Wisdom: Pondering the Meaning of Life*. Colorado Springs: IBS Publishing, 1998.

Houston, James. *In Search of Happiness: A Guide to Personal Contentment*. Batavia, Ill.: Lion, 1990.

Kreeft, Peter. *Between Heaven and Hell: A Dialog Somewhere beyond Death with John F. Kennedy, C. S. Lewis, and Aldous Huxley*. Downers Grove, Ill.: InterVarsity, 1982.

————. *Yes or No? Straight Answers to Tough Questions about Christianity*. San Francisco: Ignatius, 1991.

Lewis, C. S. *Mere Christianity*. New York: Macmillan, 1943.

Percy, Walker. *Lost in the Cosmos: The Last Self-Help Book*. New York: Noonday, 1983.

Pippert, Rebecca Manley. *Hope Has Its Reasons: From the Search for Self to the Surprise of Faith*. New York: HarperCollins, 1989.

Stott, John R. W. *Basic Christianity*. Downers Grove, Ill.: InterVarsity, 1958.

Willow Creek Resources. *The Journey: A Bible for Seeking God and Understanding Life. New International Version*. Grand Rapids: Zondervan, 1996.

The Consumer

Advertising

Josephson, Susan G. *From Idolatry to Advertising: Visual Art and Contemporary Culture*. Armonk, N.Y.: M. E. Sharpe, 1996.

Lears, Jackson. *Fables of Abundance: A Cultural History of Advertising in America*. New York: Basic Books, 1994.

Marchand, Roland. *Advertising the American Dream: Making Way for Modernity 1920–1940*. Berkeley: University of California, 1985.

Savan, Leslie. *The Sponsored Life: Ads, TV, and American Culture*. Philadelphia: Temple University, 1994.

Twitchell, James B. *Adcult USA: The Triumph of Advertising in American Culture*. New York: Columbia University, 1996.

Marketing the Church

Moore, R. Laurence. *Selling God: American Religion in the Marketplace of Culture*. New York: Oxford University, 1994.

Shelley, Bruce, and Marshall Shelley. *The Consumer Church*. Downers Grove, Ill.: InterVarsity, 1992.

Webster, Douglas D. *Selling Jesus: What's Wrong with Marketing the Church*. Downers Grove, Ill.: InterVarsity, 1992.

Production, Sales, and Consumption

Ewen, Stuart, and Elizabeth Ewen. *Channels of Desire: Mass Images and the Shaping of American Consciousness*. New York: McGraw Hill, 1982.

Jacobs, Jerry. *The Mall: An Attempted Escape from Everyday Life*. Prospect Heights, Ill.: Waveland Press, 1984.

Kowinski, William S. *The Malling of America: An Inside Look at the Great Consumer Paradise*. New York: William Morrow, 1985.

The Impact of Economic and Market Thinking on Daily Life

Alcorn, Randy C. *Money, Possessions, and Eternity*. Wheaton: Tyndale, 1989.

Baritz, Loren. *The Good Life: The Meaning of Success for the American Middle Class*. New York: Knopf, 1988.

Shorris, Earl. *A Nation of Salesmen: The Tyranny of the Market and the Subversion of Culture*. New York: Norton, 1994.

Shwartz, Barry. *The Costs of Living: How Market Freedom Erodes the Best Things in Life*. New York: Norton, 1994.

Thompson, William Irwin. *The American Replacement of Nature: The Everyday Acts and Outrageous Evolution of Economic Life*. New York: Doubleday, Currency, 1991.

Wachtel, Paul L. *The Poverty of Affluence: A Psychological Portrait of the American Way of Life*. Philadelphia: New Society, 1989.

Walter, Tony. *Need: The New Religion*. Downers Grove, Ill.: InterVarsity, 1985.

The Spectator

Our Visual-Entertainment Culture

Billingsley, K. L. *The Seductive Image: A Christian Critique of the World of Film*. Westchester, Ill.: Crossway, 1989.

Boorstin, Daniel. *The Image: A Guide to Pseudo-Events in America*. New York: Vintage, 1961.

Meyrowitz, Joshua. *No Sense of Place: The Impact of Electronic Media on Social Behavior*. New York: Oxford University, 1985.

Mitroff, Ian I., and Warren Bennis. *The Unreality Industry: The Deliberate Manufacturing of Falsehood and What It Is Doing to Our Lives*. New York: Oxford University, 1989.

Schickel, Richard. *Intimate Strangers: The Culture of Celebrity*. New York: Fromm International, 1986.

Schultze, Quentin, et al. *Dancing in the Dark: Youth, Popular Culture, and the Electronic Media*. Grand Rapids: Eerdmans, 1991.

Television and Its Impact

Barwise, Patrick, and Andrew Ehrenberg. *Television and Its Audience*. Newbury Park, Calif.: Sage, 1988.

Cook, Coleen. *All That Glitters: A News-Person Explores the World of Television*. Chicago: Moody, 1992.

Gitlin, Todd, ed. *Watching Television*. New York: Pantheon, 1986.

Huston, Aletha, et al. *Big World, Small Screen: The Role of Television in American Society*. Lincoln: University of Nebraska, 1992.

Kubey, Robert, and Mihaly Csikszentmihalyi. *Television and the Quality of Life: How Viewing Shapes Everyday Experiences*. Hillsdale, N.J.: Laurence Erlbaum Associates, 1990.

Music and MTV

Bayles, Martha. *Hole in Our Soul: The Loss of Beauty and Meaning in American Popular Music*. New York: Free Press, 1994.

Goodwin, Andrew. *Dancing in the Distraction Factory: Music Television and Popular Culture*. Minneapolis: University of Minnesota, 1992.

Turner, Steve. *Hungry for Heaven: Rock 'n' Roll and the Search for Redemption*. Downers Grove, Ill.: InterVarsity, 1995.

Nintendo

Heim, Michael. *The Metaphysics of Virtual Reality*. New York: Oxford University, 1993.

Provenzo, Eugene F. *Video Kids: Making Sense of Nintendo*. Cambridge: Harvard University, 1991.

The Internet

Turkle, Sherry. *Life on the Screen: Identity in the Age of the Internet*. New York: Simon and Schuster, 1995.

Amusement Parks

Adams, Judith. *The American Amusement Park Industry: A History of Technology and Thrills.* Boston: Twayne Publishers, 1991.

Fjellman, Stephen M. *Vinyl Leaves: Walt Disney World and America.* Boulder, Colo.: Westview Press, 1992.

Communicating to a TV Culture

Decker, Bert. *You've Got to Be Believed to Be Heard.* New York: St. Martin's, 1992.

Galli, Mark, and Craig Brian Larson. *Preaching That Connects.* Grand Rapids: Zondervan, 1994.

Lewis, Ralph L., and Gregg Lewis. *Inductive Preaching: Helping People Listen.* Westchester, Ill.: Crossway, 1983.

Lowry, Eugene L. *The Homiletical Plot: The Sermon as Narrative Art Form.* Atlanta: John Knox, 1980.

Miller, Calvin. *The Empowered Communicator: Seven Keys to Unlocking an Audience.* Nashville: Broadman and Holman, 1994.

Rogness, Michael. *Preaching to a TV Generation.* Lima, Ohio: CSS, 1994.

Shaw, Mark. *Doing Theology with Huck and Jim: Parables for Understanding Doctrine.* Downers Grove, Ill.: InterVarsity, 1993.

Troeger, Thomas H. *Ten Strategies for Preaching in a Multi Media Culture.* Nashville: Abingdon, 1996.

The Self-Absorbed Individual

Individualism

Bellah, Robert N., et al. *Individualism and Commitment in American Life: Readings on the Themes of Habits of the Heart.* New York: Harper and Row, 1987.

Bly, Robert. *The Sibling Society.* Reading, Mass.: Addison Wesley, 1996.

Dworkin, Donald W. *The Rise of the Imperial Self: America's Culture Wars in Augustinian Perspective.* Lanham, Md.: Rowman and Littlefield Publishers, 1996.

Lasch, Christopher. *The Culture of Narcissism: American Life in an Age of Diminishing Expectations.* New York: Norton, 1978.

Leinberger, Paul, and Bruce Tucker. *The New Individualists.* New York: HarperCollins, 1991.

McClay, Wilfred M. *The Masterless: Self and Society in Modern America.* Chapel Hill: University of North Carolina, 1994.

Yankelovich, Daniel. *New Rules: Searching for Fulfillment in a World Turned Upside Down.* New York: Random House, 1991.

Identity and Self-Expression

Ewen, Stuart. *All Consuming Images: The Politics of Style in Contemporary Culture.* New York: Basic, 1988.

Giddens, Anthony. *Modernity and Self-Identity: Self and Society in the Late Modern Age.* Stanford: Stanford University, 1991.

Muller, Rene J. *The Marginal Self: An Existential Inquiry into Narcissism.* Atlantic Highlands, N.J.: Humanities Press International, 1987.

Taylor, Charles. *Sources of the Self: The Making of the Modern Identity.* Cambridge: Harvard University, 1989.

Turkle, Sherry. *Life on the Screen: Identity in the Age of the Internet.* New York: Simon and Schuster, 1995.

The Therapeutic Movement

Kaminer, Wendy. *I'm Dysfunctional, You're Dysfunctional: The Recovery Movement and Other Self-Help Fashions.* New York: Vintage, 1992.

Beyond God

Secularism

Barrett, William. *Death of the Soul: From Descartes to the Computer.* New York: Anchor, 1986.

Buber, Martin. *Eclipse of God: Studies in the Relation between Religion and Philosophy.* Atlantic Highlands, N.J.: Humanities Press International, 1952.

Chadwick, Owen. *The Secularization of the European Mind in the 19th Century.* Cambridge: Cambridge University, 1975.

Kazim, Alfred. *God and the American Writer.* New York: Knopf, 1997.

Technology

Ellul, Jacques. *The Technological Society.* New York: Vintage, 1964.

Marx, Leo. *The Machine in the Garden: Technology and the Pastoral Ideal in America.* New York: Oxford University, 1967.

Noble, David F. *The Religion of Technology: The Divinity of Man and the Spirit of Invention.* New York: Knopf, 1997.

Postman, Neil. *Technopoly: The Surrender of Culture to Technology.* New York: Knopf, 1992.

Creation and Evolution

Behe, Michael J. *Darwin's Black Box: The Biomedical Challenge to Evolution.* New York: Free Press, 1996.

Davis, Percival, and Dean H. Kenyon. *Of Pandas and People: The Central Question of Biological Origins.* Dallas: Haughton, 1989.

Denton, Michael. *Evolution: A Theory in Crisis.* Bethesda, Md.: Adler and Adler, 1986.

Kauffman, Stuart. *At Home in the Universe: The Search for the Laws of Self-Organization and Complexity.* New York: Oxford University, 1995.

Science and Religion

Augros, Robert M., and George N. Stanciu. *The New Story of Science: Mind and the Universe.* New York: Bantam, 1984.

Brooke, John Hedley. *Science and Religion: Some Historical Perspectives.* Cambridge: Cambridge University, 1991.

Humphries, Nicholas. *Leaps of Faith: Science, Supernaturalism, and the Search for Supernatural Consolation.* New York: Basic, 1996.

Polkinghorne, John. *Science and Creation: The Search for Understanding.* Boston: New Science Library, 1989.

Ross, Hugh. *The Creator and the Cosmos: How the Greatest Scientific Discoveries of the Century Reveal God.* Colorado Springs: NavPress, 1993.

Staguhn, Gerhard. *God's Laughter: Physics, Religion, and the Cosmos.* New York: Kodansha International, 1992.

Swinburne, Richard. *Is There a God?* New York: Oxford University, 1996.

Tilby, Angela. *Soul: God, Self, and the New Cosmology.* New York: Doubleday, 1992.

Sharing Faith and the Scientific Worldview

Blamires, Harry. *The Secularist Heresy: The Erosion of the Gospel in the Twentieth Century*. London: SPCK, 1956.

Boyd, Gregory A., and Edward K. Boyd. *Letters from a Skeptic: A Son Wrestles with His Father's Questions about Christianity*. Wheaton: Victor, 1994.

Gibbs, Eddie. *In Name Only: Tackling the Problem of Nominal Christianity*. Wheaton: Victor, 1994.

McGrath, Alister E. *Intellectuals Don't Need God and Other Modern Myths: Building Bridges to Faith through Apologetics*. Grand Rapids: Zondervan, 1993.

Moore, Peter C. *Disarming the Secular Gods: How to Talk So Skeptics Will Listen*. Downers Grove, Ill.: InterVarsity, 1989.

Newbigin, Lesslie. *Foolishness to the Greeks: The Gospel and Western Culture*. Grand Rapids: Eerdmans, 1986.

Percy, Walker. *Lost in the Cosmos: The Last Self-Help Book*. New York: Noonday, 1983.

Polkinghorne, John. *The Faith of a Physicist: Reflections of a Bottom-Up Thinker*. Princeton: Princeton University, 1994.

Zacharias, Ravi. *Can Man Live without God?* Dallas: Word, 1994.

Beyond Right and Wrong

Morality and Ethics

Bauman, Zygmunt. *Life in Fragments: Essays in Postmodern Morality*. Cambridge, Mass.: Blackwell, 1995.

Delbanco, Andrew. *The Death of Satan: How Americans Have Lost the Sense of Evil*. New York: Farrar, Straus and Giroux, 1995.

Diggins, John Patrick. *The Promise of Pragmatism: Modernism and the Crisis of Knowledge and Authority*. Chicago: University of Chicago, 1994.

Himmelfarb, Gertrude, *The De-Moralization of Society: From Victorian Virtues to Modern Values*. New York: Knopf, 1995.

Kane, Robert. *Through the Moral Maze: Searching for Absolute Values in a Pluralistic World*. Armonk, N.Y.: North Castle Books, 1996.

Larmore, Charles. *The Morals of Modernity*. New York: Cambridge University, 1996.

Lewis, Hunter. *A Question of Values: Six Ways We Make the Personal Choices That Shape Our Lives*. New York: Harper San Francisco, 1990.

MacIntyre, Alasdair. *After Virtue: A Study in Moral Theory*. 2d ed. South Bend, Ind.: University of Notre Dame, 1984.

Nietzsche, Friedrich. *Beyond Good and Evil*. Translated by Walter Kaufmann. New York: Vintage, 1966.

Turnbull, Colin M. *The Mountain People*. New York: Simon and Schuster, 1972.

Wilson, James Q. *The Moral Sense*. New York: Free Press, 1993.

Morality and Contemporary Culture

Anderson, Digby, ed. *The Loss of Virtue: Moral Confusion and Social Disorder in Britain and America*. New York: National Review, 1992.

Bennett, William J. *The Index of Leading Cultural Indicators: Facts and Figures on the State of American Society*. New York: Touchstone, 1994.

Bloom, Allan. *The Closing of the American Mind*. New York: Touchstone, 1987.

Derber, Charles. *The Wilding of America: How Greed and Violence Are Eroding Our Nation's Character*. New York: St. Martin's, 1996.

Gurstein, Rochelle. *The Repeal of Reticence: A History of America's Cultural and Legal Struggles over Free Speech, Obscenity, Sexual Liberation, and Modern Art*. New York: Hill and Wang, 1996.

Whitehead, Barbara Dafoe. *The Divorce Culture*. New York: Knopf, 1997.

Zacharias, Ravi. *Deliver Us from Evil: Restoring the Soul in a Disintegrating Culture*. Dallas: Word, 1996.

Evil and Sin

Fairlie, Henry. *The Seven Deadly Sins Today*. South Bend, Ind.: University of Notre Dame, 1978.

Katz, Fred E. *Ordinary People and Extraordinary Evil: A Report on the Beguilings of Evil*. Albany, N.Y.: State University of New York, 1993.

Virtue

Carter, Stephen L. *Integrity*. New York: Basic, 1996.

Schlessinger, Laura C. *How Could You Do That? The Abdication of Character, Courage, and Conscience*. New York: HarperCollins, 1996.

Spencer, Anita. *A Crisis of Spirit: Our Desperate Search for Integrity*. New York: Plenum Press, 1996.

Beyond Meaning and Purpose

Postmodernism, Its Expressions, and Its Challenges

Allen, Diogenes. *Christian Belief in a Postmodern World: The Full Wealth of Conviction*. Louisville: Westminster/John Knox, 1989.

Anderson, Walter Truett. *The Future of the Self: Exploring the Post-Identity Society*. New York: Tarcher/Putnam, 1997.

———. *Reality Isn't What It Used to Be: Theatrical Politics, Ready-to-Wear Religion, Global Myths, Primitive Chic, and Other Wonders of the Postmodern World*. New York: Harper San Francisco, 1990.

Anderson, Walter Truett, ed. *The Truth about the Truth: De-confusing and Re-constructing the Postmodern World*. New York: Tarcher/Putnam, 1995.

Barrett, William. *Irrational Man: A Study in Existential Philosophy*. New York: Anchor, 1958.

Cheney, Lynne V. *Telling the Truth: Why Our Culture and Our Country Have Stopped Making Sense—and What We Can Do about It*. New York: Simon and Schuster, 1995.

Dockery, David S., ed. *The Challenge of Postmodernism: An Evangelical Engagement*. Wheaton: Bridgepoint, 1995.

Hardison, O. B. Jr. *Disappearing through the Skylight: Culture and Technology in the Twentieth Century*. New York: Viking, 1989.

Harvey, David. *The Condition of Postmodernity: An Enquiry into the Origins of Cultural Change*. Cambridge: Blackwell, 1989.

Lundin, Roger. *The Culture of Interpretation: Christian Faith and the Postmodern World*. Grand Rapids: Eerdmans, 1993.

Newbigin, Lesslie. *The Gospel in a Pluralist Society*. Grand Rapids: Eerdmans, 1989.

Phillips, Timothy R., and Dennis L. Okholm, eds. *Christian Apologetics in the Postmodern World*. Downers Grove, Ill.: InterVarsity, 1995.

Sass, Louis. *Madness and Modernism: Insanity in the Light of Modern Art, Literature, and Thought*. Cambridge: Harvard University, 1992.

Religion and Spirituality in the United States

Berger, Peter L. *A Rumor of Angels: Modern Society and the Rediscovery of the Supernatural.* New York: Anchor, 1969.

Bloom, Harold. *The American Religion: The Emergence of the Post-Christian Nation.* New York: Touchstone, 1992.

Carmody, Denise Ardner, and John Tully Carmody. *The Republic of Many Mansions: Foundations of American Religious Thought.* New York: Paragon, 1990.

Douglas, Mary, and Steven Tipton, eds. *Religion and America: Spirituality in a Secular Age.* Boston: Beacon, 1982.

Ellwood, Robert S. *The Sixties Spiritual Awakening: American Religion Moving from Modern to Postmodern.* New Brunswick, N.J.: Rutgers University, 1994.

Greeley, Andrew M. *Religious Change in America.* Cambridge, Mass.: Harvard University, 1996.

Hoge, Dean R., Benton Johnson, and Donald A. Luidens. *Vanishing Boundaries: The Religion of Mainline Protestant Baby Boomers.* Louisville: Westminster/John Knox, 1994.

Keen, Sam. *Hymns to an Unknown God: Awakening the Spirit in Everyday Life.* New York: Bantam, 1994.

Kosmin, Barry A., and Seymour P. Lachman. *One Nation under God: Religion in Contemporary American Society.* New York: Harmony, 1993.

Wuthnow, Robert. *Rediscovering the Sacred: Perspectives on Religion in Contemporary Society.* Grand Rapids: Eerdmans, 1992.

———. *The Restructuring of American Religion: Society and Faith Since World War II.* Princeton: Princeton University, 1988.

The Generations and Their Differences

Barna, George. *The Invisible Generation: Baby Busters.* Glendale, Calif.: Barna Research Group, 1992.

Celek, Tim, and Dieter Zander. *Inside the Soul of a New Generation: Insights and Strategies for Reaching Busters.* Grand Rapids: Zondervan, 1996.

Coupland, Douglas. *Life after God.* New York: Pocket, 1994.

Ford, Kevin Graham. *Jesus for a New Generation: Putting the Gospel into the Language of Xers.* Downers Grove, Ill.: InterVarsity, 1995.

Hahn, Todd, and David Verhaagen. *Reckless Hope: Understanding and Reaching Baby Busters.* Grand Rapids: Baker, 1996.

Long, Jimmy. *Generating Hope: A Strategy for Reaching the Postmodern Generation.* Downers Grove, Ill.: InterVarsity, 1997.

Mahedy, William, and Janet Bernardi. *A Generation Alone: Xers Making a Place in the World.* Downers Grove, Ill.: InterVarsity, 1994.

McIntosh, Gary L. *Three Generations: Riding the Waves of Change in Your Church.* Grand Rapids: Revell, 1995.

Murren, Doug. *The Baby Boomerang: Catching Boomers as They Return to Church.* Ventura, Calif.: Regal, 1990.

Rushkoff, Douglas, ed. *The GenX Reader.* New York: Ballantine, 1994.

Russell, Cheryl. *The Master Trend: How the Baby Boom Generation Is Remaking America.* New York: Plenum, 1993.

Strauss, William, and Neil Howe. *Generations: The History of America's Future, 1584 to 2069.* New York: William Morrow, 1991.

INDEX

Dr. David W. Henderson earned a degree from Miami University of Ohio before pursuing a career with Procter and Gamble in marketing and brand management. After his call to ministry, Henderson earned masters and doctoral degrees at Gordon-Conwell Theological Seminary, where he studied preaching under Dr. Haddon Robinson, recently named one of American's ten best preachers. He has completed independent studies at Westminster College in Cambridge, England, and is now senior pastor of Covenant Presbyterian Church in West Lafayette, Indiana. Henderson has served widely as a conference and chapel speaker on three continents, is a regular contributor to *Discipleship Journal,* and has written numerous articles and editorials.

When he is not pastoring or writing, you are likely to find Henderson spending time with his wife and four children, romping through the outdoors, or browsing the "Just Arrived" stacks at the local bookstore.